COMMUNITY SUPERVISION FOR OFFENDERS

To Carolyn

Alex, Tim and Jenny

Community Supervision for Offenders

A New Model of Probation

PHILIP WHITEHEAD

Research and Information Officer
Cleveland Probation Service

Avebury

Aldershot · Brookfield USA · Hong Kong · Singapore · Sydney

Published by
Avebury
Gower Publishing Company Limited
Gower House
Croft Road
Aldershot
Hants GU11 3HR
England

Gower Publishing Company
Old Post Road
Brookfield
Vermont 05036
USA

British Library Cataloguing in Publication Data
Whitehead, Phillip, 1952-
   Community supervision for offenders: a new model of
probation.
   1. Great Britain. Probation services
   I. Title
   364.6'3'0941

   ISBN 0-566-07129-0

Printed and Bound in Great Britain by
Athenaeum Press Ltd., Newcastle upon Tyne.

Contents

List of tables

Foreword

As a social work manager, practitioner and academic, my concern has always been with outcomes. Nowhere is this more important than in the Probation Service: ideological debates about care and control, organisational debates about casework or community work, and practice debates about group therapy or behaviour therapy are all engaging and usually entertaining. However, these debates are concerned primarily with the process of service delivery, but it is the outcome which is critical. I see little point in well intentioned care for an offender if the outcome is that the offender is sent speedily into custody. Therapy, of whatever form, which fails to produce changes in behaviour is self-indulgent particularly if it is the 'offending' behaviour which has led the individual to seek therapy willingly or under duress.

It is against this personal background that I welcomed the Home Office Statement of National Objectives and Priorities. A clear statement of what the objectives of the probation service are, allows monitoring and performance review to follow. Through these processes it can be established whether or not the service is achieving its objectives and consequently, whether interventions by probation officers in the lives of clients are having positive outcomes.

However a national statement whilst a starting point, guarantees little, if any, change at local levels. It is the commitment and enthusiasm to pursue these objectives at the local level which will determine whether change occurs. Cleveland Probation Service has set about the task of developing a Statement of Local Objectives and Priorities and in doing so inevitably hit upon a number of obstructions. These include: the inevitable inertia in any bureaucratic service; the established beliefs of staff that past ways were better and should be retained; pressure from other agencies such as the courts to accept the 'new image' of the probation service. However, Cleveland also had a positive advantage in the form of one of their officers, Philip Whitehead, who chose to research aspects of the change particularly as they affected the moves to reduce custody rates by more focussed community supervision. In undertaking this task Philip Whitehead has illuminated some of the problems of change but not solely in a desriptive fashion but also by empirical analysis of the effectiveness of one area of the probation officers' work.

Finally, on a personal note, it is not often that one's career allows one to observe outcomes. However, I have been fortunate firstly to be involved in training Dr Whitehead on his initial training when I continually stressed the concept of practitioner as researcher. It was with great pleasure, therefore, when some eight years later I was involved in examining his doctoral thesis, and now introducing his first major publication. Dr Whitehead has proved the concept of the practitioner-researcher is achievable.

This book not only provides important insights into current developments in the probation service, but serves as a model of what can be achieved by practitioners.

Professor Norman Tutt
Director, Leeds Social Services

Preface

The Probation Service finds itself facing a future in the 1990s with greater uncertainty than perhaps in the whole of its history. The political, social and economic changes of the last decade have had a profound effect on the world in which we live. The basic values of care and compassion with which the service is synonymous are now less discernible in our society. One consequence of this has been to put pressure on the service to deliver in value for money terms, which is the contemporary ideology.

Dr Philip Whitehead's book enables us to put recent events into the historical context of a whole range of service developments since the days of police court missionaries. His first two chapters provides a background for an examination of the impact of SNOP, since when the service has had to cope with being exposed to political dogma about management. Furthermore Dr Whitehead has reviewed events in Cleveland to illustrate a process begun in each of the fifty-six probation areas, that of developing a corporate management strategy. Arriving as I did as ACPO in Cleveland at the beginning of 1984, I can reflect on the events which were part of a process of changing a laissez-faire and paternalistic management style to one which assumed greater responsibility for service performance. It is for all of us a process which is far from complete.

The management metamorphosis has taken place against a background of social change. Throughout the last decade sentencers have been exposed to a rigorous law and order debate, captured by headline writers in terms of crime being a threat to society. More recent discourse has linked the growth in the prison population with the issue of confidence in the probation service, and this book illustrates that there is a real challenge for the service in winning the hearts and minds of sentencers. To do this the probation service must retain confidence in its own ability to innovate and to shape performance in a way that ensures that furture funding is not in doubt.

We are left to contemplate the future being reminded that the ultimate challenge is for the service to ensure that its traditional values are part of the contemporary criminal justice system, which is something this book does not lose sight of.

Roger Statham
Chief Probation Officer
Cleveland Probation Service

Introduction

The last few years have seen a number of important issues being
discussed within the probation service during a period of growth,
change and development, particularly in relation to the probation
order which is the central concern of this book. Primarily the
service has experienced diversification of its practices and shifts in
its ideological perspectives. Furthermore arguments and disagreements
have surfaced in the axiological sphere, otherwise known as the care-
control debate and it seems unlikely there will ever be a satisfactory
resolution of this dilemma. Consequently the elements of probation
practice, ideological perspectives and value orientation, are three of
the central reference points threading their way through this book in
both the theoretical and empirical sections.

Accordingly these various dimensions of the probation order will be,
firstly at a macro level, theoretically analysed from academic,
bureaucratic, professional and local standpoints. Subsequently at a
micro level the second section will present, on the basis of empirical
research, a quantitative and qualitative worms eye view of the
practice and philosophy of probation supervision, the operating value

system, including a consideration of the social work methods utilised by a number of probation officers in the North-East of England in the second half of the 1980's. This section also contains a chapter on the views of sentencers concerning the credibility of the probation order as an alternative to custody for the more serious offender.

I consider the climate within the probation service conducive to undertaking this research because, having worked as a probation officer from July 1981 to December 1987 in the organisation where this research was carried out, I had gradually become aware of a state of confusion, specifically in relation to the purpose of probation supervision. It seemed less than clear what comprised the elements of probation practice (or what probation officers actually do with probationers) and even more doubtful whether or not a clear underlying ideology and rationale supported practice (or why they practice in the way they do.). It also seemed there was a degree of confusion concerning whether officers were attempting to either care for or control offenders, or do both at the same time, and whether they were consciously operating with a specific social work methodology.

It will be argued that this state of affairs has been created, to some degree, by the decline of consensus in the probation service which is a consequence of the collapse of the rehabilitative ideal. It appears that from 1876 to the late 1960's there was a high degree of consensus concerning what the probation service was doing and why, with probationers. Accordingly from 1876 and for the next sixty years it was saving souls; and from the 1930's until the late 1960's it was preoccupied first with moral reformation and later 'scientific' rehabilitation. Therefore the first chapter will set the scene by historically tracing how the service has arrived at its present position by discussing both the rise of consensus given credence by the ideology of rehabilitation and its subsequent fall from grace.

Since the 1970's (and before) the rehabilitative ideal in probation has been criticised from different standpoints, but it should be acknowledged that it has been seriously undermined by empirical research which has questioned the efficacy of probation treatment to prevent recidivism. This precipitated a number of what may be loosely termed academic responses, discussed in Chapter 2, which have attempted to reconceptualise probation work in the post-rehabilitative era. Even though these models represent a disparate and diverse collection of viewpoints, most of them would agree that the probation order should be used as a vehicle to divert offenders from custodial sentences, an objective which provides the service with its raison d'etre in the post-rehabilitative period. Moreover if the rationale of the probation service in the 1980s is to manage, contain and control relatively serious offenders in the community rather than saving souls or rehabilitation, it may be asked whether any of these models help to achieve this objective?

An important development in the mid-1980's was the way in which the Home Office attempted to elucidate the future direction of probation in its Statement of National Objectives and Priorities which appeared in April 1984. It will be argued in Chapter 3 that SNOP, which constitutes an additional and competing model to those considered in Chapter 2, is a unique document in the history of the probation service. In addition to considering aspects of probation supervision I will also draw attention to the importance SNOP attaches to dealing with as many offenders as possible in the community, especially in cases where custodial sentences would otherwise be imposed. Moreover the way in which SNOP differs from previous reviews of the service contained in several Departmental Committee reports will be explored, because there can be little doubt that SNOP constitutes a landmark in the history of the probation system. This is attempted because I do not think that these issues have been adequately considered in the literature so far produced on SNOP.

However not everyone associated with the probation service would accept that SNOP is the definitive model for the future. In fact SNOP raises a number of important professional issues in relation to probation ethics, morals and values, which are taken up in Chapter 4. Here the views expressed by different probation services, individual probation officers and the National Association of Probation Officers are considered.

The last chapter in the first part of the book begins to examine the response made by one probation service to Home Office proposals in its Future Directions Document, which introduces the service in which empirical research was undertaken. Interestingly the definitive policy document produced by senior management concerning the future aims and objectives of the Cleveland Probation Service actually resorts to the language of rehabilitation when discussing the rationale of probation supervision, in addition to affirming that the service should be diverting offenders from custody.

But, it may be asked, how do probation officers themselves against the theoretical background sketched in Chapters 1 to 5 articulate their understanding of the various aspects of probation supervision at Hartlepool and Redcar probation offices? This question is answered in Chapter 7. Moreover the way in which probation officers are attempting to promote the probation order as an alternative to custody will be considered empirically in Chapter 8.

Finally in addition to presenting empirical data based upon probation records and interviewing probation officers, the research included discussions with Magistrates and Judges, Clerks and Recorders, on the viability of probation as an alternative to custody for the more serious offender. These findings are presented in Chapter 9.

To summarise, the purpose of this research is to discover, against the background of the rise and fall of consensus in the probation service, disparate academic models, the prescriptive model of SNOP, the professional concerns of NAPO and the views articulated in the policy document of the Cleveland Probation Service, what constitutes the elements of probation practice, ideology and rationale, the value orientation and the social work methods used by probation officers with probationers. It also considers the degree to which probation is being offered by officers and used by courts as an alternative to custody. For if the future of the probation service depends on its ability to provide realistic and credible alternatives to custody and therefore to manage the more serious offender in the community, it appears that this has radical implications for the practice and philosophy of the probation order itself. This will be considered towards the end of the book.

Acknowledgements

This book would not have been possible without the help of many people. Therefore I'd like to thank Bob Roshier of Durham University who supervised the PhD upon which this book is based, and acknowledge the help provided by David Byrne.

During the early stages of the research Robert Harris, David Faulkner, Cecil Fullwood and Bill Beaumont gave me some of their valuable time to talk about the probation service. By this time they have probably forgotten just how much they helped.

John Macmillan has also been a good friend and helper since I came to Cleveland in 1981.

I am particularly indebted to my friends and colleagues Roger Statham, Peter Sugden and Alistair Morrison for the constant encouragement they have given to me over the last few years, and for showing an interest in this project. I must also thank all probation officers in the the Cleveland probation service, especially those at Hartlepool and Redcar, without whom this book would not have been possible.

Finally, Carolyn has managed to provide the rare commodities of time

and space. This has not been easy because this project coincided with
the responsibility of having to look after three young children.

Despite all this help I have to accept that any errors contained in
this book are mine.

1 From saving souls to the decline of rehabilitation

Emergence of Probation

The probation system in Europe emerged against a background of dissatisfaction with the principles of classical criminology, exemplified in the writings of the Italian scholar Beccaria in the 18th century. The system of justice which prevailed in this classical period endorsed the concept of equal punishments for equal crimes, without taking cognizance of the unique circumstances of the individual offender or the particular situation in which offences were committed. Eventually classicism evolved into neo-classicism and later still into positivism (Garland, 1985a; 1985b). But as Smykla argues (1984, p61) it is against the background of neo-classicism and positivism that one discovers the emergence of probation through a series of practices which included judicial reprieve, bail and the recognizance.

Firstly judicial reprieve, or the temporary suspension of sentence for a period of time, was a practice which apparently began in England. Its purpose was to allow a temporary stay of punishment thus enabling the defendant to make application to the Crown for a pardon.

Secondly bail was used in the early 19th century to ensure that an offender reappeared before the court. Furthermore the sureties who stood bail had a vested financial interest in ensuring that the defendant abided by the instructions of the court, and this practice also involved a degree of supervision over the defendant.

Thirdly, and importantly, the recognizance was a bond made by a defendant to refrain from doing some particular act for a specified period of time and to appear before the court when ordered. This practice was first used in America in 1830, but the recognizance had its roots in English common law involving the defendant entering into a bond (with or without sureties) and pledging not to reoffend. Smykla (1984) argues that in the practice of recognizance the elements of the probation order can be identified : the suspension of sentence; freedom in the community; and possible revocation of this freedom if the conditions of the recognizance are breached. It should also be added that in England the Juvenile Offenders Act, 1847, the Criminal Law Consolidation Act, 1861, the Summary Jurisdiction Act, 1879, and the Probation of First Offenders Act, 1887, made provision for certain offenders to enter into recognizance to appear for judgement when called upon to do so. But in the meantime they had to keep the peace and be of good behaviour.

The use of the recognizance in the United States predated the work of John Augustus, a Boston bootmaker, who is acknowledged as the father of probation and who initiated probation reform in the Police Court of Boston in 1841. Augustus and other reformers worked with those on the fringes of society such as drunks, prostitutes, beggars and wayward children. Ideologically they were motivated by a religious concern and their main task was to put the wayward back on the right path which meant instilling in them a middle-class morality in the hope of redeeming and reforming them. By 1878 the first statutory provision for probation was passed by the Massachusetts legislature.

During the time that Augustus worked in Boston in the 1840's a magistrate in England, Matthew Davenport Hill, introduced the practice of suspending sentence and releasing offenders under supervision into the community. He also established a register of voluntary helpers

2

or 'guardians' to take charge of young offenders convicted by his court whom he released into their care. Even though the ideas leading to the creation of the probation system in England largely emanated from America, the English system was influenced by the work of reformers like Davenport Hill in Birmingham and Edward Cox in Portsmouth. However, it was the work of the police court missionaries which was particularly significant.

In 1876 Frederick Rainer, a Hertfordshire printer, made a suggestion to the Church of England Temperance Society which had been formed in 1873 to promote the virtues of temperance, that it should extend its work to the courts. Rainer hoped that the Temperance Society could organise some kind of work in the police courts and enclosed the sum of five shillings to start things off. It responded by appointing George Nelson, who was the first police court missionary. Subsequently the first move made by the magistrates to involve missionaries in work similar to that of probation (for it must be remembered that many more years were to elapse before statutory probation supervision would be available under the 1907 Act), was to use them informally to supervise offenders released on recognizances which was made possible by the provisions of the 1879 Summary Jurisdiction Act. And during the last quarter of the 19th century the tasks of the missionaries, at a time when drunkenness was a serious problem, was that of reclaiming drunkards appearing before the courts (Heasman, 1962, p181). They were also involved in matrimonial disputes, prison after-care work, helping offenders find or maintain employment, neighbours quarrels, children beyond parental control and assessing applicants for the poor box (King, 1958, p5). In fact, as more missionaries were appointed their duties were extended so that by 1889 it was recorded that

> the missionaries help all classes of persons, not those only who are charged with ill abuse or intoxicating drink, but any case that may be handed over to their charge by the magistrate. They deal principally with the first offenders, but they have, by the Grace of God, reclaimed many from the depths of sin and evil...(Heasman, 1962, p181).

Ideologically McWilliams argues in the first of his scholarly quartet of essays on the history of ideas in the probation service

(1983), which complement the historical analyses of King (1958), Jarvis (1972) and Bochel (1976), that the dominant ideology of the police court missionaries was the theological notion of saving offender's souls through divine grace. Furthermore, the concept of mercy provided the key to understanding their place in court and the reformation of the offender was a primary aim of their endeavours.

A careful reading of Leeson's book (1914) which is purported to be one of the earliest on probation ever written in England, reveals quite clearly that the missionary period, specifically after 1907, was replete with the language of reformation, reclamation and redemption, and that the concepts of treatment, the improvement of character and the development of the offender's moral fibre were also very much in evidence.   Furthermore, McWilliams discusses the missionary theological doctrine of the stumbling-block which embraced the idea that offenders, as sinners, could not receive the grace of God until all impediments to understanding the gospel had been removed. Implicit in this doctrine, argues McWilliams, was the possibility of coercing offenders to have such stumbling-blocks removed.   More importantly and significantly, however, was the way in which some missionaries arrived at the belief that the stumbling-blocks determined offending, which prevented the offender's salvation. Consequently 'Once this became widely accepted it meant that the Mission had no ultimate defence left against the determinist ontology of the diagnosticians' (McWilliams, 1983, p142).

Thus it was because of this 'ontological flaw' (1985, p257) by which McWilliams means the way in which some missionaries, albeit in a subtle manner, accepted the notion of determinism, which allowed a distinctively religious philosophy which had been influential for sixty years and based on the idea of saving souls by God's grace, to be gradually assimilated into scientific social work which prevailed during the period from the 1930's to the late 1960's.   In other words the missionary period, populated by men and women with strong evangelical beliefs, gave way to a more scientific and secular approach to offenders dominated by the concept of diagnosis (Heasman, 1962, p182).

The concept of diagnosis was only one facet of the treatment-based

4

philosophy which was emerging in the probation service, but it seems that diagnosis had a central place. From the late 1920s both social workers and probation officers came to an understanding of their work which was not too dissimilar to that of a physician and the medical model provided the basis and justification for probation practice (McWilliams, 1985, p260). Support for this view is found in Le Mesurier (1935, p105) who was commissioned by the National Association of Probation Officers to edit the sequel to Leeson's book, because she resorted to medical terminology when discussing the nature of probation work, particularly with juveniles.

However, Harris and Webb (1987, p41) argue that one must be careful not to assume that the medical-treatment model, underpinned by the positivism of Lombroso and Ferri, was dominant in Britain. Consequently it is probably more accurate to say that probation officers were engaged in something much more modest than aiming to effect a radical change in the offender's personality (Davies, 1972, pp317-318). Nevertheless, these were the dominant ideas which, on the whole, sustained the practical and theoretical basis of probation work after the 1930s, remaining influential until the late 1960's.

Probation, rehabilitation and casework

From 1876 to the present day probation officers have tried in various ways to reform, remake, remould and restructure the lives of offenders into good, honest, law-abiding citizens. The point has already been established that the concept of moral reformation has a long history in probation, a point reinforced by Garland who reminds us that from as early as the 1779 Penitentiary Act, the moral reformation of the offender had been one of the aims of penality (1985a, p16). Moreover, Bottoms states that reformation was still important in the penal system between the wars when the probation service was steadily expanding, becoming more professional and taking training much more seriously. However, Bottoms continues by saying that 'In the post-war period, reform became rehabilitation - that is, religious and moral impulses in reformation became secularised, psychologised, scientised' (1980, pp1-2).

The period following the second world war was a time of great optimism in the efficacy of social work with offenders to achieve the 'perfectibility of man' and probation officers in the 1960's were part of a criminal justice system which was moving towards the rehabilitative ideal (Raynor, 1985, pp3-4). Additional support for this view can be found in a Home Office document of the period (1959) which reflected the idea that the wider criminal justice system, particularly within penal institutions, operated with the goals of reformation and rehabilitation. It was also accepted at this time that a penal policy could be developed which would correct many of the personal and social ills which were considered conducive to crime. This would be a penal policy based on research, individualised sentencing, classification, diagnosis and treatment (Morgan, 1979, p2).

Consequently it may be argued that prior to 1970 there were two distinct ideological phases or unifying symbols in the probation service, which provided a high degree of consensus. Subsequent chapters will suggest that consensus no longer exists because of the collapse of the rehabilitative ideal, which was first experienced in the institutional sector of the penal system. However, it should be acknowledged at this point that casework was the social work method by which the rehabilitation of offenders was attempted. Even though casework, particularly in the post-1945 period, became the medium through which the assessment, diagnosis, treatment and cure of offenders was attempted, other methods subsequently emerged. In more recent times probation officers have increasingly resorted to other social work methods such as group work, community work, task-centred work, contracts, family therapy, transactional analysis and behaviour modification, to name but a few, which have emerged and developed since the 1960s during a period of 'acquisition' (Howe, 1987, p20; see also Coulshed, 1988).

To summarise, the conceptual framework of the probation service which dominated the rationale of practice in the 1950s and 1960s comprised the goal of rehabilitation which was to be achieved by the method of casework. Through a one-to-one relationship with the offender the officer proceeded to impart insight (with its Freudian overtones) and understanding, which is what offenders apparently

6

lacked. The probation officer concentrated on the 'intra-psychic conflict within the client' (Raynor, 1985, p4) and through a process of 'coercive soul transformation' (Bottoms, 1980, p21) and by focusing on the client's 'faulty psychic plumbing' (Cohen, 1985, p126), he would be rehabilitated into a law-abiding citizen.

Moreover operating with a medical model of crime and delinquency, which stressed the importance of assessment, diagnosis and treatment, the offender would eventually be cured of those psycho-social factors responsible for his malfunctioning and pathology. Ideally the offender would be restored to a state of harmony with society, a society understood in consensus terminology in that it was perceived to benefit all its citizens alike. Only more recently have the insights of sociology suggested that offending may not be a consequence of faulty individuals but rather a consequence of the individual's location within a faulty social structure. However changing individuals rather than society has always been the major preoccupation of the probation service.

Care, control and the decline of consensus
As one now reflects on what appear to be the halcyon days of consensus in the probation service, both practice and philosophy seemed relatively unambiguous. This perspective gains in credibility when it is also realised that the period in question was not intellectually paralysed by the problem of reconciling care and control, an issue which remains bothersome in the contemporary service and which will be considered in more detail later. For now it is sufficient to say that it has been argued in the past that society through the courts has given the probation officer the duty to both care and control, to blend benevolence with authority. Moreover it was believed that care and control complemented each other, so that if authority was used in the best interests of the client then it was considered legitimate. But who, it must be asked, decides what is best for the client? (Monger, 1964, pp12-14). It has also been stated that the exercise of authority and compulsion is simply another aspect of care and that care is demonstrated through control (King, 1969, p102); and Hunt has argued that the process of casework may be enriched by enforcement

7

(1964).

The rationalisation for this perspective seemed to be that it was legitimate to 'force' the offender into a relationship with the probation officer because it was believed that treatment would be good for him, is undoubtedly what he needs to cure offending behaviour, which must therefore be in everyone's best interests. Furthermore the exercise of authority towards the offender may be exactly what is required to resolve his authority problems and enhance his maturation (Hunt, 1964). Once again, though, it is the individual and not society who is perceived to be at fault and who needs to be changed through a casework relationship with the probation officer who acts as a moral yardstick and arbiter of right and wrong on behalf of the courts and society. Consequently from the missionary period which saw how some missionaries came to believe that the stumbling-blocks in the way of an offenders salvation could be forcibly removed, to the period of diagnosis and treatment whose apogee was in the 1960's which expressed the view that coercion and enforcement can be exercised in the best interests of the client, social control has been a salient feature of probation work. Furthermore control is unlikely to experience a diminution in the contemporary penal climate with its emphasis on law and order (Box, 1987).

Whatever the merits and demerits of the constellation of ideas associated with the period of rehabilitation through casework in the probation service, it must now be acknowledged that this consensus ideology no longer prevails. It is now extremely difficult to seriously maintain the view that the probation service is contributing to a criminal justice system moving rapidly towards a golden age of rehabilitation, or that the rationale of probation supervision can be articulated in terms of 'preventing further crime by a readjustment of the culprit under encouraging supervision of a social worker...' (Radzinowicz, 1958). Over the last few years a considerable amount of empirical research into the efficacy of probation as a successful treatment for crime has produced rather negative results.

Therefore if the service was reasonably clear about its aims and objectives prior to the 1970's, which is a view postulated in this chapter, it is highly unlikely that this remains the case today. One

8

of the concerns of this book is that the years of consensus within the probation service, particularly in relation to the supervision of offenders on probation orders, have been replaced by confusion, diversity and fragmentation. Of course the vacuum created by the collapse of the rehabilitative ideal has been responded to in a variety of ways and at varying levels of theoretical complexity. Furthermore since the collapse of rehabilitation it would be wrong to assume that the probation service has been devoid of ideologies, unifying symbols, or justifications for its work. For example, the ideology of decarceration, community correction (Haxby, 1978) and managerial, radical and personalist ideologies (McWilliams, 1987), have been articulated. Moreover the goal of offering the courts alternative disposals to custodial sentences is a central concern of the Home Office, thus providing an important rationale for contemporary probation work. But it would be interesting to know, for example, if individual probation officers operate probation orders with a specific ideology, if a clear rationale underlies practice and if they are offering probation orders as an alternative to custody in the 1980s. It is against the background of a collapsed consensus that this book will proceed to analyse, both theoretically and empirically, various aspects and dimensions of the probation order. Before explaining the decline of consensus more fully by turning to a number of research reports in the final section of this opening chapter, this historical overview would not be complete unless I considered in a little more detail than hitherto the probation order from a historical standpoint.

The tenets of probation supervision

It has already been established how the English probation system emerged out of the work of the police court missionaries, in addition to being indebted to American influences. Even though probation was legislated for in Massachusetts as early as 1878 and albeit the missionary practice of informal supervision in the years after 1876 in this country, the English probation system had to wait until the 1907 Probation of Offenders Act which combined statutory supervision with the existing practice of binding over offenders on their own

9

recognizances or the sureties of others. In 1907 the duties of probation officers when supervising offenders on probation orders were:

To visit or receive reports from the person under supervision at such intervals the probation officer may think fit; to see that he observes the conditions of his recognizance; to report to the Court on his behaviour; to advise, assist and befriend him; and when necessary, to endeavour to find him suitable employment.

Amendments were made to the 1907 Act in the Criminal Justice Administration Act, 1914, before the Criminal Justice Act, 1925 and the Criminal Justice Act, 1948, consolidated the development of the probation order. Today the legislative basis of probation is contained in the Powers of Criminal Courts Act, 1973, sections 2 to 13, reinforced by the Criminal Justice Act, 1982. It is an order available to offenders aged 17 years and over and is made instead of sentencing him. It can be imposed for a minimum of six months and a maximum of three years, so long as the consent of the offender has been secured. The probation order includes a number of normal requirements to be of good behaviour; keep in touch with the probation officer; notify him of any change of address or employment; and to report to the officer on his instuctions and receive visits at home by the probation officer. Moreover the Criminal Justice Act, 1982, has provided under Schedule 11 for additional requirements in probation orders. New sections 4A and 4B were added to the 1973 Act to allow: Section 4A (1)(a) specified activities at a particular location and Section 4A (1)(b) specified activities not at a fixed location, both for a maximum of 60 days. It is also possible under Section 4A (1)(b) to include a negative requirement to prevent, for example, an offender attending a football match on a Saturday afternoon, where the maximum of 60 days does not apply. Finally, Section 4B has provided for attendance at Day Centres, again for a maximum of 60 days. Importantly, and this seems to be one of its most distinguishing features, the probation order, as an alternative to a court sentence, cannot be located at any one specific point on the tariff of court disposals, but may be used at any stage during an offenders criminal career depending on the personal and social circumstances appertaining at the time. It therefore continues a long historical tradition of individualised sentencing (For full details concerning all aspects of probation orders see Weston, 1987, Chapter 3).

Today the probation order has progressed beyond being purely a disposal for inebriates or first offenders because the Home Office has articulated the view that community supervision should be used for more serious offenders as an alternative to a custodial sentence. A subsequent chapter will examine in some depth recent Home Office thinking concerning community supervision so I will not spend much time discussing these views here. Moreover Betteridge, a Home Office Inspector of Probation, has said that the modern probation order represents a challenge to adult offenders to remain clear of trouble for a period longer than was possibly achieved in the past and that it is specifically intended to prevent or contain reoffending. He also said that the probation order is rehabilitative in character (1984). But this is where problems begin to emerge because it is now extremely difficult to justify probation supervision on the grounds of rehabilitative efficacy. I am surprised that Betteridge needed to mention rehabilitation with its questionable connotations of individual treatment for personal pathology. It should also be noted that as long ago as the late 1960's and early 1970's various developments were taking shape which were conducive to a critique of rehabilitation because, firstly, labelling theory articulated the view that treatment could make matters worse by reinforcing deviant behaviour and secondly, treatment was not reducing the crime rate. Consequently rehabilitation was criticised by left wing civil libertarians because it interfered too much in the lives of individuals; by liberal due-process lawyers who drew attention to the problems of injustice which stemmed from indeterminate sentencing; and by the right wing, law and order lobby, who felt that rehabilitation was soft on crime (This paved the way for the emergence of the Justice Model of corrections, which is fully discussed by Hudson, 1987, Chapter 1). Moreover rehabilitation was undermined by empirical research which will now be considered in the final section of this chapter.

Research and the questionable efficacy of probation

In 1958 the results of a survey undertaken by the Cambridge Department of Criminal Science was published. Nine thousand records of offenders placed on probation for indictable offences in London and Middlesex were examined and the research tested the effectiveness of the satisfactory completion of the probationary period and the avoidance of further offending for three years afterwards. It was found that 73.8% of adults and 62.4% of juveniles were successful and that the success rate was higher for women than for men and for older than younger probationers. It was also found that success diminished with the more previous convictions one had.

However in the same year that Radzinowicz claimed that probation prevented crime in the Preface to the report just cited, a study by Wilkins into the results of probation arrived at rather less optimistic conclusions (1958). Wilkins found that there were no significant differences in the reconviction rates of two matched samples of probationers and other offenders, most of whom were sent to prison or borstal. He concluded by suggesting that, firstly, a large proportion of offenders currently being committed to penal institutions could be dealt with by probation without affecting the reconviction rate. Secondly and more importantly, he said that 'The negative result of this study is challenging. Why did undoubtedly different treatment policies make little or no difference in subsequent criminal activity'? (1958, p207).

There is little doubt that Wilkins raised important questions about the efficacy of treatment methods for offenders, particularly probationers, and his study was partly responsible for the emergence of a Home Office study into probation in 1961 which was undertaken by the Home Office Research Unit. This study lasted for eight years and was designed to discover whether particular types of treatment were more effective than others when dealing with different types of offenders.

The National Study of Probation, which was the central part of the Probation Research Project, consisted of several projects of which the main one was concerned with 17 to 21 year old males who were placed on probation in 1964 in eight large cities. In addition other supporting research was undertaken at the same time which included methods of predicting reconviction (Simon, 1971), stresses in the lives of probationers (Davies, 1969), group work in probation (Barr, 1966) and probation hostels (Sinclair, 1971). Even though the results of all this research into different aspects of probation was far from being completely negative, a point to which I'll return shortly, it seems reasonable to conclude that probation was not found to be significantly more effective in preventing reconviction than other disposals. Further support for this conclusion was found in a study by Hammond of the Home Office Research Unit, who produced the results of research into the reconviction rates of offenders who had received a range of different sentences by the courts. The information for this study emerged from research into all convicted offenders in the Metropolitan Police District during March and April, 1957. When evaluating the effectiveness in preventing reoffending of different types of treatment given to first and recidivist offenders, one of Hammond's main findings was that probation, on the whole, was just as likely as other sentences to result in reconviction. Subsequently Hood and Sparks (1970) concluded after considering both the findings of Hammond and Wilkins, in addition to other studies, that 'It must be emphasised, however, that the research just discussed cannot be interpreted as showing that probation is especially effective as a method of treatment' (pp 187–188).

Furthermore after considering the research of Hammond, Raynor commented that Hammond's findings 'held little encouragement for those who regarded effective rehabilitation as the main justification for probation orders' (Raynor, 1985, p12).

Finally, reference should be made to one other significant research study, significant because it was the last major research project carried out by the Home Office Research Unit on the probation order, thus bringing to an end the Probation Research Project started in 1961. This was the IMPACT study – Intensive Matched Probation and After-Care Treatment (Folkard et al, 1974; 1976).

The IMPACT experiment was designed to test whether more intensive treatment directed at the situational problems of 'high risk' offenders (that is problems relating to family, school, work, leisure and peer group) would produce better results in terms of reconviction rates. The research was carried out in close collaboration with the probation services of Dorset, Inner London, Sheffield and Staffordshire and was influenced by the research already completed by Davies (1969) and Folkard (1974), which showed that 'situational' problems were strongly related to reconviction rates in probationers. Furthermore Clarke and Cornish (1983, p26f) said that IMPACT took account of the main findings of 'Types of Offender and Types of Treatment' research, the purpose of which was explained in Probation Research : A Preliminary Report (Folkard et al, 1966) and whose results were summarised in the first volume of the IMPACT study (Folkard et al, 1974), where it was stated that 'Many of the negative findings might seem to suggest that treatment has no effect or even that it makes offenders worse rather than better' (pp9-10).

Consequently IMPACT took account of all this previous research when the empirical work commenced in 1972. A number of probation officers in the selected areas were given substantially reduced caseloads (20 instead of the usual 40 to 45) in the hope that more intensive treatment would produce better results. However once the research was completed the main negative finding was that there were 'no significant differences in one year reconviction rates between the experimental and the control cases, therefore producing no evidence to support a general application of more intensive treatment' (Folkard et al, 1976, pp22-23).

All the findings of the IMPACT research were not completely negative, but IMPACT did nothing to suggest that treatment delivered to offenders within the context of a probation order was particularly effective at preventing recidivism. This raised fundamental questions concerning the rationale of probation supervision, the implications of which the probation service has perhaps not rigorously enough considered. IMPACT was so embarrassing that the service would rather forget about its negative findings, which led Clarke and Corinsh to conclude that

> Given the results of their own earlier researches and the
> increasing scepticism amongst many criminologists about the value
> of probation treatment, the directors of IMPACT would hardly have
> been surprised by its largely negative results... The project's

main significance for them may have been that it marked the end of the probation research programme which had begun in some optimism fifteen years before, and which, in the search for effective treatment, had proceeded up so many inviting avenues only to discover they were dead ends (1983, pp28-29).

The largely negative findings into probation treatment have been, to some degree, replicated in a number of other empirical studies, the results of which will now be briefly mentioned.

Martinson, in Viewpoint on Rehabilitation (Carter and Wilkins, 1976, Chapter 4) explained that in 1966 a comprehensive New York State survey was commissioned to discover what was known about rehabilitation. A massive number of research reports were collected on the subject which had been published between 1945 and 1967, until eventually 231 reports were considered suitable for analysis. When the evaluation was completed the results were thought to be so damaging that publication was nearly suppressed by those who had originally commissioned the study. However the results were eventually published in 1975 by Lipton, Martinson and Wilks. Prior to this, in 1974, Martinson produced a summary of the main findings concluding that 'With few and isolated exceptions, the rehabilitative efforts that have been reported so far have had no appreciable effects on recidivism' (p25).

This conclusion was based on an evaluation of rehabilitative methods which included small probation caseloads, intensive supervision in specialised caseloads, casework and individual counselling and many others. Similar conclusions were also arrived at by Clarke and Sinclair (1974) who had undertaken research into the effectiveness of treatment on behalf of the Council of Europe and who said that 'there is now little reason to believe that any one of the widely used methods of treating offenders is much better at preventing reconviction than any other' (1974).

Furthermore Brody (1976) in his analysis of nearly 70 studies from different countries, cast doubt on the rehabilitative efficacy of different treatment programmes, particularly if probation is used for first offenders and confirmed recidivists.

It is also interesting to consider the Cambridge-Somerville Youth Study which was a randomized experiment began by Richard Clark Cabot in 1939 and lasted for a period of five years. The experiment aimed to examine the effects of a treatment programme on a number of predelinquents in Boston, some of whom were assigned to the treatment programme, and others to a control group. What is interesting about this particular programme is that during 1975-1976 McCord traced 488 of the original 506 members of the experiment (McCord, 1978). McCord discovered from the records she studied that there were no differences between the men who received 'treatment' and those who received none. Moreover

> a higher proportion of criminals from the treatment group than of criminals from the control group committed more than one crime...Among the men with criminal records from the treatment group, 78% committed at least two crimes; among the men with criminal records from the control group, 67% committed at least two crimes(p286).

Therefore, it appears that treatment may sometimes do more harm than good.

Nevertheless even though a large number of studies produced negative findings, there are some positive features. For example, Hood and Sparks (1970, p191f) refered to a study by Bailey in 1966 which indicated some positive features of treatment and Brody (1978, p135) recognised that treatment was shown to be effective when applied to certain types of offenders, when adapted to the particular requirements of individuals and when it was aimed at modifying aspects of behaviour such as addiction or aggressiveness. Moreover Pease has stated that there is some empirical evidence which suggests that offenders may be changed in ways which can affect the likelihood of reoffending (1985, p74). This has found some support in Nigel Walker's consideration of the figures produced by the six year follow-up study of Philpotts and Lancucki, which reveals that when probation is used for men convicted for the first time and after many previous convictions, the results are not encouraging in terms of preventing reconviction. Nevertheless some positive findings were discovered when probation and fines were used with men with a few previous convictions (1983). Even Martinson subsequently modified his initial negative conclusions (Cullen and Gilbert, 1982, p170f).

Finally the IMPACT study produced a 'differential treatment effect' in the sense that those offenders who did better under more intensive supervision (in the experimental group) were those with relatively low criminal tendencies but had many personal problems which had been identified by using the Mooney Problem Checklist. Conversely those who did better under 'normal' probation supervision (the control group) were those offenders who had relatively high criminal tendencies and an average to low number of personal problems, although it must be said that the results did not achieve statistical significance. Therefore one may conclude that the results of all this research discussed above are somewhat equivocal and that it would be wrong to state categorically that 'nothing works'. It seems that some treatments do work sometimes for certain offenders, but there is no one particular treatment which works equally well for all offenders (Hudson, 1987, p28f; Walker, 1987, Chapter 8).

Conclusion

Even though academic criminologists, some officials at the Home Office and some probation practitioners, have acknowledged the research which has questioned the treatment efficacy of the probation order, there is still some evidence to show that the notion of treatment will not be completely abandoned in day-to-day practice situations. In fact, there is some empirical support for this claim in the research of Boswell who, after interviewing one hundred probation officers in three different area services, discovered that they frequently referred to the language of treatment in the sense of diagnosing client problems with a view to eradicating them from the client's personality (1982, p113). Moreover it is rather interesting to note at this stage that the probation service in which this research was undertaken appears committed to some notion of rehabilitation in the mid-1980s. But more of this later.

Notwithstanding the qualifications which have been made in relation to the largely negative research findings which have now been considered, one is forced to conclude with the former Chief Probation Officer (now Chief Inspector) who said that the 'critical findings about the general outcome of treatment cannot be ignored - the evidence is too strong. The certainties of our traditional knowledge

17

base have gone and we must live with the uncertainties of empiricism..'(Thomas, 1978, p30).

This situation has resulted in Croft posing the question: 'Will this challenge evoke a response by prison and probation officers by the invention of new approaches and methods'? (1978, p4).

To some degree the question asked by Croft, specifically as it applies to the probation service, has elicited a response. Consequently what follows in the next chapter is an analysis of the way in which the decline of consensus in probation work has been responded to and reconceptualised by academics, most of whom have worked as probation officers earlier on in their careers, by focusing mainly on the probation order in terms of practice, ideology and rationale, care and control. By systematically considering the work of Harris, Bryant et al, Bottoms and McWilliams, Raynor, advocates of social control in probation and the Marxist thesis of Walker and Beaumont, it will be established that there are a rich diversity of views on probation supervision. At this stage it is important to focus on the dimensions of practice, ideology and axiology, before saying more about the theme of probation as an alternative to custody, which will assume greater significance later on.

2 The post-rehabilitive era in probation: academic models

'Pure' social work-assistance model

In two papers produced by Robert Harris (1977, 1980) he argued that since the mid-1960's the probation service has experienced rapid change and expansion in the functions it performs, resulting in the service being drawn to the centre of penal policy. This has created a complex situation in which different probation tasks have different underlying philosophies, culminating in a problem of occupational meaning (1980, p164) and an accentuation of occupational stress, a consequence of probation officers trying to hold together an increasing number of conflicting and competing functions. Therefore Harris argued that probation officers experience dissonance at three levels. Firstly, there is moral dissonance, which is the gap between the justice ideology of society and the welfare ideology of social work. Secondly, technical dissonance is the gap between the task of reducing crime through supervision and the failure, in reality, to do so. For Harris clearly accepts that the probation service is not at all successful at reducing or preventing crime, nor does social work training equip the probation officer to do so. Finally, there is operational dissonance, which concerns the complex relationship between care and control. It is argued that probation officers have responded in various ways to stress and dissonance but the point is that dissonance is more probable now than was the case in the 1960's.

One of his central arguments is that the probation service should no longer attempt to simultaneously hold together its caring and controlling functions, rather they should be distinctly separated. It is also worth noting that Satyamurti, towards the end of the 1970's, believed that the 'crisis in social work' was a result of attempting to reconcile care and control within the occupational role of the local authority social worker (1979).

To support the argument Harris also considered that the relationship between the probation service, magistrates and the public requires reconceptualisation, for there is a gap between what the public and courts are getting from the probation service and what they perceive they are getting. For example, the probation order includes various requirements, as we have already seen. The officer should ensure that the probationer adheres to these requirements, but often turns a blind eye thus not rigidly enforcing them by returning the offender to court.

It is the contention of Harris that the probation service should no longer be entrusted to carry out the statutory orders of the court. This role should be undertaken instead by a different agency whose function would be to provide community based punishments, free from the pretension of giving help or treatment to offenders. At the present time the probation officer experiences role conflict when trying to balance the demands of magistrates to carry out the statutory duties of court orders and the expectation to work with offenders in a way that is consistent with his training as a professional social worker. Therefore the solution to the problems, stresses and conflicts is to unambiguously separate care and control. Accordingly the service should be transformed into a court-based social work service

> to provide a highly trained, caring and effective social work
> service to a disadvantaged section of the community :   the

offender. It can help him with accommodation, social security, jobs; it can give him counselling with many personal problems; it can teach him social skills; it can help with marital or family difficulties (1977, p436; 1980, pp180-181).

Such a clear separation of care and control would ensure, argued Harris, in magistrates getting what they want and expect from community punishments, which would enable the probation service to focus on providing a caring service to all those in need within the criminal justice system on a voluntary basis. In other words, one should explicitly dissociate treatment from punishment (1977, p441), which can only result in both the courts and clients getting the best out of the probation service.

In conclusion, Harris said that the present system is ineffective because compulsory supervision makes little difference to the likelihood of reoffending; it is also inappropriate because non-social work magistrates control client referral to trained social workers; it denies many offenders the provision of social work help in cases where statutory court orders have not been imposed; it is also dishonest because magistrates do not always get from the probation service what they expect; and it does not allow trained social workers to practice their professional skills because of time spent performing tasks for which they were not trained (1977, p441).

I suspect that a number of probation officers would be sympathetic to the analysis of Harris concerning role conflict, the stress of reconciling the conflicting philosophies of different functions, the reality of confusion and dissonance, whilst probably not arriving at his conclusions. However in the penal and political climate of the late 1980's which is more conducive to the development of a range of community-based punishments as opposed to government funding for the social work, caring service advocated by Harris, it is as unrealistic to believe that his theoretical arguments will be translated into practice as it is to believe that custodial sentences will be abolished for juveniles, or that the adult prison population will be drastically reduced. Conceptually the model eliminates many contemporary problems and dilemmas and is attractive at this level, but as a prescription for future probation practice it seems destined never to get off the ground. To be fair, Harris acknowledged this problem when he concluded that

> The model is not offered as a blueprint for action and I do not suggest that it could be quickly or easily implemented. Accordingly I am more concerned with its theoretical and ethical assumptions than with immediate practicability and I do not deal with organisational questions or with issues of political realism (1980, p179).

Even though Harris does not retain the probation order within his reconceptualised probation service, his model should be included in this chapter as an example of the practice and philosophy of probation work divorced from the statutory orders of the court and based purely on a voluntary social work-assistance approach to individual offenders in need.

Two contract model

If the model of Harris finds no place for the statutory probation order, Bryant et al (1978) argued for a reconceptualised probation order which is concerned with aspects of practicability. The probation officers who proposed this model accepted the research which questioned the efficacy of supervision to reduce crime and concluded that it is therefore necessary to separate the legal requirements of the probation order from its social work component into two distinct contracts.

Firstly, the 'primary contract' would be made by the court and include the court and offender. If the court considered an offender could be appropriately dealt with by supervision in the community then the court would impose the order, specifying its length and frequency of reporting. If the offender subsequently reported as directed by the court to the probation service, he would fulfil all statutory requirements which could be verified by checking the reporting record sheet kept at the reception desk at the probation office.

Secondly, it would also be possible to include a 'subsidiary contract' which would be made between the probation officer and probationer. This would consist in the offer of help and provision of social work assistance, but which would be requested by the client and not imposed as treatment by the probation officer. This means that a failure to comply with the subsidiary contract would not constitute a breach of the primary contract. Within this model no longer will social work be enforced onto unwilling clients, but a range of welfare services will be made available to clients should they wish to make use of them. These services would include individual counselling, help with family problems, group work, education, welfare rights advice, development of work skills, information about jobs, day training centres and hostels. Accordingly this model has been described as the 'shop window' approach.

Bryant et al intended that this approach would encourage clients to deal with their own problems, treat them as responsible individuals and preserve the principle of self determination. The authors also considered that magistrates would have more faith in probation orders if they could determine the length and frequency of reporting. In saying this it answers some of the criticisms of Harris, but whereas Harris argued for a clear separation of care and control resulting in the probation service being identified with the former rather than the latter, Bryant et al argued for retaining both care and control within the statutory probation order, but on the basis of redefining their parameters and the basis upon which both would be provided. Consequently probation becomes a punishment on the tariff of court disposals, but social work assistance will be on offer to clients should they choose to take advantage of such facilities.

One of the potential problems of this model is that the probation order could degenerate into a rigid exercise of monitoring and perhaps inconveniencing clients, by accentuating surveillance and routinisation at the expense of help and befriending clients, which are traditionally associated with probation supervision (James, 1979). Furthermore Beaumont has criticised the Sentenced To Social Work? model because the social work element appears too impersonal and passive. Beaumont argued that probation officers need to be more positive when offering and providing assistance than this model seems to advocate (1984a, p29).

Notwithstanding these criticisms, one of the architects of the model returned to the debate against the background of criticisms and misconceptions by reaffirming that Sentenced To Social Work? was primarily concerned to clarify the various dimensions of the probation

23

order. It was not concerned with more control or a proposal for a 'beefed-up' form of probation. After reviewing and elucidating the model Coker stated that it 'retains the best of probation practice, meets contemporary criticisms of the Service and describes a better service to courts and clients' (1984, p125).

Non-treatment model

Perhaps the best known reconceptualisation of probation practice amongst practitioners is the non-treatment paradigm of Bottoms and McWilliams (1979). Their programmatic is clear:

> We believe there is a need for a new paradigm of probation practice which is theoretically rigorous; which takes seriously the exposed limitations of the treatment model, but which seeks to redirect the probation service's traditional aims and values in the new penal and social context (1979, p167).

The authors discuss the main elements of probation practice by claiming that the four basic aims of the service have been and should continue to be:

The provision of appropriate help to offenders
The statutory supervision of offenders
Diverting appropriate offenders from custodial sentences
The reduction of crime.

Where the first aim is concerned, Bottoms and McWilliams argue against treatment provided by social work experts which is understood as something forced onto offenders without prior consultation and which is paternalistically delivered after a one-sided process of assessment and diagnosis. They also state that

> both overt moral correctionalism and the 'objective attitude' are to be eschewed if the aim is an adequate understanding of clients as real people - and such an understanding may well be an essential prerequisite to offering clients adequate help (p171).

The word 'help' is one of the central concepts of the model. Probation officers may be involved in helping clients with various practical and emotional problems, but the important feature of help here is that it must be defined by the client. The rationale of practice based on the principle of help is that it faces the problem of the collapse of treatment whilst retaining the traditional values of respect for persons and hope for the future. The authors also argue that the provision of help as opposed to treatment is more

24

likely to facilitate a response to the expressed needs of clients (p174). Consequently in this model treatment becomes help; diagnosis becomes shared assessment; client's dependent need as the basis for social work action becomes collaboratively defined task as the basis for social work action. Moreover the authors tentatively suggest that there is a little evidence that providing help may even reduce crime.

After examining the practice and philosophy of help as opposed to treatment, Bottoms and McWilliams proceed under their second aim to look at the statutory supervision of offenders. It is clear to the authors that probation officers cannot escape the dimension of control and surveillance when supervising clients on probation orders. In fact, they affirm that a law-enforcement role is a legitimate aspect of the job. But there are two important points which should be emphasised. Firstly, the authors stress the importance of probation officers discussing with offenders, prior to attending court, all the possible sentencing alternatives the court might consider which are commensurate with the offences committed. If probation is then offered to the court by the probation officer as the disposal by which to deal with the offender, it must be done with the offender's full knowledge of what the order implies concerning how much control and surveillance will be imposed. The offender must also consent to the order. Secondly, and at this point Bottoms and McWilliams duplicate the position of Bryant et al, it is stated that the court should decide the length and frequency of reporting when client's are placed on probation. However, within the context of such an order the client should have the right to accept or reject social work help. And to the question, why should courts place offenders on probation, the authors reply that

> if courts can be persuaded to see that probation meets the community's wish for surveillance, whilst also allowing the client to select appropriate assistance if desired, then indeed there are sound reasons to make such orders (p179).

The third aim explores diverting offenders from custody and the final aim discusses the elusive goal of crime reduction.

These, therefore, are the main elements of the non-treatment paradigm delineated by Bottoms and McWilliams against the background of the collapse of rehabilitation, which has created a considerable vacuum within the probation service. Throughout they have emphasised the client's perspective, the centrality of help which must be defined by the client and the maximisation of client choice. Specifically where probation supervision is concerned, control is seen as a legitimate aspect of probation work but this does not mean that probation should simply be a form of containment or surveillance. On the contrary, probation must offer clients the opportunity to receive positive help and assistance. And as offenders must consent to the imposition of probation orders, so too must offenders choose whether or not to receive social work help which is offered by the probation service.

Conflict management and problem solving model

Peter Raynor (1985) also believes that the concept of help is important. He accepts that rehabilitation through casework is now a redundant unifying ideology in the probation service, a point established by the end of the first part of his book. Subsequently (from chapter 4) he reconceptualises the social work task in relation to offenders and the wider criminal justice system, taking as his starting point the concept of help as it is articulated by Bottoms and McWilliams. Raynor also argues that negotiation, client responsibility and informed choice, are principles which should be emphasised rather than coercion or imposed diagnosis, which leads him to delineate the details of social work practice consistent with these principles.

One of the central features of this model is the social work value of respect for persons by which Raynor means respect for people as moral agents, rational beings and as ends in themselves. Therefore if social work is to be consistent with this value orientation it will have to commit itself to endorsing client choice and self-determination as opposed to directive and coercive work. After discussing the arguments of Plant, Halmos, Downie and Telfer, Raynor claimed that

> Respect for persons seems to require that interference be strictly limited to the minimum amount necessary and that attempts to influence should rely not on one-sided processes like coercion or imposed diagnosis, but on two-sided participatory processes

resembling negotiation and dialogue (p96).

The argument is then developed by examining the literature on approaches to dialogue and negotiation which has influenced social work, notably the concept of 'conscientization' in Freire and 'problem-solving' in Burton. This leads Raynor to suggest that instead of understanding the role of the probation officer as providing expert diagnosis and a treatment for crime, in future the officer's role should be understood in terms of a negotiator and mediator between all those affected by crime (p105). Accordingly the probation service has something useful to offer the criminal justice system by contributing to and improving its functioning. However probation officers find themselves involved in making demands on clients and the question must therefore be asked : when are directives and demands issued by probation officers consistent with a model which is stressing negotiation and non-coercive problem solving? In other words, how does Raynor approach the problem of reconciling care and control?

If we consider care and control in relation to the probation order specifically, Raynor would argue that the social work principle of respect for persons can be reconciled with the demands and controlling elements inherent in such orders. In language reminiscent of Bottoms and McWilliams he says that probation officers must be open and honest with offenders when all dimensions and implications of probation are being discussed. This means clarifying the reasons why the order is being suggested, ensuring that the client consents to the order after being made explicitly aware of its requirements, in addition to the likely courses of action available to the court should the offender not consent to probation. The principle being articulated here is 'choice under constraint' (p116) and when justifying control Raynor argues that

> probation officers... can make demands on offenders within the context of a court order not because offenders are inherently incapable of self-direction but because, and only in so far as, the nature and scope of the demands have been agreed in advance. Such principles are consistent with moral assumptions about respect for persons and the importance of client's choices (p123).

The model of probation work in a reformulated criminal justice

27

system articulated by Raynor is a participatory, problem solving, dispute management model, in which negotiated and agreed outcomes are preferred to imposed goals and one-sided procedures (p136). Like Christie (1982) he takes us beyond both punishment and treatment to a position where the probation officer can help offenders, victims, the court and the wider community (an enlarged negotiation system), who may all be involved in criminal disputes, to work out a more rational and satisfactory way of putting matters right. And in what I consider to be an important passage in the book, Raynor makes his position clear by stating that

> We should no longer simply ask ourselves 'Are we providing effective treatments?' or 'Are we inflicting consistent punishment?', but should consider whether we are providing opportunities for those involved in and affected by offences to be dealt with in ways that respect their perceptions, responsibilities, needs and potential contribution to setting matters right. The institution of criminal justice then appears not as a set of arrangements for eliminating crime (which it cannot do) but as a system whose outcomes can contribute to a more satisfactory way of living with the consequences of crime. Possibilities of this kind seem to lie in the pursuit of the two linked aims of promoting constructive participation and reducing avoidable coercion (p142).

Finally, Raynor makes out a case for probation orders with extra conditions, which he refers to as 'enhanced' probation (p190f). However enhanced probation orders should not be used unless they meet certain specific criteria which may be summarised as follows:

1) Making extra demands should reflect the greater perceived seriousness of the offence.
2) Probation orders with extra conditions should not be solely punitive but provide opportunities for constructive help.
3) Help provided to clients must be based on joint assessment and therefore relate to client problems.
4) Extra conditions should be negotiated and agreed and have the consent of the client.
5) Such programmes which involve extra conditions should be monitored and evaluated to determine whether or not actual practice conforms to the above criteria.

I have spent some time presenting the essential features of Raynor's model because it is perhaps the most comprehensive response so far to the 'where are we going now' probation debate, precipitated by the collapse of rehabilitation. He attempts to redefine the role of the probation officer in a reformulated criminal justice system and argues forcibly for a reduction of coercion with a corresponding increase of those humanitarian values which focus on the notion of respect for persons, thus preserving the social work dimension of probation work. Consequently Raynor endorses certain humanitarian values which comes as a timely reminder when the probation service is being pushed in the direction of overt social control in order to survive in the contemporary penal climate, and in order to appear as a credible organisation which can offer the courts viable alternatives to custody. It is feared that more control will result in the diminution of social work values, culminating in the service becoming simply an adjunct of the state's law and order services. In some respects Raynor's philosophy is swimming against the flow of recent developments. Therefore at this point one must turn to consider in some detail the growing concern with the issue of control in probation, before finally examining the views of those who have theorised on the elements of a radical or socialist probation practice which unambiguously opposes the drift towards more control.

Control model
Over recent years coercion and control have been making inroads into the probation service which has thrown into sharp relief the tension between care and control, producing a voluminous literature throughout the 1970's, as well as generating confusion concerning the future direction of the probation service, its professional identity, and its place within the criminal justice system. Essentially the problem has been articulated in the following way

> The service has to be continually aware of the dichotomy between the demands arising from its place in social work with objectives concerned with the well-being of individual offenders and demands arising from its place in the criminal justice system concerned with the preservation of law and order in society (Thomas, 1978, p29).

This seemingly unresolved tension has culminated in the dimension of control being accentuated in the 1980's, even though social work values have not been completely abandoned. To understand how the service has arrived at this point requires a brief historical

29

excursion. The following analysis also provides a preamble to the discussion in the next chapter on the Home Office plan for the future of the service.

In 1966 the probation service assumed responsibility for prison welfare and after-care, followed in 1968 by parole which involved the service in the regulation, surveillance and control of offenders. Further developments following the 1972 Criminal Justice Act brought the service into the arena of delivering punishment with the inception of community service, although this sentence includes a reparative element. But when Jordan (1971) reflected on developments within the service during the 1960's, he began his analysis by quoting from the Morison Report of 1962 which said that the probation officer was a professional caseworker who employed skills shared with other social workers, in addition to being concerned with the protection of society. Jordan argued that this reflected the conflicting functions which the probation officer was trying to hold in balance at this time but which, since Morison, had been disturbed, forcing the service to choose between its two roles. How did Jordan account for this?

Firstly the Longford Report of 1964 recommended that young offenders should receive treatment thus preventing the stigma associated with the penal system. Because the probation service was closely identified with the courts, Longford envisaged that the local authority social worker would replace the probation officer in this area of work. Secondly Seebohm presented the service with a profound dilemma. If it resisted the plans for a combined social services department it ran the risk of no longer being in the mainstream of social work by becoming more and more identified with the penal system. However if it cooperated with Seebohm it risked losing its autonomy (which happened to the service in Scotland). In short, the service objected to Longford, including the 1965 White Paper and refused to be integrated with social services, which led Jordan to comment that

> Instead of seeking new ways to improve the treatment of offenders, the probation service has devoted its energies to opposing the changes advocated by the Labour Party, and in doing so has taken on the appearance of being one of the established interests of the legal system.

Therefore

> How can we account for these changes in probation officer's attitudes? Why did the probation service turn away from the body of social work in which it was pre-eminent and stress its uniqueness and the prime importance of its legal setting?

Jordan answered by arguing that as social work developed a more family-based approach in the 1960's, the probation service continued working on a one-to-one basis. It even persisted with this style of working after developments in sociology had directed attention away from the individual offender to the social structure, which should have resulted in more community involvement. Jordan claimed that probation remained predominantly an individualistic enterprise, preferring the safety of the court setting and the legal definitions of their work that this provides. His argument was that throughout the 1960's the service developed in the direction of the penal system rather than local authority social work. It preferred parole with its legally defined sanctions to voluntary after-care, which was divorced from the courts and juridical setting. The service also preferred the legally enforceable conditions of the probation relationship. Jordan is probably at fault for overstating his case and by generalising too much. Moreover there were those in the service who opposed controlling developments in the 1970's. However it is probably correct to say that the contemporary dilemma concerning care and control can be traced to these events in the 1960's, whose ramifications were to be experienced throuhgout the 1970's and up to the present day.

In 1972, one year after Jordan's analysis, Davies said that in the past the service had mainly provided oversight of offenders. Reflecting on the future he claimed that something more than oversight would be required if more offenders were to be dealt with in the community. By this Davies meant that if offenders with many personal and social problems were to be supervised in the community they will 'need to be supervised in a more positive sense than has traditionally been possible for probationers' (p321).

By the 21st May 1974 perhaps the kind of development Davies envisaged appeared in the proposals contained in the report of the Advisory Council on the Penal System - Young Adult Offenders (Home

31

Office, 1974). This report was the culmination of a review of the treatment of offenders aged between 17 and 21 years, which began in April 1970 under the chairmanship of Sir Kenneth Younger. The two main sentencing proposals were firstly, a custody and control order, which would be imposed in cases where a custodial sentence was unavoidable. Secondly, and more importantly, was the proposal for a supervision and control order which would enable a greater measure of control over the offender than a probation order. Immediately the probation service was worried about the control implications of these proposals.

Turning to the supervision and control order specifically, a new form of control in the community was envisaged which would have been stricter than traditional probation supervision. Moreover offenders would not be required to consent to the imposition of the order. What seemed to cause the service most consternation was the proposal to give the probation officer the power to obtain a warrant to effect the detention of an offender for up to 72 hours in situations where it was considered the offender was in danger of breaching the requirements of the order, where a breach had already occurred, or where a probation officer believed the commission of a further offence was likely.

In December 1974 a special issue of the Probation Journal appeared which contained a selection of articles on Younger's proposals. One was by Younger himself who, after acknowledging the controversial nature of some of the proposals, threw down a challenge to the service by asking how it proposed to deal with more serious offenders in the community as an alternative to custody if not by exercising more control which was a prerequisite for obtaining the support of the courts and public? Once again the issue of control was raised, an issue which has been the achilles heel of the probation service over the last twenty years.

Irrespective of the logic of Younger's proposals it must be acknowledged that the report was controversial and that it touched a nerve which resulted in the service resoundingly rejecting Younger. Moreover it was met with 6 notes of reservation or dissent involving two-thirds of the ACPS membership which had produced the report. Subsequently NAPO asseverated that

32

there is already negative reaction to the proposed 72 hour detention within the Supervision and Control Order to suggest that this would be unacceptable to the majority of the service... Even without the 72 hour detention, there would be many reservations about the proposed Supervision and Control Order (Probation Journal, 1974, p117).

Notwithstanding the rejection of Younger, in the mid-1970's the possibility of developing a more tough form of probation was not entirely abandoned, which has elicited the comment that the defeat of Younger was only a temporary setback in the development of the community control of offenders (Harris and Webb, 1987, p44). For in 1980 the Kent Control Unit, which emerged out of the Close Support Unit (intensive supervision for juveniles) was opened. This required probationers to attend a specified place for six days per week for a period of six months as a condition of a probation order. The Unit emphasised deterrence and containment rather than assessing the needs of the individual client or the provision of appropriate help, which elicited criticism from those probation officers who saw in such developments a breach of social work traditions (see discussion in Spencer and Edwards, 1986). When the Kent Control Unit was established, probation powers were defined mainly by the Powers of Criminal Courts Act, 1973. Section 4 of the Act provided for the attendance of a probationer at a Day Training Centre as a condition of probation, and attendance was strictly limited to 60 days at those centres established in London, Liverpool, Sheffield, and Pontypridd. However, Section 2 stated that

a probation order may in addition require the offender to comply during the whole or any part of the probation period with such requirements as the court... considers necessary for securing the good conduct of the offender...(S2 (3)).

It was Section 2 (3) that Kent claimed as the authority to justify offenders attending the Control Unit and there is little doubt that what was happening in Kent became the focus of attention of the care-control debate within the service. But was the Control Unit a legitimate use of the provisions of Section 2 or was the probation service overreaching its powers?

In 1981 an interesting and significant development occurred which temporarily decelerated the spread of control. A probationer who had been ordered to attend a Day Centre (not a Day Training Centre) as a condition of a probation order was prosecuted for failing to attend. She appealed on the grounds that such a condition was invalid which was surprisingly upheld by the Divisional Court. Even more surprising, perhaps, was that the House of Lords endorsed the decision of the Divisional Court and clarified that the condition was invalid, there being no power under Section 2 (3) of the 1973 Act to include a condition in a probation order to attend a Day Centre. Subsequently the Rogers v. Cullen judgement in 1982 gave rise to two major amendments to the power to impose a probation order after Lord Bridge said that

> the power to impose requirements (under S.2 (3) of the 1973 Act) must be subject to some limitation in at least two respects. First, since the making of a probation order is a course taken by the court to avoid passing a sentence, a requirement imposed under S.2 (3) must not introduce such a custodial or other element as will amount in substance to the imposition of a sentence. Secondly, since it is the court alone which can define the requirements of the order, any discretion conferred on the probation officer pursuant to the terms of the order to regulate a probationer's activities must itself be confined within well defined limits (Stone, 1988).

Consequently because courts could no longer include a requirement to attend a Day Centre as a condition of probation and because breach proceedings for failure to attend could not be brought against offenders, the opportunity was taken during the passage through Parliament of the Criminal Justice Act, 1982, to give courts additional powers.

It may be strongly argued that the dimension of control within probation has been escalating over the last two decades. Control has its supporters within the service who believe that it will make the process of supervision more credible to the courts, result in more probation orders being imposed, and because it is expected that closer control in the community will achieve a diminution of the prison population. For it has been stated in the 1980's that the service should provide

> a non-custodial disposal that will be seen not only as an acceptable option to prison, but as a punitive, retributive and controlling facility in its own right, hard enough to replace prison as the preferred short-term sentence...(Davies, 1982).

34

We have also heard a former Chief Probation Officer articulate a policy of probation supervision based on discipline, containment and surveillance (Griffiths, 1982a, 1982b). Furthermore a review of articles contained in the Probation Journal over the last decade or more reveals how the issue of control has generated interest, debate and controversy (Beaumont, 1976; Chapman, 1977; Burnham, 1981; Drakeford, 1983; Jordan, 1983).

To conclude this lengthy but necessary analysis of the development of control and by way of introducing the authors whose views counter such developments, Walker and Beaumont have perceived a 'coercive tilt' within the service (1981, p152) and claimed that 'there can be little doubt that a slow shift towards the use of more coercive measures and greater restrictions on both clients and probation officers is continuing' (1985, p14). It is to Walker and Beaumont that one must finally turn in this chapter for arguments which oppose the development of control.

Radical model
After considering the four major tasks of the service in Probation Work-Critical Theory and Socialist Practice (1981), identified as social enquiry reports, probation orders, prison welfare and after-care, and after differentiating between 'official' and 'practice' accounts of these four tasks, the authors present a Marxist perspective of probation work in the theoretical section of the book. Walker and Beaumont begin their analysis by examining the connections between probation and wider economic, structural and political factors within society. They discuss the State and specifically the function and ideological role performed by welfare services and the criminal justice system, in the way both apparently preserve and promote a capitalist economic system.

Walker and Beaumont argue that the role of the probation service should be understood in a similar way, because it is involved in the reproduction of capitalist social relations, the individualisation of crime and the promotion of integration and consensus in society. To illustrate their argument they claim that probation officers reproduce capitalist social relations by pressurising offenders to conform to the norms of society, encouraging them to find work, to accept authority, to use leisure time constructively and the way in which capitalist sexual relations are maintained. Therefore the authors say that 'A fundamental conclusion of our analysis is that probation officers are paid to do a particular job for the state and that this role is generally supportive of capitalism' (1981, p160).

Consistent with this analysis is the way the probation service has, throughout its history, concentrated on the individual offender, which of course dominated the period of rehabilitation through casework in the 1950's and 1960's. This conceptual framework is rejected because its

> focus on the individual all but obscures the class issues involved in the law and its enforcement - for example the unequal distribution of wealth, the way the law bears heavily on working-class dishonesty and the effects of discriminatory policing. This concentration on differentness hides common causes and redirects possibilities for collective action into the search for individual solutions (1981, p148).

Notwithstanding this interpretation, Walker and Beaumont acknowledge that contradictions exist within probation work, because many of these pressures are resisted by probation officers when working with clients. This results in officers finding themselves in the invidious position of being both "in and against the state" (1981, p158). Accordingly there is some room for manoeuvre and the scope to develop a socialist probation practice within a service which, so it is argued, performs tasks conducive to capitalism, which is explored in the final chapter of the book (1981, p162). Within the context of an approach characterised by resisting a correctionalist perspective, taking the opportunity to discuss the oppressive nature of the criminal justice system and being open and honest with clients, the authors proceed to discuss six areas of progressive practice in relation to the three spheres of personal practice, the agency and the union. The following are examples taken from the sphere of personal practice.

Firstly there is defensive work which means defending clients against the criminal justice system and advocating the minimum use of custody, in addition to the minimum use of breach and recall procedures and resisting the use of extra conditions in probation orders.

Secondly is helping, understood as providing help clients themselves require, which may include both practical and emotional help. This is the way in which Bottoms and McWilliams understood the concept of help.

Next educational work and, fourthly, the development of useful services which specifically meet the needs of clients.

Fifthly community involvement, which could mean involvement with local tenants organisations and claimants unions to broaden the ability to struggle within the state and to take criminal justice issues into the working-class movement.

Finally there is campaigning action which could mean campaigning for social change and changes within the criminal justice system.

Beaumont expanded on the meaning of 'progressive' practice elsewhere (1984) and later Walker and Beaumont developed their ideas when editing a collection of essays on various aspects of probation work (1985). Here the task was to consider in more detail than in their earlier book a socialist practice of court work, probation supervision, day centre work and prison work. Whilst it is accepted that the political climate of the 1980's is not conducive to the practices advocated by the authors, nevertheless they conclude by saying that 'Persistence is needed to defend against oppressive encroachments, to provide useful help to clients, to resist and expose injustices and to exploit opportunities for constructive developments' (1985, pp140-141).

The analysis of Walker and Beaumont deserves careful consideration because it challenges the service to understand itself not in a vacuum, but in relation to the state in a capitalist society, the wider socio-economic structure and the political machinations of the criminal justice system. And even though many probation officers may not be able to identify with the Marxist theoretical framework of the authors, it is possible that they are involved in the kinds of progressive practices discussed above. There is no place in this analysis for the individualisation of what are argued to be social problems, the rehabilitation of offenders back into a society which is considered to be riddled with injustice and conflict, a correctionalist perspective, or the excessive use of surveillance, control and punishment. For by concentrating on the individual offender the authors argue that attention is being diverted away from the fundamental necessity to radically change the nature of society which is responsible for crime, thus overlooking that crime is a political and social construct.

Radicalism within the probation service is a relatively new phenomenon, because it was only in the 1970s that a number of probation officers began to acquire a political consciousness (Hugman, 1980). The book by Walker and Beaumont belongs to this tradition and whilst not explaining the aetiology of all offending, should be seriously considered as a model for probation work, particularly the prescriptions in the final chapter of the book (1981) which delineates the elements of a socialist probation practice. In the last analysis, it is important to the authors that

> there are probation officers prepared to state publicly that prison is destructive, that there are unjust laws, that law enforcement is discriminatory and even that the probation service cannot cope with the poverty and hardship our work uncovers (1981, p169).

Summary and conclusion

This chapter has considered a number of academic responses to the decline of faith in treatment within the probation service since the 1970's, particularly in relation to the probation order. The rationale of probation based upon rehabilitation through casework provided probation officers with the goal of reintegrating offenders back into a law abiding society where once more they could lead a normal life. And even though the language of rehabilitation and treatment is still heard and casework methods practiced (Boswell, 1982), from numerous theoretical and empirical standpoints it has been noticed that rehabilitation is now a questionable goal. Consequently out of the ideological vacuum has emerged a number of models which attempt to reformulate probation work in a changing epistemological, penal and political climate.

The elements of probation practice and underlying ideologies within the models have been touched on. However one of the most significant

38

features of these models which should be emphasised in this concluding section is how they may be located at different points on what may be described as a social work-social control continuum. Such is the diversity of views within the contemporary probation service that located at one extreme of the continuum is the 'pure' social work-assistance model of Harris, whilst at the opposite extreme is the control and punishment model of Davies and Griffiths. According to one model the morality, humanity and unconditional value of care and concern for offenders is explicit within a system which has abolished the statutory probation order. To the other the goals of containment and punishment are significant.

In the 'real' world of everyday practice it seems reasonable to assume that neither of these two models, located at opposite extremes of the continuum, accurately portrays the framework within which probation officers have operated. In other words, probation work is not a clear cut choice between care or control, but a complex combination of the two. There is some empirical support for this view in Fielding's research, based on interviewing 50 probation officers in 3 different services. He introduces the notion of the 'collapsed dichotomy' when discussing care and control. What I think he means by this is that both care and control become conflated in practice situations, in that caring involves controlling clients and that through control one demonstrates care and support. Fielding found that his respondents expressed difficulty in rigidly differentiating control and care. They did not see control and care as opposed ideologies (1984, p167). Therefore it is more likely that officers have operated probation orders within the framework of a model which occupies what may be described as the 'middle ground', represented by the models of Bryant, Bottoms and McWilliams, Raynor, Walker and Beaumont. These four models should not be seen in isolation or opposition because at certain points they overlap, complement and reinforce each other. One unifying characteristic is the way these four models are committed to providing social work help whilst acknowledging that a degree of social control is ineluctable within probation supervision.

To briefly recapitulate, Bryant et al considered that the court should specify the legal requirements of probation which would be monitored by the service. However a range of welfare services would be made available to clients on a voluntary basis, a view shared by Bottoms and McWilliams, and Raynor. This conceptual distinction is clarified by Raynor when commenting that the authority to make demands on clients comes from the court, but that the authority to help comes from the client (1985, p156). Where the concept of help is concerned Bottoms and McWilliams believe it addresses the collapse of treatment, yet retains the values of hope for the future and respect for persons (1979, p172). Moreover Bottoms and McWilliams, and Raynor, tentatively affirm that providing help may reduce crime. However to achieve this it seems important that there should be a high degree of consonance between what clients want and what the probation service offers (Raynor, 1985, p37). It is also useful to refer to Boswell again at this point because she found that, for some officers, helping offenders was important (1982, p112) and Willis discovered in his study of young adults on probation that the probation process was mainly concerned with providing welfare help rather than exercising social control (1986, pp162f).

Because Bottoms and McWilliams, and Raynor, attempt to balance both care and control in probation, their models can be located at a point midway between the two extremes of the continuum. However Bryant should be located nearer the control end of the continuum because this model could potentially develop into court imposed surveillance. Alternatively Walker and Beaumont may be located nearer the care end of the continuum because of their opposition to control, particularly the development of the widespread use of extra conditions. It is therefore possible to schematically present a typology of these models in Table 2.1 at the end of this chapter.

Given the diversity of academic ideas which have contended with each other over recent years, probation officers could be forgiven for feeling confused and uncertain about the nature of probation practice and philosophy and consequently their role in the post-rehabilitative era. Furthermore one must begin to question whether these models go far enough in their prescriptions of probation work which will convince the courts that the probation service can deliver credible

40

alternatives to custody for relatively serious offenders. For it may be postulated here that if the probation service is to provide realistic alternatives to custody in order to manage, contain and control more serious offenders in the community, then there will have to be something more than the contracts of Bryant et al, more than Bottoms and McWilliams' suggestion for a reformulated social enquiry report and more than an approach based on participation, problem solving and a reduction of coercion and control, proposed by Raynor and Walker and Beaumont respectively. It may well be the case, given the way the probation service is developing towards the end of the 1980s, that the models considered in this chapter do not adequately answer the question posed by Younger in the mid-1970s concerning how the probation service proposes to deal with the more serious offender in the community, as an alternative to custody, in cases where the standard probation order does not appear to be suitable.

Since the mid-1980's the Home Office has taken the initiative to reformulate probation practice which could have far reaching effects on the supervision of offenders in the community. In fact the Statement of National Objectives and Priorities could make a considerable difference to the issue of the probation service providing alternatives to custody. It is to this document that I turn in the next chapter.

Table 2.1
6 models of probation supervision

Model	Advocates	Practice	Ideology	Care/Control	Continuum
'Pure' Social Work	Harris	A social work service which helps with client problems	Care	Care and control should be separated	Care
Radical	Walker/ Beaumont	Progressive practice means helping clients with problems	Mitigate the harsh effects of the CJS	Minimum control	
Non-Treat't	Bottoms and McWill's	Client defined help	Retain the values of hope for the future and respect for persons	Balance between care and control	
Problem Solving	Raynor	Help; negotiation; participation; shared assessment; respect for persons	Manage conflicts	Balance between care and control	
Two Contract	Bryant et al	2 contracts; clients can receive help from welfare services	Increase confidence of the courts and encourage clients to deal with their own problems	Probation is a punishment but help is available on request by the client	
Control	Davies Griffiths	Punishment, control and surveillance	Enhance credibility with the courts	Emphasis on control	Control

3 SNOP and probation: a bureaucratic model

Introduction

The Statement of National Objectives and Priorities-SNOP (Home Office, 1984a) published by the Home Office in April 1984 is central government's plan for the probation service and is a direct response to what is known as the Financial Management Initiative (FMI). In fact SNOP is the document through which the principles underlying the FMI will be applied in the probation service during the second half of the 1980s and beyond. This may be explained by saying that during its first three years the Cabinet Office Efficiency Unit, established in 1979 under Sir Derek (now Lord) Rayner, conducted 135 scrutinies and 6 government inter-departmental reviews with a view to promoting greater efficiency (Fullwood, 1984). Consequently the background to the FMI as it relates to the probation service should be seen in the way the FMI was applied to the civil service and government departments which, it has been estimated, has saved the Conservative government well over £1 billion (Harris in the Observer, 21.02.88).

After coming to power in 1979 the Conservative government produced 3 White papers on efficiency in July 1981, September 1982 and September

1983, and the work of Rayner was important within this context. The underlying principles of FMI are: economy, efficiency and effectiveness; a critical questioning of the role of the public sector; changing management practices to improve performance; greater accountability; cash limits and value for money; objectives, priorities and targets. Furthermore it has been clarified that

> The principle on which the present government operates - across the whole field of public expenditure - is that resources must determine the policy and not that the policy can determine resources. This means that each service or programme is given a budget and is expected to get on and do the best job that can be done with it (Faulkner, 1984, p3).

Moreover the aims of the FMI are: a) A clear view of objectives with the means to assess these and where possible to measure they have been achieved; b) A well-defined responsibility for making the best use of resources including the emphasis on value for money; c) The need for information about costs, relevant training and access to expert advice to help exercise responsibility (Butler, 1983).

Therefore against the background of the emergence of the FMI, it may be argued that SNOP is a unique document when examining the relationship between the Home Office and the service. No other document to have emerged from within the Home Office on probation has remotely resembled SNOP in the sense that it is the first ever official definition of what the service should be doing. Even though it may be accurately claimed that the Home Office has attempted in the past, albeit in a more piecemeal fashion, to determine service objectives in the development of, for example, prison after-care, parole and community service, it has never before been attempted on such a grand scale. For the first time the Home Office is attempting overtly to direct and determine the objectives and priorities of the service and to require each local service to set its own objectives and priorities in accordance with them. Whilst acknowledging that each area service may have to respond to its own unique local problems and take initiatives which reflect local conditions and concerns, from now on it is intended that local developments will take place within the clearly defined parameters established by Home Office civil servants and Ministers. However by the summer of 1986 the Home

Secretary, Douglas Hurd, remarked that there was still a long way to go to achieve the objectives of the Home Office which largely depends on area services being more determined to accept the discipline of central government priorities delineated in SNOP (Hurd, 1986a, p7).

Having initially acknowledged the unique character of SNOP, particularly within the context of the FMI, it is appropriate that the starting point for this chapter should be to elucidate the main points of the document itself. The discussion will then continue by examining Home Office reviews of the probation service prior to SNOP, which were contained in a series of Departmental Committee Reports. It will then be argued that in terms of process, content, ideology and Home Office control over the service, SNOP is fundamentally different from these previous Reports and therefore unique.

SNOP

After a succinct introductory preamble the Statement considers certain objectives and priorities for the probation service in seven sections. The first section locates the service within the wider context of the criminal justice system, as did the Working Paper on Criminal Justice (Home Office, 1984b), an approach subsequently endorsed by the Home Secretary in 1986 (Hurd, 1986a, p7; and in speech to ACOP, 1986b). The Statement emphasises the importance of a planned and coordinated response to crime and that in future the service will have a duty to the whole community, not just individual offenders, to ensure that the law is enforced and society protected (Faulkner, 1983). The second section delineates the central purpose of the service which is the supervision of offenders in the community. Section three restates the principal statutory tasks of the service, enumerated as advice to courts through the provision of social enquiry reports, the supervision of non-custodial orders including both probation and community service orders, through-care and statutory after-care, which is followed by a fourth section dealing with the seperate statutory tasks arising from civil work. Section five describes several specific objectives related to the tasks of the preceding two sections categorised as:

A) Working with the Courts

45

B) Supervision in the Community
C) Through-care
D) Other work in the community (including civil work).

The final two sections, six and seven, delineate service priorities and consider the appropriate allocation of resources to achieve service objectives.

Because the focus of this book is the probation order and also because the main priority of SNOP is the ability of the service to supervise as many offenders as possible in the community, especially in those cases where a custodial sentence is considered to be a real possibility, it is unnecessary to examine in detail every section of SNOP. Consequently attention will now be given to section V B (iii) to (v) of the document which deals specifically with how the Home Office understands the elements of probation supervision.

Section V B (iii) begins by stating that each area probation service should be able to put into effect as many orders as the courts decide to make, especially in cases where custodial sentences would otherwise be imposed. Lloyd considered that there are two major influences which have culminated in the Home Office stressing the theme of alternatives to custody in the 1980's. Firstly the prison system is vastly overcrowded; secondly imprisonment is excessively costly compared with community programmes for offenders (1986, p4). Therefore the probation service has a clear mandate to supervise in the community those offenders who have extensive criminal records and/or those who have been found guilty of relatively serious offences.

In 1983 the Draft Home Office document which preceded SNOP was explicit when it used the language of 'the service's capacity to cope with offenders with comparatively serious records of crime' (Home Office, 1983a, 5 (v)). Even though the 1984 Statement was less explicit, it was still stated that 'The first priority should be to ensure that, wherever possible, offenders can be dealt with by non-custodial measures...' (VI (a)), a view reiterated by Leon Brittan when he was Home Secretary in an interview given to the Probation Journal (1984a, p6). To this end SNOP says that the service should provide social enquiry reports where there is a statutory requirement,

46

where the court is likely to consider making a probation order and where an alternative to a custodial sentence is being advocated by the writer of the report (V A (i)).   Accordingly   as priority (b) in section VI explains, the service will have to be more selective in future when preparing reports to achieve the goal of reducing reliance on custodial facilities.

Section V B (iv) proceeds by stating that to achieve the objective of community supervision for as many offenders as possible, a range of facilities will have to be provided which 'used in conjuction with probation and supervision orders in suitable cases, will increase their effectiveness and thereby the Service's capacity to cope with the widest possible range of offenders'.

This means providing facilities such as hostels and day centres as adjuncts to probation orders through the development of additional requirements or extra conditions. By resorting to extra conditions it is hoped that the courts can be convinced that the service is able to deal with more serious offenders, that community supervision will be more efficacious in achieving a diminution of offending and that the public will be adequately protected.

It has already been discussed in the previous chapter how it is now possible to develop and expand the use of extra conditions, because of the opportunities provided by Schedule 11 of the 1982 Act.   It has also been suggested how some probation officers might feel anxious about   the attendant dangers of an accentuation of social control, considered implicit within both the 1982 Act and SNOP.   To allay such fears David Faulkner stated that this document was not intended to bring about 'a significant shift towards exercising new measures of social control or towards the ideas associated with a correctional service...' (1984, p4).   However in the same speech at York to an audience comprised mainly of probation officers, references were made to the need to emphasise 'firmness in the sense of insisting on offenders observing the requirements of their orders', and the notion of 'more intensive supervision for those who have been more heavily convicted, who have committed more serious offences or who are judged to be more seriously at risk' (p4).   Furthermore the new measures being proposed are expected, according to the Home Office Working

47

Paper, to 'make real demands on offenders' (1984b, p21) and the Home Office expects that swift action will be taken against those who do not comply with the requirements of community supervision orders. One may therefore speculate that the development of extra conditions attached to probation orders, albeit differences of emphasis from service to service (Lloyd, 1986, p14f), has the potential to create problems, ethical dilemmas and axiological conflicts in relation to the approach and orientation of probation work for some probation officers in their dealings with clients. These issues will be explored in more detail in Chapter 4.

The third feature of supervision which requires little elucidation is described in Section V B (v) as

> ensuring by clear planning and follow-up action that the supervision, support, advice and guidance available to offenders under probation or supervision orders, through the exercise of social work skills and use of available facilities, are applied as efficiently and effectively as possible in each case so that the risk of offending is reduced, to the benefit of the offender and of the community.

The themes to draw attention to here are the principles of efficiency and effectiveness, which echoes the principles of the Financial Management Initiative. Within the current climate it is vital that the probation service provides value for the money provided by the taxpayer (Home Office, 1984b, p21). Accordingly because the first priority of the service is the supervision of offenders within the community, an increasing proportion of each area service's resources is expected to be reallocated to achieve this goal.

These, then, are the salient points within SNOP concerning the future of community supervision and there can be little doubt that SNOP is an important document, with potentially far reaching implications for the future of the probation service. Before explaining these dimensions of probation supervision in more detail within the context of discussing the way in which SNOP is unique compared with previous reviews of the service, it is first of all necessary to introduce those Departmental Committee Reports of 1909, 1922, 1936, and 1962.

Departmental Committee Reports

On the 8th of March 1909 the Home Secretary, Herbert John Gladstone, appointed a Departmental Committee consisting of five members to enquire into the workings of the Probation of Offenders Act, 1907, which had come into operation on the 1st of January, 1908. Compared with later Departmental Committee Reports the 1909 Report was relatively short. This may be largely explained by the fact that the system it reported on was only a little over one year old and because it focused mainly on developments in the London area, although it has to be said that some evidence was received from further afield. By the 23rd of December, 1909, the Committee reported back to the Home Secretary (Home Office, 1909).

At this inchoate stage of development in the history of the probation service, some courts were using probation orders more than others which resulted in the Committee recommending that the Home Office should write to all magistrates with a view to encouraging a greater use of probation. The Committee also considered and made recommendations in respect of the appointment and remuneration of probation officers and anticipated the creation of the National Association of Probation Officers in 1912. It also considered the duties of officers in relation to attending court, explaining the meaning of probation orders to new probationers, record keeping and visits, and providing reports to magistrates on the conduct of probationers when asked for by the court. Ideologically probation was perceived as a powerful instrument for the reformation of individual offenders and also for the prevention of crime, and it is also evident that the Home Office had an influential role in the creation of the probation system, which was to have important implications for the future.

It is important to recognise that the Bill which culminated in the Act of 1907 was sponsored by the Home Secretary himself, but the only element of central Home Office control at the stage the Bill was progressing through Parliament was a Government amendment giving the Home Secretary the power to make rules for carrying the 1907 Act into effect. Bochel's interpretation of this is that

There seems to have been no question at this stage of a government grant towards the service—and, therefore, no justifiable reason for giving the Home Secretary substantial controlling powers. But the power to make rules did vouchsafe to the Home Office some possibility of influencing the way in which the system was to develop (1976, p30).

In fact the 1909 Committee recommended that there should be one official at the Home Office with responsibility for keeping in touch with probation work and providing information in relation to it (p13).

Eleven years later, on the 22nd of November 1920, another Departmental Committee was appointed by the Home Secretary, Edward Short, to enquire into the training, appointment and payment of probation officers (Home Office, 1922). Even though this Report was more comprehensive than its predecessor and the Committee held more meetings and received evidence from nearly twice as many witnesses (49 as opposed to 29), it still comprised five members, the same as in 1909. By the 30th of January, 1922, the Committee reported back to the Home Secretary with its findings and recommendations.

Once again the Report of 1922 recorded that the use being made of probation orders was uneven. It recommended, for example, that probation officers should continue to be appointed by the courts and paid by the local authorities. Officers were not to be given too many cases and, in comparison with the way in which probation orders are being encouraged in the 1980s for the more serious, up-tariff cases, the Committee recommended that probation should be used early on in an offender's criminal career. Moreover where it had failed it should not be tried again (p22). By this time the importance of probation officer training was being acknowledged and an increase in salaries was being advocated. The Committee also reinforced the underlying ideology of probation which had been articulated in 1909 as a means of reformation. Therefore the main recommendations of the 1922 Committee may be summarised as follows:

firstly, every court should have a probation officer at its disposal;

secondly, remuneration should be improved;

thirdly, central government should provide a grant towards the cost of the service - and it is this recommendation which should be considered in more detail because of its implications for future Home Office involvement in the business of probation.

It is interesting to note that the Howard League had repeated, having first made the suggestion in 1909, that the administration of the probation service should be in the hands of a paid Commission. The 1922 Committee rejected this suggestion, but accepted the continued need for a Central Authority (which was soon to be assisted by an Advisory Committee), whose duties would be discharged by the Home Office. It was also acknowledged that the Children's Department of the Home Office, which was concerned with the service, should have more staff in order that more time could be devoted to probation matters. Again it is Bochel who explains that

> Although the Committee did not recommend any immediate extension of central government control over the local administration of probation - except through the extension of advisory and information services - one of its most important recommendations did foreshadow an increase of supervision from the centre. This was the recommendation for which the Home Office had looked when the Committee was set up. The time had now come, the Committee considered, for the institution of a government grant towards the cost of probation (1976, p88).

By way of qualification it should also be acknowledged when considering the provision of a government grant and the corollary of an accentuation of Home Office inspection and control, that a Circular issued by the Home Office at the time stressed that central control would be kept to a minimum to encourage local initiatives and responsibilities (King, 1964, p18). This seems to be a significant point to bear in mind when the degree of Home Office control being exercised through SNOP is considered below.

On the 9th of October, 1934, the third Departmental Committee for consideration was appointed by the Home Secretary, Sir John Gilmour. It was comprised of nine members who proceeded to examine many aspects of probation. On completing their work the Committee reported back to the new Home Secretary, Sir John Simon, on the 13th of March, 1936 (Home Office, 1936). Undoubtedly this was a major review of the service and the Report of 1936 established the basis of probation work for the next 25 years. In addition to examining a wide range of issues, such as matrimonial work and the supervision of offenders, the

51

Committee also recognised the necessity for properly trained officers who had acquired the skill and knowledge to operate as court social workers. It also considered the creation of a probation inspectorate, which occurred shortly afterwards, salary increases and the appointment of principal probation officers to provide oversight of the day-to-day work of the service.

It has already been stated above how the reformation of the offender was the underlying ideology of probation supervision in the 1909 and 1922 Reports. The 1936 Report reinforced this ideology and explicitly stated that 'The object of probation is the ultimate re-establishment of the probationer in the community and the probation officer must accordingly take a long view' (p58).

One of the most significant developments in the 1936 Report was the degree of influence and control being advocated that the Home Office should exercise. The Committees of 1909 and 1922 had reflected on the important role played by the Home Office in the creation and development of the service. This was reiterated in 1936, but it may be argued that the role of the Home Office was becoming more important and assuming greater significance. The Report of the 1936 Committee supports this claim where it stated that

> In its present stage, the probation service, which is now developing rapidly, needs the direction and guidance of an active central authority to ensure efficiency, to act as a clearing house for new ideas and to co-ordinate the work of the various authorities. There is much to be done in the next few years and no step is more likely to contribute to the development of an efficient service than that the Home Office should accept greater responsibility for its general administration, supervision and direction (para 152).

Subsequently the notions of 'efficiency' and Home Office responsibility for the future 'direction' of the service were to acquire new significance during the 1980's with SNOP.

On the 27th of May, 1959, the Home Secretary R A Butler and J S Maclay, Principal Secretary of State for Scotland, appointed a Departmental Committee under the chairmanship of R P Morison to enquire into all aspects of probation work in England, Wales and Scotland. When the Committee presented its comprehensive Report in

52

March 1962, it had considered the issues of recruitment and training, organisation, administration, pay and conditions of service, as well as the practice and philosophy of probation supervision. There can be little doubt that this was a major enquiry covering all important aspects of probation work in the early 1960's and, on the whole, the Committee approved the existing functions and organisation of the service, recommending that it should continue along the lines proposed by the 1936 Committee (Bochel, 1976, p206). Moreover the Morison Report continued the traditional understanding of probation ideology articulated in the three previous Reports, endorsing the perception that probation is concerned with treatment, reformation and the rehabilitation of offenders (Home Office, 1962, paras 8to24 and 53to59).

It has also been considered how the influence of the Home Office had gradually increased from 1909 through to the 1936 Report. Morison confirmed this but added that

> Our enquiry has left us in no doubt that the activity of the Home Office and, in particular, of the probation inspectorate...has been a major cause of the remarkable development of the service since the 1936 Committee reported (para 178, p71).

However the Morison Report went on to say that over the last few years the relationship between the Home Office and probation committees, and between the Home Office and service had been strained (para 180, p71f). This predicament had apparently four main causes and, interestingly, one or two of these have a degree of contemporary significance.

Firstly, there had been an increase in the volume of work within the service. Secondly, in the interests of national economic policy the salary claims of probation officers had been resisted by the Home Office. Thirdly, the Home Office had exercised financial controls over the service which had apparently created problems for probation committees. Finally, strain was caused because of the perception that the Home Office had failed to show sufficient interest in the service. Notwithstanding these problems, where the issue of Home Office control over the service is concerned, the most significant statement of the Morison Report was that

> We have already indicated that the Home Office should, in our

view, exercise a degree of control and guidance which reflects the legitimate national interest in the service...Home Office control should serve one or both of two ends - the efficiency of the service; and the safeguarding of a substantial Exchequer interest (para 194, p76).

It is important to maintain a sense of balance because it must be acknowledged that because the probation committee system was working satisfactorily, a number of Home Office controls in relation to organisational and administrative matters could be abolished (Bochel, 1976, p212f). In conclusion it appears that the Morison Report was greeted with general approval by all vested interest groups.

Prior to SNOP in 1984, the Morison Report of 1962 was the last major review of the probation service. It will now be argued that in terms of process, content, ideology and Home Office control, SNOP is fundamentally different from the four Departmental Committee Reports just considered.

Process

By process I mean the procedures which were in operation to produce the various documents under discussion and the way in which their recommendations were put into effect. The process involved in the Departmental Committee Reports from 1909 to 1962 consisted in the Home Secretary appointing a relatively independent group of people to collect evidence on certain aspects of probation work. Subsequently after the Committees had completed their work they reported back to the Home Secretary with numerous observations and recommendations, some of which were given effect by legislation at a later date. For example the 1922 Committee, which examined the training, appointment and payment of probation officers, had its main recommendations included within the Criminal Justice Act, 1925, amended by the Criminal Justice (Amendment) Act, 1926.

But when sometime after the Conservative party had been elected to governmental office in 1979 it was considered a reappraisal of the service was necessary, the process initiated to achieve this was fundamentally different from that of previous years. Contrary to popular wisdom that it was Home Office officials who were primarily responsible for initiating a review of the service, the reality of

54

what actually happened appears much more subtle and complex. This claim is made because, in June 1986, I interviewed the Departmental Under Secretary of State who was mainly responsible for SNOP at the Home Office, to collect information for this Chapter. On this occasion, and subsequently confirmed by correspondence, David Faulkner (1986) pointed out that, in a sense, Home Office officials were only responding to the call for a reappraisal which had already been put forward by the representative organisations and what was therefore judged, by the Home Office, to be the collective sense of the service that one was needed.

Some support for such an interpretation of events can be found in the way that, for example, the Hampshire Probation Service was reorganised in the mid-1970's. One of the initiatives of this reorganisation was that the Southampton probation office established a working party on 'objectives' in the autumn of 1977 (Hil, 1986). Moreover it appears that a number of other probation areas had local statements of objectives and priorities which predated SNOP, including the Greater Manchester Probation Service which had produced such a document during 1980. It should also be reiterated that from the mid-1970s, symbolised by the 1976 Criminal Justice Policy Review, and against the background of developments and changes in the probation service, wider social change, a growing fiscal crisis and prison crisis in the early 1980s (Whitehead, 1987), the probation service had been attempting to redefine its rationale. Therefore it may be said that the initiatives of the sort just referred to in Hampshire and Manchester on the issue of future service objectives, was gradually leading to a careful reappraisal of what the service was doing and where it was going, which inevitably involved the Home Office at a later date.

When the review began it was hoped that it would be a joint exercise between the Home Office and the service, working through its representative organisations consisting of the Central Council of Probation Committees (CCPC) as the employers, of which all probation committees are members and whose objectives are to consider all aspects of training and recruitment, organisation and administration, duties, pay and conditions of service; the Association of Chief

Officers of Probation (ACOP) as service managers, comprising CPO's, DCPO's and ACPO's; and the National Association of Probation Officers (NAPO) which is a trade union and professional association drawn from all ranks of the service. It was also hoped that a report or statement would eventually be published to which the Home Office and all the representative organisations would be equal parties. Only later did this hope turn out to be impracticable because, as Faulkner explained (1986) the degree of agreement necessary to produce a joint statement could not be achieved, which culminated in a document produced by the Home Office after consultation. This change coincided with the Draft of August 1983. It is also worth mentioning that in addition to meeting with the CCPC, ACOP and NAPO, Home Office officials consulted with Chief Probation Officers (CPO's). For in May 1983, prior to both the appearance of the Draft and the pending general election, officials from the Home Office met with CPO's at Bournemouth where they gave their attention to a manifesto for the future of the service. Subsequently a paper emerged from within the Home Office which was a direct outcome of the Bournemouth meeting which set out 'for further discussion, a possible pattern for future planning and consultation between the Home Office and the probation service on the current issues of probation policy and practice' (Home Office, 1983b).

It concluded by saying that a statement of national principles and intentions, possibly in the form of a White Paper, could appear by the beginning of 1984.

Notwithstanding the problems involved in disentangling the complex threads of the degree to which the Home Office and other organisations were involved at the beginning in initiating the SNOP process, what is more clear is that the Home Office itself eventually assumed full responsibility for reviewing the service. No Departmental Committee was appointed, which in itself signalled an end to the consensus approach of these previously appointed Committees. Perhaps one should not be too surprised at this departure from previous practices and traditions because it is indicative of and reflects what can only be described as a particular style of government which operates with a 'we know best' attitude, a characteristic of the Conservative government in the post-1979 period. A good example of what I mean by style of government and this 'we know best' attitude, may be found in the Conservative government's decision after 1979 not to reappoint the Advisory Council on the Penal System (ACPS) after it had been dissolved in March 1978 (Morgan, 1979). The ACPS had been in existence since 1966, having replaced the Advisory Council on the Treatment of Offenders, which had been formed in 1942. The function of both the ACTO and ACPS was to advise the government of the day on penal policy. From 1966 to 1978 the ACPS produced 9 reports, beginning with Detention of Girls in a Detention Centre in 1968 and ending with Sentences of Imprisonment in 1978. Moreover if the ACPS is considered no longer necessary, then neither is the Advisory Council on Probation and After-Care (ACPAC), which has not existed since 1976 (Morgan, 1979, p13). Undoubtedly referring the issue of the future of the service to the ACPS, the ACPAC, or a Departmental Committee, would have resulted in a considerable delay before a report was produced and the Home Office may not have received a report much to its liking. Furthermore by the time an independent Committee had reported the political complexion of government might have changed resulting in a much less urgent need to prioritise the service along the lines eventually proposed by SNOP.

Be that as it may, what is clear is that during the early 1980's when the review had been launched, the Home Office became primarily responsible for preparing a Draft document of National Purpose and Objectives which appeared in August 1983. The Draft was then circulated to the representative organisations who proceeded to respond during the autumn of 1983. ACOP, for example, officially responded to the Draft in September 1983 and stated that

> Since its issue in August 1983 the Home Office draft Note has received intensive consideration within ACOP over a short period of time. It has been considered in meetings of all our 8 regional groups, as well as in Chief Officer's Teams at area level. It has also been considered by the Committee of Regional Representatives and the General Purposes Committee. In this way the Note has received serious attention from a substantial majority of ACOP members (ACOP, 1983).

After taking account of these responses the Home Office produced revised versions of the initial draft which were intensively discussed

57

before, once again, they were circulated to the organisations. Once refinements had been made the final Statement appeared in April 1984, which has become the definitive statement upon which local probation areas have to plan their work. I said earlier that it was considered at one stage that the final statement might be in the form of a White Paper. However by January 1984 it had been decided that this would be a mistake because a White Paper would be too restrictive, particularly if it required amending in the light of the idiosyncratic nature of local probation services.

Therefore it may be forcibly argued that the process which created SNOP was very different to the process employed by the Home Office in previous years to produce the Departmental Committee Reports. Even though one could spend much time debating the intricacies of who was the prime mover in initiating the process which culminated in SNOP, the end result was a Home Office 'in house' review, which broke with the consensus traditions and practices of the past. It was a review undertaken by civil servants with the approval of Ministers and eventually endorsed by Leon Brittan who was Home Secretary at the time.

Content

The differences between SNOP and the Departmental Committees from the standpoint of content may be dealt with succinctly. After reading SNOP one is immediately struck by the brevity and narrow parameters of the document. SNOP is not concerned, for example, with matters relating to organisation, administration, recruitment, training, salaries or conditions of service, in the way that Morison was in 1962. On the contrary, SNOP is specifically concerned with the purpose, tasks, objectives and priorities of the probation service in the five spheres of court work, the supervision of offenders in the community, through-care, community work and civil work. In other words it is a statement about what the service should be doing.

Accordingly because some areas of work are now considered to be more important than others, which is an inevitable consequence of prioritisation, the influence of SNOP will be profoundly more wide ranging than previous Reports if it is rigidly applied by local area services.

Ideology

SNOP is different from previous Reports ideologically. From 1909 to 1962 it has already been made clear that the ideology and rationale of probation work, particularly in relation to probation orders, was encapsulated in the concepts of reformation, treatment and eventually rehabilitation. It is worth repeating what was stated in the 1936 Report and echoed by the other Departmental Committee Reports, in that the object of probation supervision was understood in terms of re-establishing the offender in the community (Home Office, 1936, p58). Even though there is one reference to the treatment of offenders in the first paragraph of SNOP, the concept of treatment being alluded to here does not have the same connotations which prevailed in previous years. In fact it is fairly accurate to claim that, on the whole, the conceptual framework provided by the medical-treatment model of probation which experienced its apotheosis in the 1950's and 1960's has been largely abandoned by the Home Office over recent years (Home Office, 1977, pp48-49). It is true that SNOP affirms that the probation service will continue to concern itself with reducing crime, but it is now accepted in official circles that the business of permanently transforming offenders into non-offenders is extraordinarily difficult. Therefore more modest goals are necessitated which elicits the question: what seems to be the dominant ideological theme in SNOP?

There is not one simple or unambiguous answer to this question because, on the one hand, if SNOP's priorities are rigidly applied and resources mainly employed in future to supervise as many offenders as possible on community supervision orders which are understood to be clear alternatives to custodial sentences, particularly where serious offenders are concerned, this implies more control over offenders by the probation service. This has been made possible by the provisions contained in Schedule 11 of the 1982 Act, which were referred to earlier. The intention seems to be that resorting to extra conditions will make supervision more credible to sentencers thus providing

59

realistic alternatives to custody, enable offenders to live more satisfactorily, thereby benefiting both offenders and communities. Moreover Jock Young (1986) has argued that mainstream British criminology in the 1960's was characterised by positivism and correctionalism. However positivism has now been displaced within the criminological establishment, represented by the Home Office, by what he calls administrative criminology which is associated with a disparate collection of academics including Ernest van den Haag, James Q Wilson, Norval Morris and Ron Clarke, the latter being formerly at the Home Office Research Unit. Notwithstanding their different political views it seems that these academics are united in their antagonism to the notion that crime is determined by social circumstances, display a lack of interest in the aetiology of crime and rehabilitation, accept that offenders freely choose to offend and advocate deterrence. These views have also permeated the juvenile criminal justice system (Pitts, 1988).

Where all this becomes relevant for the probation service is if Young's analysis is correct in the way that the Home Office has abandoned the search for the aetiology of crime and given up the goal of rehabilitation, thus focusing instead on the management, control, surveillance, policing and the more effective containment of offenders. For if we are not sure what causes crime or how to rehabilitate offenders who are located both in institutions and the community, what else is left except a penal policy based on more effective containment and control? Undoubtedly SNOP could be interpreted to justify more control over offenders, but it is interesting how area services in their responses to SNOP have apparently betrayed conflicting opinions on this important issue. Lloyd's research discovered that probation areas were ambivalent concerning the development of control and coercive practices (1986, p65).

On the other hand, it is both naive and incorrect to assume that SNOP is simply a blueprint for more social control, as though the Home Office is deliberately engaged in something covertly sinister, SNOP being but one element in a wider process set in motion by central government to control working class offenders. The reality of what is

60

happening to the criminal justice system in the 1980's is much more complex, subtle and ambivalent than this, as one can observe by reading, for example, the Home Secretary's speech to ACOP in September 1986. It is also a misconception to assume that the Home Office is working towards abolishing the principles and values of social work, even though it has not endorsed such principles and values as fervently as it might have, leaving organisations like NAPO feeling threatened. It has to be remembered that SNOP, when discussing supervision in the community, refers to the provision of support, advice and guidance to offenders and uses the language of exercising social work skills. It also advocates crime prevention, mediation and reparation which are seen as tasks that probation officers can legitimately perform. Consequently there are some features within SNOP which do not co-exist easily with an interpretation of the document solely in terms of advocating more control, which reveals just how much the language of penal politics is replete with contradiction, inconsistency and ambiguity.

Notwithstanding these ideological contradictions, it must be reiterated that the ideology and rationale of probation work which, in the post-war era, found expression in the notion of rehabilitation through casework, is no longer applicable or justifiable on either theoretical or empirical grounds. It may also be argued that it is pragmatic nonsense to pursue a policy of rehabilitation when the vast majority of probation clients live in increasingly disadvantaged inner city areas, exist on meagre welfare benefits, are unemployed with little prospect of finding work again and have little investment in contemporary society. Of course the rhetoric of rehabilitation may continue to flow in the blood stream of agencies like the probation service, remain vital for legitimatizing its existence, through which it convinces itself that it is engaged in something worthwhile by striving to achieve some desirable utilitarian end. But the point should be made that, from a left wing perspective, the reality of rehabilitation to probation clients may mean nothing more than being pressurised to accept things as they are, being happy with their lot in life, living happily in poverty and learning to conform to injustice and inequality. It seems illogical to talk about clients

61

being reintegrated back into local communities when the conditions which prevail in those communities may sometimes be conducive to offending in the first instance and to which offending may be interpreted as a logical and rational response.

Therefore for these and other reasons SNOP is not ideologically committed to rehabilitation, but to achieving a reduction of crime during the period the offender is under supervision only. Thus the dominant ideological shift is from permanent transformation and cure towards a more modest diminution of offending during the period a probation order is in operation by using a variety of techniques. The Draft document was clear that this was the goal of supervision in the community, and even though SNOP was not as explicit as the Draft, Lloyd accepts that SNOP should be interpreted in the same way (1986, p22). Of course it is this goal which potentially lends itself to the development of more control over offenders and the point is worth considering that SNOP continues the tortuous arguments of the 1970's concerning the choice between care and control in probation. In fact the whole care-control debate is more acute in the late 1980s than at any other previous period.

It has already been acknowledged that the Home Office has not abandoned the social work values of care and support for offenders in its plans for the future of the service, but I would argue that there can be little doubt that the emphasis in future will be on developing aspects of control in the community. Consequently the debate within the probation service no longer focuses on choosing between care and control, but in deciding how much control the service is prepared to accept and exercise at the same time as it tries to hold on to notions of respect for persons and client self determination. For as Brittan said in a speech to ACOP some six months after SNOP had been published within the context of discussing probation orders

> Not only do I regard the power to include specific requirements in probation and supervision orders as useful and important in their own right; they also exemplify the direction in which I believe the use of probation should go and in which it will have to go if the courts are to be persuaded to use probation for the more serious offender (Brittan, 1984b).

In the last analysis it's all a question of emphasis, but it will be important to monitor how area services balance their caring role with the demands of the criminal justice system to be more controlling. Finally, what about Home Office control over the service?

Home Office control

As a consequence of SNOP Home Office control over the probation service has increased and is qualitatively different to that level of control proposed or envisaged in previous Departmental Committee Reports. In discussing the Bill which culminated in the Probation of Offenders Act, 1907, it was said that the only element of central control at this stage was a government amendment giving the Home Secretary the power to make rules for putting the 1907 Act into effect. Even though the proposal for a government grant towards the cost of the service in 1922 foreshadowed an increase in central control, a Circular issued at the time stressed that this would be kept to a minimum to encourage local initiatives. Both the 1909 and 1922 Committees acknowledged the important role played by the Home Office in the creation and development of the service. This was reiterated in 1936, but by this time it may be argued that the role of the Home Office became more important and was to acquire greater significance. Finally the Morison Committee argued that Home Office control should ensure that the service is efficient and that the interests of the Exchequer are safeguarded.

Throughout the period covered by the four Departmental Committees, albeit the strains and tensions at the time of Morison between the Home Office and Probation Committees (Home Office, 1962, p71f), it may be said that even though control from the centre gradually increased over the years, a delicate balance was maintained between the Home Office, local probation committees and area services. However it is reasonable to assume that because of SNOP, strains and tensions will emerge between Home Office civil servants and Ministers, the Probation Inspectorate and area services, as the Home Office continues to impose its priorities on a service traditionally characterised by a relatively high degree of autonomy.

It is worth reiterating, but this time from a different perspective to that discussed in the section above on Process, that SNOP is mainly a product of the Thatcher government's first and second term of office, the process beginning when Whitelaw was Home Secretary. On visiting the Home Office to collect information for this chapter, I was told that during the 1979-1983 period there were those officials at the Home Office who seemed to believe that the probation service was able to manage its own affairs and get on with the job without too much interference from central government. And even though it was during Whitelaw's tenure as Home Secretary that the service was slowly coming under official scrutiny, it does not appear that this was provoking too much concern. It was also about this time that David Faulkner took up his new post (having been at the Home Office since 1959), which resulted in him becoming primarily responsible for SNOP.

Subsequently when Brittan replaced Whitelaw as Home Secretary in June 1983, which coincided with those changes in the emergence of SNOP discussed earlier which saw the Home Office becoming responsible for the Draft once a joint statement between the Home Office and the representative organisations became impossible, the atmosphere and mood seemed to change perceptibly. Without wanting to caricature what happened or to overtly personalise the issue, it is nevertheless possible to develop the argument that from the easy going, mild mannered, liberal and affable Whitelaw, the service came under the critical scrutiny of the tough minded, no-nonsense, cost effective and management by objectives Brittan. In fact this change in style, tempo and mood in the dealings of the Home Office under Brittan with the probation service finds some support in what Brittan himself said to ACOP:

> During my term of office as Home Secretary I have sought to articulate, more clearly perhaps than has been done in the past, the policies, objectives and priorities which within my own sphere of responsibility I think it right to pursue for the criminal justice system as a whole (Brittan, 1984b),

which of course includes the probation service. There is further support for this change of tone, ethos and attitude at the Home Office in Stern's book (1987) where she analyses what happened at the Home Office after Brittan became Home Secretary in relation to the politics of imprisonment. Stern claims that throughout the 1970's and early 1980's there was consensus between the parties on using prison more sparingly. But with the installation of Brittan attitudes changed, particularly in relation to parole. On the one hand, Brittan said that no one sentenced to more than five years imprisonment for an offence of violence would be released on parole, except in exceptional circumstances. On the other hand, he said that parole would be introduced for prisoners serving ten and a half months or more after one third of the sentence had been served.

Even though the powers of the Home Secretary in relation to the probation service are limited, relying more on persuasion and influence rather than statutory powers in getting area services to endorse the principles of SNOP (Grimsey, 1987, p6), it is clear that a number of centralising initiatives have occurred over recent years. I have already referred to the FMI and SNOP, but one could also mention the following: the rise and development of managerialism (McWilliams, 1987); the Financial Management Information System (FMIS) currently being devised by Deloitte, Haskins and Sells, who are a firm of management consultants appointed by the Home Office to create a system to help senior probation managers better relate resources to measurable outputs (ACOP, 1986); the Grimsey review which examines ways in which the Inspectorate can contribute in future to the economy, efficiency and effectiveness of the probation service (1987); the development of clear policies, targets and performance indicators to measure performance, and cash limits. All these may be cited as examples of a centralising thrust from Queen Anne's Gate (Fullwood, 1987).

Finally, as a way of encapsulating these centralising developments, reference should be made to a speech made by Brittan's successor, Douglas Hurd, after he had been made Home Secretary in September 1985. Hurd asseverated that 'There must be a greater readiness to accept the discipline of priorities and, nationally, the Home Office will continue to try to secure a greater harmony of the local statements with the National Statement' (Hurd, 1986a).

Conclusion
It may be argued that SNOP breaks new ground in the history of the probation service, a claim I have attempted to justify by considering

the notions of process, content, ideology and Home Office control over the probation service and as such heralds a new chapter in the history of the service in the 1980s. Furthermore it is important to reiterate that the central concern of SNOP is the supervision of as many offenders as possible in the community, particularly those offenders who have been more heavily convicted and who have committed serious offences, to reduce the numbers being sent into custody and thus save money. But as I began to question the efficacy of some of those models to achieve this objective towards the end of the previous Chapter, so one must also question whether SNOP goes far enough to convince the courts that the probation service has credible alternatives to offer. It may well be the case that SNOP provides the basis for the development of more intensive forms of supervision in the community, but again one may speculate that the courts require more than improvements in social enquiry reports and more than the development of extra conditions which includes specified activities, Hostels and Day Centres.

After the publication of SNOP each area probation service responded by producing a local statement of objectives and priorities, concerning how they propose to give effect to the national document. These responses reveal a rich diversity of views and opinions which suggest that not everyone associated with the service uncritically accepts that SNOP is the definitive model for the future. Consequently the analysis will continue in the next chapter by looking at some of these responses and reflecting on some of the professional concerns which have been articulated by organisations like NAPO. Before doing so Table 3.1 presents a summary of SNOP as a model for supervising offenders in the community on probation orders.

Table 3.1

The SNOP model of probation supervision

The 2 central themes of SNOP are:
Firstly, the management of resources more
economically,efficiently, and effectively.
Secondly, the supervision of as many offenders as
possible in the community, especially in cases where
custodial sentences would otherwise be imposed.

ELEMENTS OF PROBATION PRACTICE
To be part of the criminal justice system and to work
with statutory and voluntary agencies to plan a
coordinated response to crime. To use social work
skills to link offence with offender and to locate
the offence within its social context.

VB (iii) To put into effect probation orders,
especially in cases where custody is a possibility.
(iv) Maintain a range of facilities as adjuncts to
probation, under Schedule 11 of the 1982 Act.
(v) Provide support, advice, guidance to offenders
and to use social work skills to reduce the risk of
reoffending.

IDEOLOGY AND RATIONALE
The rationale of practice is to reduce crime and
enable offenders to live more satisfactorily. To
increase the effectiveness of supervision to the
benefit of both offender and community.
The ideological shift is from rehabilitation through
casework, towards greater management and control in
the community to prevent and reduce crime during
the period of supervision.

CARE/CONTROL
Social work concepts have not been abandoned in SNOP.
However, it may be hypothesised that if the central
task of the probation service is to deal with more
serious offenders in the community, then the service
will have to convince the courts that probation is a
credible option. This could involve resorting to
extra conditions, enhanced control, a tougher and
firmer attitude, thus making real demands on offenders.

CONTINUUM
CARE

HARRIS

WALKER
AND
BEAUMONT

BOTTOMS
AND
McWIL'MS

RAYNOR

BRYANT

SNOP

DAVIES
GRIFF'S

CONTROL

4 Responses to SNOP: a professional model of probation

Introduction

The Statement of National Objectives and Priorities will exercise a powerful pressure on the probation service in future years, because central government has some responsibility to shape and determine the practice and philosophy of a public sector service to which it contributes 80% of its finances. However in addition to those bureaucratic and administrative responses made by the Home Office discussed in the previous chapter, including those academic responses considered in Chapter 2, to the question of supervising offenders in the community in the post-rehabilitative era, the analysis will now continue by first of all turning to the views of the National Association of Probation Officers (NAPO).

The NAPO was one of those organisations consulted by the Home Office when the Draft and final Statement were being prepared. But it is interesting to contrast NAPO's response to the 1936 and 1962 Departmental Committee Reports with which it was largely in agreement, with its response to SNOP where it had fundamental differences with the Home Office concerning the practice and philosophy of probation and other related issues. Consequently after considering NAPO's response to the Home Office Draft and final Statement in the first part of this chapter, the discussion will be expanded to incorporate NAPO's understanding of the supervision of offenders in the community. Subsequently the way in which probation officers have responded to SNOP in the Probation Journal will be considered, before concluding with an analysis of how area probation services initially articulated their responses to SNOP which are important when considering the provision of credible alternatives to custody.

NAPO, the Home Office Draft and SNOP

Reference has already been made to the Home Office Working Paper on Criminal Justice (Home Office, 1984b) in which the then Home Secretary, Leon Brittan, proposed that the criminal justice system should be based upon three main themes - balance, maintenance of public confidence and greater efficiency and effectiveness. According to NAPO, this Working Paper constituted a punitive policy towards offenders because it was based on increasing the use of imprisonment. One year later in May 1985, NAPO produced its Alternative Criminal Justice Strategy in which it discussed a wide range of issues including public attitudes to crime, police powers, courts, criminal law reform, prisons, crime prevention, victim support and reparation (NAPO, 1985). This document emphasised that many offenders currently being dispatched into custodial facilities could be feasibly dealt with in the community. In other words, both probation and community service orders should be used more than prisons. This proposal had implications for resources, a theme to which NAPO returned when it responded to the Home Office Draft of August 1983.

Essentially NAPO objected to the Draft because it failed to commit itself to providing additional resources to the probation service, because it failed to adequately affirm support for social work values and because it failed to consider that through-care, after-care and civil work were as important as community supervision. Notwithstanding these objections, it should be acknowledged that NAPO's response was not completely negative. Accordingly it agreed with the Home Office on using probation orders for more serious

69

offenders as an alternative to custody and less for offenders appearing before the courts for the first time. On balance, NAPO concluded by stating that it had 'sought to contribute positively to the Home Office discussions on the Future Direction of the Probation Service. We are disappointed at what we perceive as the rather negative tone of this draft statement' (1983a, p8).

As NAPO criticised the Draft for its 'negative tone', so it subsequently found the final Statement 'deeply disappointing' (1984, para. 1), primarily because the Home Office had failed to commit itself to strengthening the service and because SNOP strongly implied a reduction of resources in certain areas of work. Once again though, NAPO's response was not totally negative because it was able to discover broad areas of agreement with the Home Office, the main points of which may be summarised as follows.

Firstly, and to reiterate its position of 1983, NAPO agreed with the Home Office that probation orders should be used more for offenders at risk of custody and less for those who have committed relatively minor offences. Secondly NAPO agreed that the preparation of social enquiry reports should be undertaken more selectively. This would mean terminating the preparation of pre-trial reports on juvenile offenders, pre-trial reports where offenders are pleading not-guilty at the Crown Court and fewer reports on those appearing for the first time and where offences are of a relatively minor nature. Finally NAPO acknowledged a role for the service in the community, crime prevention and victim support schemes.

Alternatively NAPO once again strongly objected to the Home Office stance on resources, arguing that it would be more cost effective to provide additional resources to the service in order to deal with many more offenders in the community, rather than resorting to expensive custodial institutions. NAPO is making an important point here and its argument is sound because probation is much less expensive than prison, is more humane and no less effective at preventing recidivism, as Wilkins and others suggested earlier (see Chapter 1). Regarding the costs of different facilities, the Home Office itself estimated in 1986 that the average weekly cost of an offender in prison was £218. In comparison the average weekly cost of an offender on probation was

£11 and for community service £10 (Home Office, 1986, p101). But the attitude of government to penal policy is much more complex and ambivalent than this, because it is not based solely on the arguments of cost effectiveness or the findings of empirical research, but more on political expediency, including emotive appeals to the demands of law and order. Accordingly the probation service is affected by the prevailing socio-economic climate (Box, 1987, Chapters 5 and 6), the influences and pressures of law and order concerns, and by wider political considerations. However it also has a professional identity of its own which is grounded in social work and expressed in a humanitarian concern for offenders, which NAPO sedulously defends.

NAPO has therefore cogently argued that if more resources were provided to the service it would be enabled to follow a programme of increasing the use of probation and community service orders; provide more accommodation for homeless and unsettled offenders; provide more bail hostels and facilities for alcoholic, drug dependent and mentally disordered offenders; increase its involvement in community projects to prevent crime and assist victims; to give more attention to young adult offenders involved in motor crime and burglary offences; and to strengthen the provision of voluntary after-care to break into the cycle of repeated imprisonment for petty offenders. It may be said that such a comprehensive programme would probably reduce the number of offenders currently entering prison and that for many offenders would provide a more logical and humane response to their problems. Unfortunately given the mood of the Home Office, the political climate, the arguments considered in Chapter 3, the emphasis on the 'justice model' rather than welfare (Hudson, 1987) and the priorities of the Exchequer in the mid-1980's, it seems unlikely that NAPO's programme will be implemented. Therefore the fear grows 'that services might be pared down to a narrow range of tasks of proven cost effectiveness and applied on a principle of offenders' reduced eligibility and from considerations of social control' (Day, 1987, p23).

To summarise, NAPO's main criticisms of SNOP are that:
it fails to plan for the growth of the service;
it gives a low priority to after-care;

71

the low priority given to civil work; and,

its failure to provide a positive programme for the future development of the service. Accordingly NAPO has argued that at the first opportunity this negative statement should be replaced (1984, para. 18).

Having reflected on NAPO's response to the Home Office Draft and final Statement, the discussion will now be expanded to incorporate the way in which NAPO understands probation practice and philosophy. This will include considering the issue of extra conditions in probation orders which, once again, brings to the surface the care-control dichotomy, the increasingly important issue of the future value orientation of the service and its ability to provide credible alternatives to custody.

NAPO and probation supervision

In a policy paper approved at the 1982 AGM (NAPO, 1982) the Association stated that the two main elements of the probation order are, firstly, the supervision of offenders and, secondly, the duty to advise, assist and befriend. This helps to clarify NAPO's position concerning the underlying rationale of probation, in that it is perceived as a disposal available to the court which is based on social work principles and values. This is reflected primarily in NAPO's concern to preserve the adage first articulated in 1907, which is to advise, assist and befriend. According to NAPO the probation order should be a flexible and multi-purpose order which is available to provide positive help, support, advice and guidance to offenders. If probation supervision comprises these elements, which are delivered particularly through a one-to-one relationship between offender and probation officer, it is believed to have the efficacy to be useful and beneficial to clients. Furthermore the practical elements of probation practice should consist in providing a range of counselling and welfare services.

Again such facilities should provide useful help to clients which echoes the approach of Bottoms and McWilliams, and Raynor, encapsulated in the notion of client defined help. Such facilities would include social skills training for offenders, family therapy,

72

courses on the use of leisure and recreation, help to find employment, adult literacy courses, advice on welfare rights and group work. Moreover these facilities may well be provided and delivered within the context of Day Centres (NAPO, 1983b, para. 4.9). NAPO also considers that probation practice could include the use of volunteers who would be entrusted with the role of befriending clients. But, it may be asked, why should the probation service deliver a range of facilities which are designed to help offenders within the context of probation orders? In other words, how does NAPO articulate its understanding of the ideology and rationale of probation supervision?

In the document already referred to which presents NAPO's Alternative Criminal Justice Strategy to the Home Office Working Paper on Criminal Justice (1985), it was stated that probation orders should be more 'effective' at reducing and preventing crime (pp15-17). On this both NAPO and the Home Office would agree. It has also been discussed in the previous chapter how SNOP understands that probation is intended to reduce and prevent crime during the period the order is in operation. Similarly because NAPO eschews the language of rehabilitation and treatment when articulating its views on the ideology of probation, it may be hypothesised that it would agree with SNOP in attempting to make probation orders more effective during a specified period, rather than expecting probation to have the efficacy to permanently transform offenders. Accordingly NAPO has stated that

> The purpose of the probation order is to enhance the offender's self-responsibility. Such an order can be offered at all stages of an offenders criminal career making the order as valid for serious and persistent offenders as for more marginal offenders who exhibit social and personal problems (1985, p15).

Perceptive readers will observe what appears to be a discrepancy in NAPO's position regarding which offenders are eligible for probation. For it has already been said that NAPO and SNOP are agreed that probation orders should be used for more serious offenders and less for those not at risk of custody. But in its 1985 document NAPO is expressing the view that probation may be offered at any stage in an offender's criminal career. Notwithstanding this apparent inconsistency in NAPO's position, the social work bias of NAPO is here being expressed when it is articulated that probation may help with the personal and social problems of minor offenders. In fact it seems that this is the way in which probation orders have been predominantly used in the past (Raynor, 1985, p188).

Even though the question of eligiblity for probation raises crucial issues, particularly where the issue of values is concerned and to which I'll return with a more detailed consideration below, NAPO seems concerned to reinforce the view that the rationale of probation should enhance the offender's self-responsibilty. As such Probation is a humane approach to crime related problems (1982, para. 2.8). Furthermore offenders should be treated as individuals who are confronted with choices concerning their behaviour and that a period of probation should help to enhance the ability of offenders to deal with their own personal and social problems (1982, para. 3.3). Probation should be based on a meaningful and positive relationship between the officer and probationer which should provide support, help clients face up to their situations, focus on attaining limited but achievable goals, to deal with specific problems and assist clients to acquire a greater understanding and acceptance of themselves (1983b, para. 4.9). Probation is also about enhancing self-esteem and increasing client choices, so that they may begin to act in ways which are less injurious to themselves, families and communities (1982, para. 3.8, p6). Therefore if the emphasis of NAPO is on the development of a relationship between the probation officer and client within the context of a probation order, through which constructive assistance and help can be given to clients to enable them to assume greater responsibility for their own lives, where does this leave the issue of extra conditions and requirements in probation orders? In other words, what about the contentious issue of control and authority?

In NAPO's response to the Home Office Draft document it was stated that

> it is unequivocally in the public interest that probation officers engage constructively with those under supervision, maintain useful relationships with them, to encourage trust and to exercise a positive influence over them. This is a skilled and difficult task requiring a careful balance between the use of authority and concern for the individual (1983a, para. 13, p4).

74

Whilst accepting that probation involves a degree of control, contained in the 'standard' probation order, NAPO is decidedly unhappy about the drift towards the use of extra conditions, control, surveillance and containment. According to NAPO, extra conditions are unnecessary, unhelpful and inhibiting because they 'would disrupt the balance necessary for effective supervision and reduce the degree of influence which can be exercised' (1983a, para. 14, p4)

Subsequent to the publication of the 1982 Criminal Justice Act, NAPO objected to the inclusion of night restriction orders and negative requirements in probation and supervision orders, advising members not to be associated with them by refusing to recommend them in their reports to the court (1983c). Nevertheless it accepted that Day Centres could be used as adjuncts to probation orders. At first sight this may appear as though NAPO is duplicating SNOP's position, but there is a fundamental difference between NAPO and the Home Office. Whereas SNOP implies that Day Centres will increasingly be used as a condition of probation orders, NAPO advocates that attendance should be on a voluntary basis. NAPO seems forced to pragmatically accept that resorting to Day Centre provision as a condition of probation is likely to increase as a consequence of SNOP and the 1982 Act (there were 60 approved Day Centres in 1986; Home Office, 1986, p35). Accordingly in its Policy Document on the use of conditions in probation orders (NAPO, 1983b), it made its position clear on what is an important issue within the probation service.

Firstly NAPO's argument against extra conditions is that they will not prove more effective in preventing crime, that they could inflict damage on the social work dimension of probation supervision thus adversely affecting the relationship between the officer and probationer and that they could result in an escalation of breach rates. If the increased use of extra conditions resulted in more offenders being breached for non-compliance with probation orders, then supervision in the community may subsequently appear less rather than more credible to the courts, culminating in the opposite effect to the one originally intended. In other words, conditions attached to probation orders could become a 'backdoor' into prison. However there is a body of opinion which believes that extra conditions will

75

culminate in an increased use of probation orders. NAPO rebuts this by arguing that extra conditions are by no means a pre-requisite to increasing the use of probation orders, because between 1979 and 1981 there was a 29% increase in the use of probation orders - from 27,584 to 35,700 - without any significant change in the approach of the service to the supervision of offenders.

Secondly if it is the case that in future extra conditions are going to be used much more than they have been in the past, when should they be imposed? The principles advocated by NAPO which should be considered prior to resorting to extra conditions are:
Only resort to extra conditions when the offender is considered likely to reoffend;
when the offences are serious;
when there is a record of persistent offending;
when there has been a lack of response to previous disposals; and,
when there are extensive personal and social problems which indicate a high risk of further offences (1983b).

Finally, and to return to the issue of Day Centres, under what circumstances should these facilities be used? NAPO postulates the following criteria: Firstly prior to advocating a condition to attend a day centre, careful assessment is necessary to ensure that such a condition is an essential adjunct to probation. Secondly the probation officer and client should engage in a joint process of assessment to determine the client's problems and to decide whether they can be alleviated by attending a day centre facility. Thirdly the nature and demands of such an order should be made clear to the client. Fourthly the grounds for breaching clients who attend such facilities should be established. Finally extra conditions must be appropriate and relevant given the nature of the client's problems and have the explicit agreement and consent of clients. NAPO affirms that strict criteria should be applied by probation officers prior to suggesting the use of extra conditions, such as attendance at day centres, in order to ensure that they are used appropriately.

It is therefore important to reiterate NAPO's position in relation to working with clients within a framework of extra conditions, because NAPO's position is different to that of the Home Office in

SNOP. NAPO believes that extra conditions should not be used solely to impose control or to contain clients, nor should probation be an exercise in court imposed surveillance. On the contrary, if extra conditions are considered unavoidable they should primarily facilitate the positive provision of social work help which should benefit offenders. Consequently NAPO policy has been summarised in the following way:

> We do not welcome the use of extra conditions in probation orders believing that existing legislation allows sufficiently for the probation officer to offer the range of help and advice described above in a flexible and open manner. Good practice essentially cannot be reproduced in legislation. Our social work identity, stressed in this paper, makes it vital that we do not succumb to calls for 'tougher' approaches by the imposition of extra and unnecessary conditions. The risk to our practice is real and NAPO should continue to oppose any extension of a controlling role (1982, para. 4.11, p9).

One may applaud the way in which NAPO continues to faithfully endorse its social work values and defend its principles. The problem is that it is swimming against a current which is taking the service in a different direction as we shall see later. It may nevertheless be argued that the views of the National Association of Probation Officers deserve serious consideration within the probation service, particularly in relation to the practice and philosophy of probation supervision. It cannot be emphasised too strongly that NAPO unambiguously affirms that the probation order should be based upon the principles and values of social work, that social work principles should take precedence over social control and that the use of extra conditions should be kept to the absolute minimum. Accordingly there is this radical dimension to NAPO's views which constitutes an important element in the dialectics of contemporary probation debates concerning the future orientation of the service. Furthermore Michael Day, the former Chief Probation Officer of the West Midlands, has said that one should not be surprised if a professional group of workers, like probation officers, who are concerned with a disadvantaged section of the community, did have a radical element. He suggests an important role for NAPO by stating that

> Any service working as close to the formal system of social control as probation needs an internal reminder that it must not comply uncritically with demands made upon it. Resistance from

77

NAPO has often represented a proper caution and resulted in constuctive shifts in policy and practice (Day, 1987, p33).

Having now considered NAPO's response to SNOP and its views on probation, I turn next to the way in which the Probation Journal has been used as a vehicle through which a range of concerns have been articulated.

The Probation Journal, Home Office Draft Note and SNOP

I am surprised that the Journal has not been used more extensively than it has to feature articles on the subject of the Statement of National Objectives and Priorities, it being the instrument through which probation officers, of all grades, can express their views on probation issues. A case could have been made to publish a special issue of the Journal devoted entirely to the ramifications of the Home Office proposals, for which precedents exist. For example, a special issue of the Journal was produced in response to the Younger Report in 1974 and also in response to the inception of community service orders in 1977. Except for Raynor's article on the Home Office Draft (1984) and my own attempt to discuss the context within which SNOP emerged (Whitehead, 1987), one has to search the Journal extremely carefully to find articles relating to the final Statement. In fact in the two years following the publication of SNOP, not one article appeared which specifically concentrated on this subject. What did appear were two very short comments in the 'Personal Accounts' section of the Journal, of which only one of these, by Morrison, related to the final Statement. Therefore after acknowledging what must be considered as a significant omission in the Probation Journal on a subject which could have far reaching implications for the future of the service, the concerns articulated in the Journal may now be considered.

In March 1984 Creedon, who was then a Senior Probation Officer in the Durham service, suggested that the response of the probation service to the Home Office Draft Note should express caution. Even though the Draft presented the service with a challenge, Creedon also suggested that it contained risks. Once again concern was expressed that social work values were not discussed at any length by the Home Office and because through-care and civil work were afforded such a low priority. Creedon argued that social work help should be available equally to those offenders subjected to probation orders and those released from prison, on the grounds that both groups of offenders might have needs and problems which could be amenable to the assistance the service provides. He concluded by saying that the Home Office Draft document was primarily a product of civil servants and that it reflected their concerns rather than reflecting any understanding of the needs of clients. Therefore 'The challenge to the Service is to demonstrate that our values, our skills and our experience can provide a legitimate service to people going through the experience of Court appearances and custodial sentences' (1984, p31).

Two issues later Morrison, a Deputy Chief Probation Officer in Nottinghamshire, acknowledged that the response of the service had been one of uncertainty and apprehension, but this time in relation to the Statement rather than the Draft (1984). According to Morrison, such responses reflected anxiety about whether SNOP will promote service leadership or whether it will be used to reinforce service management. By management he meant the allocation of tasks and roles, planning, determining the most effective way of doing things and achieving certain objectives. But by leadership he meant the concern with beliefs and values which resulted in him posing the question: 'how is the Probation Service to combine these two components?'

Morrison answered by arguing that the Home Office is exercising its management responsibilities in SNOP by setting clear objectives for the service. However he also argued that the probation service itself should articulate its value base (by which, unfortunately, Morrison seems to mean the discredited rehabilitative ideal) and that these values should inform the way in which objectives are defined and pursued. His most interesting comment was to suggest that there could develop a division within the service between, on the one hand, Chief Probation Officers and Probation Committees who are mainly concerned with management and objectives and, on the other hand, main grade probation officers and NAPO who are mainly concerned with service values. It seems that there is the potential for such a division to emerge, but Morrison's analysis fails to account for the fact that the

79

situation within the service is complex, in that it is incorrect to assume that all management grades will automatically or unthinkingly work to assiduously apply the principles of SNOP, or that CPO's and ACPO's are not concerned with social work values. Morrison concludes by appealing to CPO's to give professional leadership and, to step outside the Probation Journal for a moment, perhaps Jenny Roberts would be considered to be doing just that in the thoughts she articulated at a NAPO Conference at York in 1984.

As the Chief Probation Officer of Hereford and Worcester, Roberts emphasised the importance of the service making clear to all those it associated with what it stands for (1984, p15). She acknowledged that certain values are being threatened in the post-SNOP era because the cost of helping the vulnerable and less competent is being questioned. Everything seems to have its price and in such a climate Roberts encourages the service to hold fast to its values, even though this may result in a reduction of resources. In other words, 'Resources may be the price the service pays for its values' (p6). And by values Roberts means concern for all those in need within the criminal justice system, a concern for justice, individualisation and respect for the dignity of all offenders.

To return to the Journal, Beaumont has also been concerned to defend certain values in an article in which he reflected on the future of the penal system as a whole, but which also contained a brief comment on the Home Office Draft (1984b). Subsequently Beaumont took issue with the Statement at the York Conference (1984a), where he drew attention to certain issues worth consideration. The analyis of Beaumont is that the two main strands of Government thinking contained in SNOP are applied monetarism and the emphasis on control. However, and this is a significant point overlooked by some critics of SNOP who only see the document advocating an accentuation of control, there is a third strand. Beaumont argues that this third strand comprises ideas which are drawn, first of all, from the British Crime Survey, which suggested that much offending is relatively trivial, that the fear of crime is greater than its actual reality and that the public are less punitive than one is led to believe by emotive comments within the popular media. Other features of this third strand include coordinating the response of all agencies who comprise the criminal justice system, understanding crime in its social context, crime prevention, mediation, reparation and a concern for the victims of crime.

Therefore the reality of SNOP, it must be acknowledged once again, is somewhat complex because it contains conflicting and competing ideas. Accordingly in the post-SNOP era it seems that the potential exists for the probation service to develop systems of working in the community, which was suggested by Raynor (1984); to develop the more progressive programmes advocated by Beaumont (see Walker and Beaumont in Chapter 2 above); or the development of more controlling and coercive practices. Beaumont stated that SNOP

is based on contradictory ideas and contains differing possibilities. It reads as an incomplete, shallow and ultimately unsatisfactory manifesto for change. In time I think it will read very oddly indeed, as a curious product of curious times (1984a, p28).

Finally having now perused the Probation Journal for its views on the Draft and Statement, the next section of this chapter will consider the way in which area probation services initially responded to SNOP.

Area services responses to SNOP

After the publication of SNOP, the Home Office made it clear that it expected area services to respond by producing their own local statements which were intended to constitute the basis for putting the National Statement into effect. At the same time the Association of Chief Officers of Probation commissioned a study of these local statements which were collated and analysed during the last few months of 1985 at the Cambridge Institute of Criminology (Lloyd, 1986). The analysis of these local statements reveals the way in which area probation services expressed a rich diversity of opinions on SNOP, which could result in a degree of tension between area services and the Home Office in relation to certain apects of probation practice, philosophy and values in years to come. What did Lloyd's research discover?

Firstly it has been noted already how section VB of SNOP is devoted to the supervision of offenders in the community. Specifically

81

section VB (iv) resorts to the language of 'maintaining a range of facilities' which may be interpreted to mean, for example, the development of Day Centre facilities under Schedule 11 of the 1982 Act. Lloyd discovered that of the 32 areas which described the setting up of special facilities to deal with offenders as an alternative to custody, 10 areas mentioned using the requirements contained in Schedule 11. Alternatively 3 areas apparently did not resort to these requirements, ostensibly on the grounds that extra conditions will adversely affect the flexibility inherent within the probation order (p14). Once again the crucial issue of the degree to which it is considered legitimate and appropriate for the probation service to exercise control over society's deviants is encountered and Lloyd found that 'Areas are divided in their approach to the issue of control; some are keen to take on more serious offenders and develop more coercive practices, while others are less so' (p65).

Secondly the subject of SNOP's priorities elicited a variety of responses from area services (p56f), in that few areas produced a list of priorities duplicating that contained in SNOP. To recapitulate what these priorities are, section VI (a) of the Statement stated that the first priority of the service must be the supervision of as many offenders as possible in the community, especially where custody is a real possibility. Consequently social enquiry reports should be prepared more selectively (VI (b)) and only sufficient resources should be allocated to through-care in order for the service to fulfil its statutory obligations (VI (c)). Moreover sufficient resources should be allocated to community work and civil work (VI (d) and (e)). But section VII of the Statement made it clear that priority VI (a) will demand a larger proportion of each area services total resouces, which involves a reappraisal of sections VI (b), (c) and (e), culminating in the possibility of a reduced level of resources in these areas of work. There are those associated with the service who perceive that this is the thin end of the wedge which could result in the probation service eventually being divested of its responsibilities for through-care and civil work. Interestingly of 51 areas analysed by Lloyd, 28 failed to include a list of priorities in their local statements; 6 areas duplicated SNOP's list of priorities;

5 areas adopted a different order of priorities, leaving 12 areas to adopt a different form of priorities altogether to SNOP.

Thirdly, and to expand the analysis of the preceding paragraph, the issue of the service having a set of priorities imposed by the Home Office logically proceeds to a discussion of values, which is perhaps the most important subject on which the Home Office and probation service could experience conflict, but which has only been alluded to so far in this chapter. The nature of the problem was introduced by Lloyd when he said that

> The implication of any process of prioritisation is that some tasks are more important than others and as a result should receive more resources. To many people involved with the Service, all the work done is important and none can be given up, due to the fact that people will suffer as a result (p62).

It is therefore reasonable to hypothesise that if SNOP's priorities are applied in area services who are under pressure from the Home Office (although Lloyd's research indicates this is not a foregone conclusion), then a situation will arise in which some areas of work are deemed to be more important than others - probation more important than through-care and civil work - resulting in certain categories or classes of offenders being potentially neglected. If it is the case that resources will be limited in future and if area services are under pressure to implement a policy based upon the principle of the most efficient and cost-effective use of resources, it is possible to speculate on the following scenario.

According to SNOP, the category of offenders primarily targeted for supervision in the community are those facing a custodial sentence, rather than those minor and/or first time offenders who are obviously not in danger of custody. In other words, if the administrative, bureaucratic and financially determined policy of the Home Office and Exchequer is applied, which involves prioritising between offenders on the basis of who is and who is not at risk of receiving a custodial sentence, then such a policy will undoubtedly clash with those social work and professional values already introduced above. The difference in approach is between a policy based on deeds compared with a policy based on individual need. For it seems that the probation service remains professionally committed, on the whole, to respond to the needs and problems of all offenders, both high and low tariff cases, who are being processed by the criminal justice system. Moreover Boswell's empirical research into the goals of the probation service, discovered that a high proportion of her sample of 100 probation officers saw the goals of the service in social work terms. This meant that phrases such as 'helping the individual', 'assisting the offender to realise his own potential', and 'to advise, assist and befriend', were being used. In other words, a commitment to social work implies helping all individuals in need, rather than selected categories of clients (Boswell, 1982, p112f).

It is not without significance that despite the relative silence of the Home Office on the concept of social work values in SNOP, many areas included a section on values in their local statements. Lloyd found that 30 out of 51 services mentioned social work ethics. It should therefore be acknowledged that the cost effective, value for money, philosophy of SNOP which is enshrined in the Financial Management Initiative, is in direct conflict with the values of a professional agency which, on the whole, refuses to abandon the values of care and concern for all offenders, irrespective of what the financial costs might be. This point finds empirical support in Lloyd's research because even though the FMI is a central theme running throughout SNOP, it was largely ignored by over a third of the local statements, which probably conveys a hidden yet powerful message to the Home Office. For as one area service remarked 'Given the need to provide a cost effective Service it would be well to acknowledge that human values cannot be assessed by financial methods of accounting alone' (p63).

Axiology and the probation service

Because the issue of values is likely to remain important when considering the future orientation of the service, it requires more detailed exploration at this juncture. Accordingly the first task is to unpack the concept of values which has been referred to several times already in this chapter. It must be said that it is one of those concepts which means different things to different people, thus raising the problem of definitional precision. And even though, as was pointed out in the previous chapter, the Home Office has not completely abandoned social work values in SNOP, it is undeniable that the Statement is based on a different value system to that which would be articulated by, for example, NAPO, perceived as the guardian of the professional value base of the service. But what is meant by appealing to the notion of social work values?

A theory of value (or axiology) concerns those things considered to be good, desirable and important, and Downie and Telfer would say that a value is something which is valued in a particular way by someone or a group (1980, p9). Therefore when probation officers resort to the term values within the context of their work with offenders, they mean a constellation of attitudes and responses directed towards offenders which are considered to be of intrinsic moral worth, fundamentally humane and to be highly esteemed as ends in themselves. Translated into spheres of action this would mean that through a process of demonstrating care and concern, helping, supporting and assisting, advising and befriending individual offenders, probation officers remain faithful to a basic core of professional ethics. Furthermore in a riposte to SNOP produced jointly by ACOP, CCPC and NAPO (Probation - The Next Five Years, 1987), probation values are articulated as respect for persons; a belief in the freedom of the individual; the capacity for individuals to change for the better; that lasting change can only come from within and not imposed from without; and a commitment to minimum intervention and to constructive, humanitarian approaches to offenders.

The values being referred to here are echoed in McWilliams' analysis of the Personalist School within the contemporary probation service (McWilliams, 1987, p110), represented by the writings of Hugman (1977), Millard (1979), Bailey (1980), Stelman (1980) and Raynor (1985). According to McWilliams, the personalist school insists that offenders should be treated as ends in themselves, rather than as means to an end. To capture the flavour of this school and also to press the point home even further, Hugman has said that

> My general thesis is that action or service of any kind, whether by social workers.... or whoever, has integrity and value only if it has regard to and respect for the unique human capacities and talents and needs of individuals (1977, p14).

However it may be argued that it is becoming much more difficult for the service to indulge itself in an approach dominated by social work values, particularly when practice based on help and 'treatment' offers no guarantee that offending will be subsequently reduced and that a social work approach to the more serious offender may do little to convice the courts or public that the probation service is offering a credible alternative to custody. Nevertheless it is interesting to speculate here on what might happen in practice situations when a main grade officer is faced with making certain decisions cognizant with the principles and values of SNOP, whilst attempting to preserve the professional value base of his social work training.

Let us consider a probation officer fully aware that, as a consequence of SNOP, he should be recommending mainly serious offenders for probation supervision who are at risk of losing their liberty. It transpires that during the course of interviewing an offender within the context of preparing a written report to assist the court to determine the appropriate disposal, that this particular offender is not at risk of losing his liberty, having committed a minor shoplifting offence. However other features require attention, which are that the offender has certain personal and social problems, including what may be assessed as welfare needs, which could be alleviated by activating the resources available to the probation service if he was the subject of a statutory probation order. Faced with these factors, will the officer be forced to explain to the offender and subsequently the court that, even though the offender has various needs, he cannot be assisted by the probation service because his deeds do not warrant statutory intervention, there being no risk of a custodial sentence? Will the Senior Probation Officer, who is responsible for his team's performance and the achievement of certain objectives delineated in SNOP and the respective local area statement, demand that the main grade officer divert 'minor' cases such as this away from valuable resources? Or will the officer ignore his Senior and the implications of SNOP by responding to the needs of the individual offender rather than conform to the impersonal, fiscal demands of the FMI? Will decisions be made on the basis of cost-effectiveness or the needs of individual

86

offenders? (I should add that senior managers in the Northamptonshire probation service started to encourage officers to avoid recommending first offenders for probation and to focus instead on more serious offenders, which led to some resistance (Parry-Khan, 1988, p16)). These seem crucial questions facing the service in the post-SNOP era, the answer to which will determine the future shape and priorities, the moral basis and value system, the diversion of offenders from custody, in addition to the kind of officers who will operate such an agency.

According to Lloyd, the questions I have just addressed concern 'human plight' situations which officers are faced with daily and it is worth quoting Lloyd in full where he concludes his discussion on values by saying that

> it is clear...that the Service is very committed to its social work values, and feels threatened by the implications of SNOP's proposals. However, as always, the response is far from unified and there are major differences between areas. Quite a large number of local Services felt it unnecessary to mention values at all, and there were quite marked differences of opinion. But the significance of these values for many areas should certainly not be underestimated. To quote one final statement, 'If practice does not fit comfortably with these values, then it is the practice which should be reviewed' (1986, p68).

How will the probation service resolve the conflict between a policy based on social work values determining the nature of practice, with a Home Office policy where, in future, limited resources will determine the policy and not where the policy will determine the resources?

Conclusion

It is therefore clear that, in future, there is the potential for conflict between the Home Office, the probation service and particularly the professional concerns represented by NAPO. Consequently it is legitimate to consider that the National Association of Probation Officers has the increasingly important task of protecting the interests of its members and client groups, in addition to preserving 'values which may seem threatened by political expediency' (Day, 1987, p22). This is because there is the danger that, in years to come, the probation service 'may give greater emphasis to social control and cost effectiveness than to the considerations of social welfare and individual need that are central concerns of a social work profession' (Day, 1987, p34).

Accordingly Table 4.1 returns to the discussion in the first part of this chapter by summarising some of the central themes of the NAPO model for the supervision of offenders in the community which, I suggest, should be seriously considered alongside those other models discussed in previous chapters. Having said that, if the probation service is to convince the courts that it has the ability to provide alternatives to custody for the more serious offender, can it achieve this by an approach which emphasises social work rather than social control?

Having considered, albeit briefly and selectively, the way in which area services have responded to SNOP through their local statements towards the end of this chapter, the next chapter, which completes the first part of this thesis, sharpens the focus even further by specifically analysing how one probation service has articulated its understanding of the various dimensions of the probation order. This introduces the probation service in which empirical research was undertaken during 1987 and 1988.

Table 4.1

The NAPO model of probation supervision

CONTINUUM

CARE

ELEMENTS OF PROBATION PRACTICE

The two main elements of practice are supervision, | HARRIS
and, advice, assistance and friendship.

Probation supervision should offer help, guidance and | WALKER
support through a one-to-one relationship. Through a | AND
variety of welfare orientated facilities, probation | BEAUMONT
should provide social skills training, family therapy,
courses on the use of leisure, recreation, and to help
offenders find employment, adult literacy, welfare | NAPO
rights advice, and group work.

Adjuncts to probation orders, such as Day Centres,
should operate on the principle of voluntarism.

The probation order may be offered at all stages of a
criminal career, but particularly for more serious
offenders who are at risk of custody.

IDEOLOGY AND RATIONALE

To make supervision effective and reduce crime during | BOTTOMS
the period of the order. A humane approach to problems | AND
based on a meaningful relationship between officer and | McWIL'MS
probationer. To enhance offenders self responsibility
and capacity to deal with personal and social problems. | RAYNOR
To confront offenders with choices concerning their
behaviour, and help them acquire more understanding and
acceptance of themselves. To behave in ways less
damaging to themselves, families, and communities.

NAPO does not refer to rehabilitation or treatment.

CARE/CONTROL AND CONDITIONS

The 'normal' probation order contains sufficient | BRYANT
conditions to allow probation officers to work
constructively with clients. On the whole NAPO
opposes extra conditions under Schedule 11, but if they | SNOP
are used then strict criteria should be applied to
limit their use.

Extra conditions should not be solely used as a means
of control, containment or surveillance, but to
facilitate the provision of social work help which | DAVIES
should benefit and constructively assist offenders. | GRIFF'S

The dimensions of care and social work values are
emphasised more than control, which means that the
NAPO model can be located nearer the care end of the
continuum.

CONTROL

5 The Cleveland service and probation: a local model

Introduction

When the Cleveland Probation Service was formed following local government reorganisation on the 1st of April, 1974, it had a total of 63 probation officers of all grades, 32 clerical staff, one ancillary worker employed in the courts and a part-time lodgings officer. It was responsible for the supervision of 2116 offenders who were the subject of probation, juvenile supervision and through-care orders. A total of 4122 criminal and civil reports were prepared for the courts and the service had the facility of an after-care hostel which was supported by a voluntary committee.

Ten years later, at the end of the year in which SNOP appeared, the Cleveland Service had 78 probation officers, 20 ancillary staff, 8 hostel warden staff, a full-time lodgings officer and 51 administrative and clerical staff. A total of 1996 offenders were the subject of probation, juvenile supervision and through-care orders, and in 1984 a total of 5017 criminal and civil reports were prepared. Moreover additional resources and the legislative provisions for alternatives to custody, a consequence of the 1972 and 1982 Criminal

Justice Acts, have provided new dimensions to the work of the Cleveland Service. For example, community service began in Cleveland in 1975 and by the mid-1980's operated 700 new orders per year, in addition to the more recent provision for 16 year old offenders. A Probation Hostel opened in Middlesbrough in 1978 providing 20 places for adult offenders subject to a probation order with a condition to reside at the hostel, followed in 1981 with a Bail Hostel providing accommodation for up to 20 offenders who might otherwise have been remanded in custody to Durham prison. Furthermore in 1984 the Day Centre moved from a dilapidated church hall into refurbished and more spacious accommodation in Middlesbrough, which afforded the facility much greater potential.

Therefore the decade 1974 to 1984 has been one of change, innovation and expansion for the Cleveland Probation Service. It is also possible that the next decade will experience further changes, particularly in the sphere of working with offenders in the community, because of the way the service attempts to give effect to the implications of the Home Office Statement of National Objectives and Priorities.

This chapter is divided into two sections. Firstly the story will be recounted of how the Cleveland Service started to engage in a process of consultation and discussion which culminated in a local statement in January 1986, which delineated how it proposed to give effect to SNOP at the local level. Secondly the way in which the local service has articulated its views on the various dimensions of probation supervision will be discussed.

The local process

In a letter sent by David Faulkner to all Chief Probation Officers which accompanied the Home Office Statement on the 30th of April, 1984, the view was expressed that the Home Secretary hoped that chief officers and probation committees would seriously consider the Statement when deciding local service objectives and priorities. Subsequently on the 3rd of October, 1984, the CPO of Cleveland said that

The Cleveland Probation Committee at its July 1984 meeting had before it the Home Office Statement of National Objectives and Priorities. It resolved that the Chief Officer should prepare a comprehensive statement for the October meeting of the Committee which would outline the methods by which the priorities identified in the Home Office Statement could be achieved in Cleveland (Cleveland Probation Service, 1984, para. 1).

This statement by the chief officer is extracted from a Consultative Document Regarding Organisational Changes published on the 3rd October 1984, which may be said to mark the official beginning of the local process which embraced all probation staff and which eventually culminated in the Future Directions Document of January 1986. From October 1984 the service was actively involved in a process of consultation and discussion on a wide range of probation issues at many different levels. This process, which was precipitated by SNOP, continued throughout the whole of 1985.

To correctly recount the story of the local process in Cleveland, historical accuracy demands that this story should begin in 1983 at a point predating both the publication of the Home Office Draft and the final Statement. To be precise, the earliest reference I was able to discover in the Cleveland probation service to those national events which involved the Home Office meeting with the representative organisations of the service which culminated in the Draft of 1983, was a Minute from a meeting of senior probation officers on the 27th of May, 1983. Some weeks later at another meeting of senior probation officers on the 5th of July 1983, one of the two Assistant Chief Probation Officers (the one who was shortly afterwards promoted to the post of CPO in Cumbria) told this meeting of middle managers that a number of factors were posing a direct challenge to the work of the probation service in England and Wales. These factors were enumerated as the nature of the incumbent Conservative Government (a comment which was not qualified), the growing emphasis on management and the concern to obtain value for money (the FMI). This meeting heard that questions were being asked, at a national level, about the deployment of resources and the need to move away from traditional roles.

Throughout the remainder of 1983 there were three further references to the Draft within the context of seniors meetings, after it had been published, once in September and twice in October. Accordingly from as early as May 1983, there were those in the Cleveland Service, particularly at senior and middle-management levels (which comprised the CPO, the two ACPO's and SPO's), who were conscious that something was happening to the service, that it was under review by the Home Office, which would have implications for the future aims, objectives and priorities of area services. Moreover what was happening had implications for the role of local management teams in relation to the allocation of resources and the monitoring of effectiveness in all spheres of probation practice, specifically in the sphere of community supervision.

The chapter on SNOP should have made it clear that it is a complex task disentangling those diverse strands which culminated in the final Statement. Similarly the local story reveals a process which involved various influences and pressures concerning the way in which the Cleveland Service started to give effect to SNOP. It is inaccurate to state that it was solely the Home Office Draft or Statement which resulted in the local service taking stock of itself and thinking in terms of objectives, priorities and management goals. Notwithstanding the undoubted influence of the Home Office, it must be acknowledged that the appointment of a new ACPO who succeeded the aforementioned ACPO who was appointed CPO in Cumbria and who commenced work in January 1984, was a significant event in the process of beginning to think in terms of clarifying and delineating local service aims and objectives. The new ACPO joined a senior management team which comprised the CPO and one other ACPO. (However it should be added that a third ACPO was appointed in August 1985 who eventually commenced work in November. Therefore at the present time the senior management team, which is based in Middlesbrough, comprises the CPO and three ACPO's).

It seems reasonable to suggest that the arrival of the new ACPO at the beginning of 1984 was significant because he came to Cleveland with clearly worked out views on the role of management which meant that the language of aims, objectives and priorities was in vogue. Furthermore it may be suggested that he breathed new life into a management structure which had remained unchanged for several years, by questioning and challenging traditional ways of thinking about what

93

the probation service was doing in Cleveland and where it thought it was going. Within several weeks of his arrival he had initiated an exercise amongst a number of senior probation officers in February 1984 which consisted in them having to examine the objectives of their respective teams. Subsequently at a seniors meeting held on the 13th of March, 1984, senior officers were reminded about the team objectives exercise and the ACPO explained that a similar exercise was taking place amongst senior management within headquarters. By March 1984, the same ACPO had produced a document for a headquarters meeting on the principles, aims and objectives of the Cleveland Service, followed in May and June by successive papers on the subject of managing the service. Of course, the production of the Home Office Draft and subsequently SNOP, must have served to sharpen the focus of the Cleveland Service on the issues of its future aims and objectives. However it may be argued that the arrival of the new ACPO during the period between the publication of the 1983 Draft and 1984 Statement, had a marked effect on getting the local service, particularly at senior and middle-management levels, to look at the implications of developing a set of local aims and objectives and the increasingly important issue of managing the service efficiently and ensuring that social work practice is effective.

By April 1984, the climate within Cleveland was conducive to responding to the Home Office Statement in a serious and positive manner. In other words, it was psychologically prepared to initiate a local process which would eventually culminate in a series of proposals designed to give effect to SNOP once the Home Office had finally made its intentions clear.

After April 1984 the local process gathered pace. On the 7th of May, 1984, SNOP was discussed at the weekly meeting of senior management in headquarters, when it was decided to circulate copies of the Statement to all probation officers. Then by week commencing the 18th of June, the Home Office Inspector for the Cleveland Service arrived from Manchester to discuss various issues with senior management, including the document prepared by the ACPO on managing the service. Even though this visit was apparently not a direct response to SNOP, the issue of future management objectives for the service was discussed. Then, over one year later in August 1985, the Inspector retured to specifically discuss how the service was proposing to translate SNOP into actual practice locally. However it was made clear to me during an interview I had with one of the participants that this meeting was conducted at a 'low-key' level, in the sense that the Inspector was not imposing directives on the local service from above. But remaining with what happened in 1984, it has already been noted that on the 17th of July, 1984, the probation committee held its quarterly meeting at which it had before it the Home Office Statement, in addition to the paper on managing the service prepared by the new ACPO. Accordingly the Committee commissioned the CPO to produce a response by the October meeting of the committee which culminated in the Consultative Document Regarding Organisational Changes on the 3rd of October, 1984.

On the day the Consultative Document was published a meeting was held between senior and middle-management to discuss its content and implications. This Document was relatively brief, no more than 500 words in length, but certain policy aims of the service were articulated. Firstly it was asseverated that the most important aim of the service was to increase the use of probation and supervision orders by developing a system of Day Care (later renamed Resource Units), with the task of providing constructive packages for probation, juvenile supervision and after-care clients on both a voluntary and statutory basis. Secondly the Document stated that a critical analysis of probation practice was necessary in future, that senior officers would be expected to exercise a greater influence over the intake of work into their teams and that reports for the courts would have to be prepared more selectively. Thirdly it was proposed to create a small Civil Work Unit and, fourthly, community service orders would continue to be used for offenders facing a custodial sentence. Finally additional resources were to be sought to finance the proposed changes. Consequently from a situation in which discussions were held between senior and middle-management, the Consultative Document widened the process to include all probation staff, which will now be considered.

During the last few weeks of 1984 a series of meetings were being organised throughout the county by headquarters which were to involve all probation and clerical staff. A letter sent to probation officers by the CPO said that 'I am very much looking forward to joining with you in a process of consultation and discussion which will influence the future working of the Cleveland Service in a major way for the next decade' (Cleveland Probation Service, 1985a).

These meetings were held at different times in different localities throughout the county to incorporate staff from the districts of Middlesbrough, Langbaurgh, Stockton and Hartlepool. At these meetings the agenda was comprised of a total of nine subjects which were considered to be important by senior management. These nine subjects were : probation packages, day care, civil work, detention centre and youth custody supervision, a district approach to probation work, court reports, juvenile justice, court work and links with the wider community. Each of the four district meetings was divided at its one day conference into three subgroups which meant that each group was expected to examine three of the nine subjects under discussion. Later on the discussions of each group were written up to produce a report which appeared in March 1985 as the Future Directions Discussion Papers (Cleveland Probation Service, 1985b).

A few days prior to the publication of these Discussion Papers, the CPO published an Interim Report concerning the process of organisational change which kept staff informed as to what was happening, particularly concerning the bid to secure additional resources (Cleveland Probation Service, 1985c). Therefore the period between January and March 1985, saw the appearance of the Discussion Papers which were circulated to every probation office in the county, with the Chief Officer's Interim Report. Moreover by this time a joint Probation Committee/NAPO/NALGO Working Party had been established to examine the proposals for change contained in the Consultative Document. This development requires analysing in some detail because certain problems emerged within the Working Party which should be mentioned, to which I'll return later. At this juncture it may be said that the Working Party was a response to a resolution passed by the Cleveland Branch of NAPO which had stated that

This Branch calls for an early JCC meeting to discuss the

96

consultative document on organisational changes as presented by the Chief Officer, with a view to setting up a Working Party of Employer, Management and NAPO, and the Working Party report to the JCC at an agreed time (Cleveland Probation Service, 1985d).

The history of the JCC (Joint Consultative Committee) in Cleveland predates the creation of the county in 1974 which was the year when almost all other JCC's were formed. It appears that the former Teesside Probation Service established a JCC in March 1973 at the initiative of the probation committee. It is comprised of probation committee members who represent the employers (magistrates) and members of staff (probation officers) providing a forum where issues of mutual interest and concern can be discussed by both parties. Consequently at a JCC meeting held on the 30th of November 1984, it was resolved that a Working Party should be established to consider the CPO's Consultative Document. The Working Party comprised four NAPO representatives, one NALGO official who represented the interests of clerical staff and some ancillaries, and three members of the probation committee. In addition the CPO, the two ACPO's and the secretary to the JCC, were to act as advisors to the Working Party which was to report any observations or suggestions to the JCC. The first meeting was held in February 1985 and a second was held in March. In addition to the work of the Working Party, throughout the whole of 1985 meetings were being held at regular intervals which involved all probation staff of all grades to specifically discuss the proposed changes.

On the 8th of May, 1985, a Further Consultative Document was published by the CPO which stated that because the service had managed to achieve some real growth in the budget which was eventually passed on the 23rd of April, 1985

we are now able to put more concrete proposals to staff about the future shape of the Service. We have particularly attempted to reflect views expressed in the Day Meetings when specialisms, packages and day care were significant areas of interest (Cleveland Probation Service, 1985e).

In practical terms this implied a degree of rationalisation which involved creating a Resource Senior Probation Officer at Hartlepool, conflating the three probation teams at Stockton, Thornaby and Billingham into two teams which would, in turn, create a second

97

Resource Senior, establishing a Civil Work team, reorganising the work of the Middlesbrough teams to create a specialist Court Team, and preparing for the appointment of a third ACPO. These proposals were discussed at further district meetings held throughout 1985. For example, the Middlesbrough District held meetings on the 16th of May and the 16th of October, 1985, at which the proposal for a restructured court team, the duties of the Resource Seniors and the work of the Resource Units, civil work and the functions of the long awaited computer, were all debated at some length.

On reflection it appears that the process of consultation initiated by senior management in October 1984, which continued throughout 1985 with a view to eliciting the views and opinions of all probation staff to the proposed changes, and in which the author of this book participated, was a positive and constructive process. On the whole, most officers made a positive and enthusiastic response. In fact the messages received within headquarters from senior officers who had discussed a variety of issues with their teams, suggested that the vast majority of officers were thinking seriously about the future of the Cleveland Probation Service.

However, to return to an earlier point, problems surfaced within the Working Party. It appears that throughout the summer of 1985 difficulties emerged between senior management and staff which were to persist until the end of the year, which resulted in the staff side of the Working Party calling for a cessation of its activities until a full meeting of the JCC had been held. It is now difficult to uncover the exact nature of the grievances which existed at the time, but the focus of the problem seemed to be that some members of NAPO perceived that the service was not being properly consulted about proposals for change. It was felt by some that the process of consultation was largely a cosmetic exercise because it was believed that headquarters had a master plan or blue print for the future of the service. It has to be said that, on the basis of documentary evidence consulted and the author's personal involvement in what was happening at this time, this claim is somewhat dubious to say the least, when the story of the local process recounted so far has stressed the reality of discussion and consultation with members of staff at every stage of the decision making process.   In fact it appears that senior management were acutely sensitive concerning the necessity to repeatedly consult with staff on proposed changes and developments, which was conducive to eliciting their cooperation.

Notwithstanding these problems, which resulted in an untimely delay before any proposals could be implemented which would affect working practices, by the end of 1985 some of the difficulties were resolved. This resulted in the publication of the definitive management document in January 1986 - Future Directions : Objectives and Priorities (Cleveland Probation Service, 1986).   This was the document which articulated the primary task, aims and priorities of the Cleveland Probation Service, in addition to delineating the policy and practice implications of five main service objectives described as community supervision programmes, criminal courts and reports, community involvement, through-care and civil work.   Because this document is the result of fifteen months hard work, by which the Cleveland Service intends to give concrete effect to SNOP and also because it will determine the shape of the service for many years to come, the priorities of the local service stated in this document may be reproduced in full:

1) The effective supervision of offenders released by the criminal courts into the community with the objective of reducing offending behaviour and rehabilitating offenders.

2) The preparation of effective reports on offenders to assist the criminal courts in the sentencing function.

3) Appropriate participation with the community in order to adopt a corporate approach towards crime prevention, the victims of crime and the rehabilitation of offenders.

4) The provision of effective through and after-care supervision for those offenders sentenced to custody by the courts.

5) The maintenance of a specialist social work service in collaboration with relevant community groups and statutory services for the civil courts in their domestic jurisdiction.

Like SNOP the Cleveland Future Directions Document considers probation work in the spheres of community supervision, social enquiry reports, work in the community, through-care, after-care and civil work. However the Cleveland Service does not duplicate SNOP's priorities because of the way in which the local service intends to fulfil its obligations to all categories of clients which will not necessitate (initially at least), a shift in resources from through-care or civil work, towards community supervision. Cleveland's policy is that through-care and civil work will be adequately resourced and, as such, reflects NAPO policy rather than SNOP. Moreover it has more in common with the joint statement produced by ACOP, CCPC and NAPO, rather than SNOP, on the development of the probation service over the next five years (Probation - The Next Five Years, 1987).

One of the reasons for this is that budget negotiations between October 1984 and April 1985 produced an increase in resources, which provided for the appointment of additional staff and obviated any necessity to prioritise resources. In fact the local service was not a little surprised at the amount of extra resources it was able to attract which occurred against a national backcloth of cut-backs, financial restraint and limited growth. The outcome is that at present and for the forseeable future, the Cleveland Service will be able to fulfil all its obligations in all spheres of work without having to reallocate resources in the way envisaged by SNOP. However the signs already exist to indicate that from 1987 onwards, it will be increasingly difficult to attract extra resources at the levels recently achieved, which suggests that the service may eventually have to reconsider what levels of resources should be devoted to different areas of work. But this concerns the future rather than the immediate present.

I have now attempted to tell the story of the local process which began in May 1983 and which arrived at some kind of conclusion in January 1986. Prior to moving on in the second section of this chapter to analyse the way in which the Cleveland Service has articulated its views on the probation order specifically, the key dates in the local process may be summarised and presented chronologically in the following way:

27 May 1983	earliest reference to the Cleveland Service being made aware of the Home Office review of probation.
August 1983	Home Office Draft published.
January 1984	appointment of new ACPO.
April 1984	SNOP published.
17 July 1984	probation committee commissioned CPO to produce a local statement on how SNOP could be given effect locally by the October meeting.
3 Oct 1984	publication of Consultative Document Regarding Organisational Changes.
Early 1985	4 District one day conferences were held to discuss nine management issues.
19 Feb 1985	first meeting of NAPO/NALGO/Probation Committee Working Party created by the JCC on 30 Nov 1984.
18 March 1985	Interim Report to staff.
March 1985	Future Directions Discussion Papers published containing reports on nine management issues discussed at the district meetings.
8 May 1985	Future Directions - Further Consultative Document appeared.
May-Dec 1985	further district meetings held to discuss proposed changes. Meetings continued to be held at all levels to further the process of consultation and discussion. Problems emerged during this period within the Working Party.
January 1986	Future Directions : Objectives and Priorities was published. Key management policy document on the future of the service concerning community supervision, the courts, work in the community, through-care and civil work.

In order to explore the way in which the Cleveland Probation Service has articulated its views on the elements of probation practice, ideology and rationale, care and control, two documents already referred to are crucially important which will now be considered in more detail. Firstly in the Discussion Papers of March 1985, two sets of papers focussed on probation packages and day care. These papers are important because they constitute the only available documentary evidence and official record of what a number of practitioners thought about probation issues at this time. Secondly it is necessary to examine in more detail the management policy document of January 1986 which contains the definitive statement on community supervision programmes. It should also be acknowledged that senior management took account of the views articulated in the Discussion Papers when formulating local policies.

Future Directions Discussion Papers:Probation Packages

By employing the somewhat esoteric concept of 'packages' the Cleveland Service appears to mean that a range of activities and facilities will be made available to offenders within the context of a probation order. These packages will be made available to offenders who are the subject of 'standard' probation orders on a voluntary basis (and also to clients of the service who have been released from a period of custody). They will also be available to offenders as a direct requirement of a probation order. Depending on the assessed needs of the offender, it is proposed that the following facilities should be made available : life and social skills training, outdoor pursuits, offending behaviour groups, art and craft groups, domestic skills courses, video groups, literary skills groups, budgeting groups, family therapy, drinkwatchers, sports and gardening groups.

The four groups of probation officers who discussed packages at their respective day meetings seemed to understand that this provision would be offered to the courts as a condition of a probation order. Accordingly Schedule 11 4A (1)(b) of the 1982 Criminal Justice Act is to be invoked so that offenders placed on probation will be required to attend, for example, an offending behaviour group for a period of up to 60 days.

It should be acknowledged that the four groups of officers who discussed probation packages did not have an unlimited amount of time to develop their thinking. At most each group could devote no more than one hour to this subject which may help to account for what at times seems little more than a superficial analysis. Furthermore time restrictions may help to explain why the reports of these groups are

102

at some points vague and ambiguous in the sense that statements are made without explanation or clarification. However as the introduction to the Discussion Papers warned 'These papers simply chronicle the first part of a considerable exercise. They are in a sense rough and uncut, but hopefully reflect some of the enthusiasm that the Service has for the task' (Cleveland Probation Service, 1985b).

Nevertheless all the groups perceived that packages will be made available to courts in those cases where offenders are facing a custodial sentence. One group remarked that even though traditional one-to-one casework type probation orders will remain for minor offenders, it was also assumed that Orders with a 'package' are to be located at the heavy end of the offending spectrum. By 'heavy' I assume that this refers to cases where offenders have committed relatively serious offences and/or have serious records of crime which has placed them at risk of receiving a custodial sentence. The reasoning is that probation orders with a package will make the process of supervision in the community more credible to magistrates who, it is believed, will be more willing to impose this kind of order as a direct alternative to a custodial sentence. It remains the case that the courts will have to secure the consent of the offender before imposing such orders, a point reinforced by one of the groups. Moreover two out of the four groups stressed that packages must benefit clients and ideally be tailored to meet the specific needs of individual offenders.

Therefore when considering the issue of packages it seems that probation officers in Cleveland demand that they fulfil at least two criteria. Firstly magistrates must perceive they are tough enough to offer credible alternatives to custodial sentences for offenders located at the heavy end of the offending spectrum. Secondly such orders must be attractive to clients and meet some of their individual needs. In other words, in addition to making probation orders appear more credible to courts by accentuating control through Schedule 11 conditions, there must also be the opportunity for clients to receive a constructive social work service which will be of benefit to them. It should be added at this point that by the 1st of April 1987, a 'Change Your Ways in 30 Days' scheme was launched under the provisions

103

of Schedule 11 of the 1982 Act. As part of a probation order offenders were required to attend a group work programme for 30 days, as an alternative to a custodial sentence.

Accordingly nearly all four groups referred to the dimension of control and authority within probation orders, in the sense that these are recognised as ineluctable components of community supervision programmes. However there was the hint of a problem concerning the relationship between care and control among some probation officers. In fact one group considered that coming to terms with care and control was a 'major problem' for probation officers, but went on to say that 'Control particularly is something that officers have avoided over the last few years and Probation, whether it be packaged or not, would be difficult to sell unless officers face up to some degree of control' (Cleveland Probation Service, 1985b).

Even though the issue of control and care has apparently presented problems for some local officers, the groups simply acknowledged this almost in passing without attempting to theorise on the reasons for this dilemma. Nor did they attempt to explore a resolution to this problem, or define what care and control actually mean, or suggest how much control is legitimate for probation officers to exercise when they are also attempting to preserve a commitment to social work values. Consequently the pragmatic position to emerge from the group discussions was that even though probation officers should continue to help and care for offenders, they should also not be afraid to exercise discipline, control and authority. They seem to be articulating that care involves control in the sense that if one really cares about a client then this will be practically demonstrated by exercising control. As such this seems to echo the findings of Fielding referred to earlier where he stated that 'My respondents expressed difficulty in rigidly differentiating control and care. They do not see control and care as opposed ideologies' (1984, p167). However because the concept of care and control was not considered in detail by the groups, this and other issues require empirical exploration within the Cleveland Service in the post-SNOP period. This is because the Discussion Papers provide only a limited amount of information on contemporary probation concerns.

104

Finally, related to the concepts of discipline and control is the issue of breach proceedings taken against those offenders for failing to comply with the requirements of a probation order. All the groups discussed potential cases of breach action affirming that there will be occasions when certain clients will have to be breached for failing to comply. And even though such action on behalf of the probation officer may result in offenders being committed to custody, which would be diametrically opposite to what was intended when the probation order was originally imposed, this may be the price to pay for maintaining the credibility of the courts. For as one group said

> It was the consensus opinion that breach was not used enough and officers really had to consider it in great depth and even more readily. It was felt that breach should be only used as a last resort but there were other mediums for better warning systems, particularly using seniors and other management staff as a 'big stick' before breach need be used (Cleveland Probation Service, 1985b).

Albeit the contradictions inherent in balancing using breach 'even more readily' and 'as a last resort', it is acknowledged that the notions of flexibility, discretion and understanding must also be considered when deciding whether or not it is appropriate to breach an offender on probation.

To summarise, the group discussions on probation packages articulated the view that such packages, which will be predominantly offered to the courts as a condition of probation under Schedule 11 of the 1982 Act, must offer credible alternatives to custody. Clients will be required to consent to these orders and it is expected that packages will benefit clients by responding to their expressed individual needs. There may be a problem reconciling care and control for some officers, but there seems, on the whole, to be a pragmatic acceptance that officers will exercise care by providing what is understood as a social work service to clients, in addition to exercising discipline, control and authority on behalf of the courts and because these are integral components of the probation order. Finally, officers must not be afraid to breach clients when necessary and appropriate in order to maintain the credibility of the service before the courts.

Day Care

The provision of day care overlaps with probation packages in the sense that the former will provide the context for the service delivery of the latter. It was envisaged that throughout the county of Cleveland specific localities would provide buildings and probation staff who would have the responsibility of providing various packages. In other words, if an offender is placed on probation with a condition to undertake specified activities which may, for example, require the offender to participate in a social skills group, he may have to attend some facility within his local community for this purpose, or attend a probation day centre.

Much of the group discussions on day care duplicated the discussions on probation packages. Therefore to avoid unnecessary repitition the content of what was said will not be reproduced here. Suffice to say that one group expressed the opinion that

> There appeared to be unanimous agreement that Day Care facilities are an essential part of our future development. Whilst there will always be a place for one-to-one casework and supervision, a variety of facilities are crucial if we are to deal with unemployment and its attendant problems and produce viable schemes to act as alternatives to custody (Cleveland Probation Service, 1985b).

Alternatively another group expressed caution at the concept of day care, suggesting that some officers are worried about the control implications of such developments. Accordingly it was stated that 'The only anxiety expressed was the fear that day care may become a form of day custody with probation officers being the custodians of the keys' (Cleveland Probation Service, 1985b).

These, then, are the views of a number of probation officers on the subject of day care and probation packages, both of which should become important features of the probation order during the next few years within the Cleveland Probation Service.

Hitherto the views of probation practitioners on probation issues have been examined. But what, it may be asked, are the views of senior management on probation supervision? To answer this question one must return to consult in more detail the definitive management policy document which was published in January 1986.

106

Future Directions:Objectives and Priorities

The list of priorities of the Cleveland Service in relation to five specific areas of work has already been reproduced above. But what was articulated as the first priority in January 1986 was in fact a repetition of what had already been stated in the Consultative Document in October 1984. Here it was stated that the first and most important policy aim of the service was 'to increase the use of Probation...Orders'. Subsequently, by January 1986, senior management were able to discuss in more detail the ideology and rationale of probation orders in addition to reflecting on the resource and development implications of such orders.

Under Objective 1 in the Future Directions Document, which deals with Community Supervision Programmes, the policy of the Cleveland Service is

> To promote the use of community supervision programmes as direct alternatives to custody through the use of probation and supervision orders. Also, when necessary, to provide additional specific programmes as requirements of orders directed towards confronting offending behaviour, making reparation and promoting rehabilitation (Cleveland Probation Service, 1986, p4).

More than anything else it seems fair to say that the Cleveland Service wants to increase the use of probation orders, as direct alternatives to custodial sentences, which duplicates the central priority of SNOP. Moreover, and this is a significant point, it is acknowledged that probation orders without extra conditions merit consideration as alternatives to custody disposals in their own right.

However special community supervision programmes will be provided to strengthen the 'normal' probation order by developing the use of extra conditions

> to provide an alternative to custody option... where there are special needs that would not be met by Community Service by offenders. The programmes would provide a concentrated challenge and work in the areas of offending behaviour, life and social skills, addictions and the problems associated with long term unemployment (Cleveland Probation Service, 1986).

The central elements of these community supervision programmes are that they must offer a clear alternative to a custodial sentence, appear credible to courts, meet the needs of individual offenders and reduce crime by rehabilitating offenders. At this juncture it is simply necessary to acknowledge the fact that the senior management policy document articulates the rationale of probation in terms of rehabilitation. Interestingly the ideology persists that social work should be efficacious in reducing crime and achieve the rehabilitation of offenders. This is a subject to which I'll return later in the empirical section of this research when considering the views of individual probation officers on the subject of the rationale of probation.

To return to the subject of probation orders with extra conditions, it is expected that offenders will adhere to whatever requirements are imposed by the courts and that there will be clearly established minimum standards of supervision. Accordingly if it is a condition of an offender's probation order to attend a day centre on a weekly basis to participate in a course of family therapy, but fails to attend as directed, the offender will be breached unless he can adequately justify his absence. It is also expected that such absences will be quickly followed up by the probation officer responsible for the probation order, which implies that a close relationship will have to develop between the supervising officer and the staff of the day centre who may be responsible for putting into effect the extra condition.

Consequently it is clear from reading the official policy document of the Cleveland Probation Service regarding its future objectives and priorities, in addition to what has been said by practitioners, that the supervision of offenders in the community will be given a high profile over the next few years. Such a policy lends itself to empirical investigation which could profitably explore a range of probation issues, both quantitatively and qualitatively, some of which have been introduced in these first five chapters. Moreover against the background of a collapsed consensus which was discussed at length earlier and articulated in terms of the decline of the rehabilitative ideal, it would be interesting to know what sense probation officers are making of a central feature of their work at a time when community supervision is increasingly seen as an alternative to custody for the more serious offender. In fact, it should be acknowledged that this

kind of research is considered desirable by the Chief Probation
Officer who stated in October 1984 that, in future, 'The work which
the service undertakes should be critically examined' (Cleveland
Probation Service, 1984). It is this statement which justifies the
research contained in this book in relation to the probation order.
Furthermore, and to return to Lloyd's research into the local
statements produced in response to SNOP, he concluded by saying that
'this has been a study of what local services have said, not what they
are doing or have done... But one is left with the inevitable, all-
important question, what is actually happening in local areas'? (1986,
p72).

Or to be more specific : what is happening in the Cleveland Probation
Service? This is the question to be explored in the remainder of
this book. Before doing so Table 5.1 summarises the way in which the
Cleveland Service has articulated its views on the three dimensions of
probation supervision.

The Story So Far

Before turning to the findings of empirical research presented in
Chapters 7 to 9, it is perhaps helpful at this point to recapitulate
on what I have attempted to say so far. Briefly, against the
background of the decline of the rehabilitative ideal which replaced
the rationale of probation work understood as saving offender's souls,
towards the end of the 1980s the service is being challenged to
understand its primary task as providing alternatives to custody for
the more serious offender. All those models of probation discussed in
Chapter 2, with the exception of the 'pure' social work model of
Harris, see the probation service providing alternatives to custody.
Furthermore, this is the central task of the service according to SNOP
in Chapter 3, a view endorsed by NAPO in Chapter 4. Finally in
Chapter 5 I considered the views of the Cleveland probation service
which also affirms that the provision of alternatives to custody is
the central task and that everything should be done to achieve this
objective. I have also discussed how these models articulate various
aspects and dimensions of probation supervision.

But the critical question which concerns me in the remainder of this book is whether or not the practices, ideologies and axiologies propounded by these different models are conducive to convincing the courts that the Cleveland probation service can provide alternatives to custody and that it can manage, contain and control offenders in the community in ways which appear credible to the courts when they are faced with having to sentence the more serious offender. In other words, because the probation service can no longer justify its existence in terms of saving souls, or curing by casework, one must seriously consider whether it has the kind of practice, ideology, values and methods to achieve the objective of reducing the custodial population. Could it be the case that the dimensions of probation supervision need to be reconceptualised in a different way to those models of probation already considerd above?

Table 5.1
The Cleveland Model Of Probation Supervision

CONTINUUM
CARE

ELEMENTS OF PROBATION PRACTICE
These consist in one-to-one casework supervision and
group work. However, through the development of
'packages' and day care resources, the elements of
practice will include providing help with life and
social skills, unemployment, addictions, in addition
to providing outdoor pursuits, family therapy, and
sports facilities.
These facilities will be provided by various resource
units to clients on a voluntary basis, and as a
condition of a probation order under Schedule 11 of
the 1982 Criminal Justice Act. Consequently, the
elements of practice are being diversified.

IDEOLOGY AND RATIONALE
The underlying ideology and rationale of probation
supervision in Cleveland is to:

make probation more credible to courts;
provide alternatives to custody;
meet individual needs and benefit clients;
reduce crime by ensuring that social work intervention
is effective;
the rehabilitation of offenders.

CARE/CONTROL AND CONDITIONS
The 'normal' probation order will still be used in
appropriate cases, but Schedule 11 facilities will be
developed for more serious offenders as alternatives
to custody
However, if the dimensions of control and authority are
to be accentuated this does not mean that probation will
become simply an exercise in surveillance or
containment. It is clear that within a framework of
extra conditions and increased social control for some
offenders, the needs of individuals will be
assessed in order to provide a social work service
which is intended to benefit them.
Cleveland's pragmatic approach seems to be that care
and control are to be held in balance, and that
they both complement each other.

HARRIS

WALKER
AND
BEAUMONT

NAPO

BOTTOMS
AND
McWIL'MS

CLEVELND

RAYNOR

BRYANT

SNOP

DAVIES
GRIFF'S

CONTROL

6 Research methods

Introduction

As the foregoing has made clear this study is concerned to provide knowledge of probation practice, ideology, values and social work methods, in relation to what has always been the central task of the probation service - the supervision of offenders in the community. It is worth reiterating that long before the statutory probation order was introduced in 1907 the police court missionaries were being used by magistrates to 'informally' supervise offenders released from the courts on recognizances (McWilliams, 1983). But by 1985, the year in which the research for this book began, 27,300 (7.1%) males and 9900 (16.8%) females sentenced for indictable offences (that is offences which may be tried at the Crown Court, as opposed to summary offences which can only be heard at the Magistrates Court) were given probation orders. It should also be acknowledged that the use of probation orders fell from 6.3% of sentences given for indictable offences in 1975 to 5.2% in 1978, but has steadily risen since then to 8.4% in 1985 (NACRO, 1987a).

Notwithstanding its decline in the 1970's and its partial recovery in the 1980's, it may be argued that the probation order has the potential to become an important disposal on the tariff of sentences available to the courts. This is because there are pressures at work within the criminal justice system to increasingly use this disposal as an alternative to custodial sentences for the more serious offender.

Stage one – Quantitative Research

According to the Statement of National Objectives and Priorities produced by the Home Office and reinforced in the Future Directions Document of the Cleveland probation service, previous chapters have discussed how the central aim of the probation service is to use the probation order as an alternative to custody. Therefore it is important to empirically assess the degree to which probation officers in the two probation teams where this research was undertaken are attempting to achieve this central objective. In other words, are the probation officers who agreed to participate in this research attempting to deal with as many offenders as possible in the community by advocating probation as an alternative to custody? This is a crucial question at the present time when concern continues to be expressed, both on the left and right of the political spectrum, at the ever rising prison population. Moreover one should not lose sight of an important historical precedent for such an approach to probation which is that the probation system was created at a time when the criminal justice system was searching for alternatives to custody towards the end of the 19th century (Garland, 1985a, p23; Boswell, 1982, p3).

To elicit this information it was decided that during the first six months of 1987 data would be collected on all those offenders being considered for probation in social enquiry reports presented to the courts in Cleveland by probation officers in the Hartlepool and Redcar teams. During the early days of the research I was still working as a probation officer and I perceived that there would be few problems securing the cooperation of these probation officers. Moreover by selecting these two teams from the North and South of the county it was virtually assured that data would be collected from all the courts in Cleveland, which are the Hartlepool, Teesside and Guisborough Magistrates Courts and the Teesside Crown Court. This, in fact, turned out to be what happened. To collect the necessary data and to ensure a high degree of construct validity (Kidder and Judd, 1986, p36) information was needed which conformed to three main criteria which may be described as:

1) Cases where a probation order was mentioned by the probation officer in his report to the court and where a probation order was imposed;

2) Cases where a probation order was mentioned by the officer, but where such an order was not made by the court;

3) Cases where a probation order was not mentioned in the report of the officer, but where such an order was considered appropriate by the court.

Data had to be collected according to the first criterion to assess how many probation orders were made following the recommendation of the probation officer and to subsequently consider how many of these were made as an alternative to custody. Furthermore this data provided a basis for detailed discussion with probation officers. But the reason for collecting data on the second criterion was because although probation officers could have been making efforts to achieve the policy objective of increasing the use of probation supervision for offenders facing a custodial sentence, this goal may not have been achieved because magistrates and judges, for whatever reasons, were unwilling to comply with the recommendation in the probation officer's report. Finally, it was necessary to allow for the courts making probation orders in circumstances where they had not been recommended by probation officers (I should point out here that only 3 cases conformed to the last criterion).

Consequently a recording schedule was designed to collect relevant quantitative data on cases which complied with the above three criteria and in relation to a number of other variables. The relevant cases were initially identified by referring to what is described as the C/Comp 1 book at the Hartlepool and Redcar probation offices which, among other things, provides a record of what probation officers are recommending in their reports to the courts and also

114

records the outcome of cases once an offender has been dealt with. Therefore it was simply a case of discovering in the C/Comp 1 book which cases had been recommended for probation and where a probation order had or had not been imposed to select appropriate cases.

After identifying the cases which complied to these three criteria the data required to complete the recording schedule was obtained by referring to additional probation records, which consisted in all cases of a social enquiry report. This document provided written information on the offender's background, family history, school and employment record, previous convictions, current offences, concluding with a recommendation for the court to consider when determining sentence. Furthermore in those cases where a probation order was imposed it was possible to consult additional probation records from within the organisation completed on offenders every three months (known as Part B assessments). In fact all the quantitative data required to complete the first stage of the research was obtained from within the Cleveland probation service itself.

It should be acknowledged that from the beginning of this study the Assistant Chief Probation Officer with responsibility for research and statistics in Cleveland was supportive in this undertaking, because it was felt it could help to inform and develop local policy and practice concerning the supervision of offenders in the community. The teams at which the research was undertaken were visited in January 1987 with the ACPO in attendance where I spelt out in detail all aspects of the research proposal. It was gratifying that there was not one note of dissent from any of the probation officers at Hartlepool and Redcar to the research. Accordingly they all provided me with easy access to the data which was required from their own records. By February 1987 the data was in the process of being collected and the officers understood that I would be interviewing them at a later stage about their own cases. At the end of the first stage of the research I had a total of 132 cases which conformed to the above criteria. The details for each officer at Hartlepool and Redcar are presented in the following Table.

Table 6.1

Probation officer cases

Officer	Number of POs Recommended	Number of POs made	Number of other non-custodial sentences	Number of custodial sentences
A	5	4	0	1
B	6	3	1	2
C	9	5	2	2
D	7	7	0	0
E	11	8	2	1
F	7	4	1	2
G	14	2	3	9
H	9	3	2	4
I	15	8	4	3
J	15	5	5	5
K	11	4	5	3
L	9	3	5	1
M	3	2	1	1
N	8	5	3	1
Totals	129	63	34	35

(It should be clarified at this point that Table 6.1 includes data on those 3 probation officers (L, M and N) referred to below who left the Cleveland service before they could be interviewed and who had between them a total of 22 cases, out of which 10 probation orders were made. Consequently the total number of cases amount to 132 even though 129 probation orders were recommended in the social enquiry report. The total number of probation orders imposed was 63, a take up rate of 48.8%).

Stage two – Qualitative Research

After visiting the two probation teams for one day every two weeks over a six month period to collect quantitative data, the second stage of the research explored this data in more detail by interviewing the probation officers concerned on how they understood the way they were using probation orders, which followed-up the theme of alternatives to custody. During the first part of these interviews each officer was interviewed in respect of all his cases by using a semi-structured interview schedule, where one of the questions asked concerned how many of the above cases had a probation order been made as an alternative to custody. Moreover the Bale Risk of Custody scale (Bale, 1986) was used to assess which offenders were at risk of custody, about which more will be said later. A total of 8 questions were asked which were designed to cover all the officers' cases, both where a probation order had and had not been made.

During the second part of the interview a more flexible approach was used as I started to focus specifically on those probation orders which had been imposed and also to probe more deeply the dimensions of probation practice, ideology, values and methods. It should be said that this unstructured qualitative approach was an important and necessary aspect of the research because it added a richness and depth of understanding to the subject matter under discussion (Reid and Smith, 1981, p90). All individual interviews were tape recorded and each lasted for approximately one hour. The four main dimensions upon which information was sought in the second part of the interviews were:

1) The elements of probation practice - or what probation officers are proposing to do with prospective probationers?

2) The ideology and rationale which underlies practice - or why officers are proposing to undertake certain tasks?

3) Value orientation - or where probation officers stand in relation to the care/control debate.

4) Social work methodology - or how officers are working with probationers?

In order to examine the four dimensions of the probation order in depth, all probation orders imposed during the first six months of 1987 in those courts which supplied work to the Hartlepool and Redcar probation teams were discussed with the appropriate probation officer. At the end of the six month period the probation officers in question had become responsible for a number of new probation orders, as Table 6.1 elucidates, which provided a basis for an in-depth analysis of these cases. Consequently between July and September 1987 each probation officer was presented with a list of his or her probation order cases. The officer was presented with a single sheet of paper in relation to each probation case, upon which was found four columns under four main headings:

117

1) Elements of probation practice.
2) Underlying ideology and rationale.
3) Social Work Methods.
4) Value orientation.

Prior to the second part of the interview I had completed the first column by drawing upon information from probation records which was subsequently presented to the officers. Next, it was the task of each probation officer to complete columns 2 to 4. To do this it was decided to use prompt cards for columns 2 and 3 (Moser and Kalton, 1985, p278f) where the officer was presented with a number of ideologies to choose from to explain why he was working in a particular way with an offender and similarly with social work methods. These prompt cards were compiled after consulting the research findings of Boswell in which her sample of 100 officers identified a number of different ideologies and methods (1982). The completion of column 4 was in response to a specific question on the issue of care and control which was: 'Are you trying to either care for or control offenders, or do both?' The format used for each probation case was as follows:

	1	2	3	4
Case No.	Elements of Practice	Ideology	Social Work Methods	Care, Control, or Both?

By using such an approach it was possible to build-up a picture of the elements of probation practice and philosophy. Once this exercise had been completed it was first thought that a Semi-structured Interview Schedule could also be used, as in the first part of the interview, to follow up the data provided in the columns and to obtain additional information on other key issues concerning probation supervision 'concerned with individual's own accounts of their attitudes, motivations and behaviour' (Hakim, 1987, p26; see also Walker, 1985).

However after giving this methodological problem more careful thought, it was finally decided that an interview schedule which was designed to ensure that the same questions were asked of all the respondents in exactly the same way could have imposed unnecessary restrictions and would have been too rigid. It was felt important that I engaged probation officers as much as possible by 'getting inside' their individual understandings and meanings of probation work. Therefore such 'insight can only be obtained if the researcher is permitted fully to engage his subjects rather than to adopt a stance of uncommitted neutrality' (Walker, 1985, pp12-13).

Consequently I decided that it was more appropriate to use an approach described by Jones as the depth interview (1985) and which Walker elucidates as 'a conversation in which the researcher encourages the informant to relate, in their own terms, experiences and attitudes that are relevant to the research problem' (1985, p4). Moreover Burgess has said that the depth interview provides 'the opportunity for the researcher to probe deeply, to uncover new clues, to open up new dimensions of a problem and to secure vivid, accurate, inclusive accounts that are based on personal experience' (1982, p107). Therefore instead of having a rigid interview schedule it was more appropriate to have an aide memoire comprising the topics of probation practice, ideology, values and methods. This was conducive to following up any interesting ideas as they emerged concerning the dimensions of probation supervision presented by officers using the prompt cards. I should also add that even though I was aware of the difficulties involved in 'seeing through the eyes' of respondents (Bryman, 1988, pp72-81), I did not feel that my presence was preventing officers from conveying an accurate picture of their work. This was because I had established a good rapport with them both prior to and during the course of the qualitative research which facilitated the process of officers openly providing information.

Initially there were 14 officers to be interviewed in-depth. But because of inevitable staff movements, by the time I came to conduct the interviews there were 11 officers remaining in the teams at Hartlepool and Redcar. However because the officers who left these three teams were replaced by probation officers straight from university and polytechnic training courses, it seemed important to elicit their views on probation as well. To do this and in order to add yet another dimension to the research, it was decided that once all the individual interviews had been completed to supplement the depth interviews with what Hedges refers to as group interviews (1985).

During the two group interviews with the Hartlepool and Redcar teams which now included the three SPOs, the intention was to allow individuals to interact with each other with a view to generating new ideas concerning probation supervision. Again I did not conduct these group interviews on the basis of using a rigid questionnaire, but had a list of topics on the subject under discussion which were to be probed in some detail. Consequently as the interviewer or moderator I was

> conducting a 'steered conversation' rather than an interview. Respondents must be left as free as possible to express themselves, and the moderator's job is mainly to nudge the conversation progressively into the more fruitful channels (Hedges, 1985, p78).

Once the second stage of the research was completed, I was ready to move into the third and final stage.

Stage three

Because the theme of alternatives to custody was important during the previous stages of the research, it became necessary to undertake further empirical work which consisted in a series of group interviews with probation officers, magistrates, judges and clerks. In addition, I was given the opportunity to interview, on an individual basis, the Clerks to the Teesside and Hartlepool magistrates and two practising Recorders with many years experience of criminal justice issues. These interviews were undertaken between January and May, 1988. In all the discussions of alternatives to custody from within the local probation service after 1984, and the development of appropriate policies, it seems that no one had considered how it would be important to systematically elicit the views of the decision makers. It occurred to me that, even though the Cleveland probation service was genuinely attempting to provide alternatives to custody by, for example, developing its use of the probation order with Schedule 11 4 A (1)(b) conditions, both magistrates and judges probably had a great deal to contribute on this subject too. To get this data I considered it was necessary to create a situation where probation officers and sentencers could discuss the theme of alternatives to custody together. Consequently the vehicles for eliciting this information already existed in the Probation Liaison Committee (PLC) and the Judges liaison meeting.

For many years known as the Probation Case Committee, it was redesignated the Probation Liaison Committee by the Criminal Justice Act, 1982, and the new Probation Rules of 1984. This committee, which is comprised largely of magistrates, has advisory and liaison functions in relation to the probation service and its duty is to review the work of probation officers (ACOP, 1985). Moreover the PLC should be used to 'afford each probation officer appointed for, or assigned to, its petty sessions area such help and advice as it can in performing his duties' (Probation Rules, Rule 19, 1984). Therefore the PLC afforded the vehicle for probation officers to meet with magistrates, where views could be exchanged and advice solicited, on the theme of developing the probation order as an effective and credible alternative to custody for the more serious offender. Similarly the judges liaison meeting, which is a bi-annual meeting at which judges and probation officers meet to share professional views and concerns, could be used to explore the same theme.

It transpired that because I worked for the Cleveland probation service it was possible to gain access to these meetings. I therefore attended 3 PLCs at Guisborough, Redcar and Hartlepool, and a Judges liaison meeting at the Teesside Law Courts, where the subject of probation as an alternative to custody was discussed in some detail and with great animation. My approach during these meetings was to give a brief introductory outline of the research, drawing particular attention to those cases where a custodial sentence had been imposed after the officer had recommended probation, and concluding with the following question to begin the discussion: 'Are there any further provisions the probation service in Cleveland can develop to make the probation order a more credible and effective alternative to custody for the more serious offender?'

Group interviews should ideally consist of between 4 and 12 people (Hakim, 1987, p27) but on occasions the groups comprised rather more than 12 people. Anticipating that this might happen I perceived that it could be technically difficult to tape record such interviews, because the groups met in relatively large premises where it would have been difficult to pick up all that was said because of poor acoustics. Therefore I enlisted the services of a professional shorthand/typist who took shorthand notes of all the discussions which were then subsequently typed. These meetings were selected on the basis that these magistrates and judges operated in the courts at which the 132 cases referred to above were sentenced. Specifically, the PLCs were those of the Redcar and Hartlepool probation teams and the judges sat regularly at the Teesside Crown Court. However the remaining in-depth interviews with recorders and clerks were tape recorded and later transcribed.

Summary of methods and scope of research

To do justice to the diverse themes running through this research and to explore the data in as much detail as possible from different standpoints, it was necessary to use a variety of quantitative and qualitative instruments which included a recording schedule, a semi-structured interview schedule, prompt cards, in-depth interviews and group interviews. The scope of the research may be clarified as follows:

Stage 1

6 months quantitative data which produced 132 cases after complying with specific criteria;

Stage 2

11 in-depth interviews of main grade probation officers at Hartlepool and Redcar;

2 group interviews of the Hartlepool and Redcar probation teams, which now included the three SPOs and several new officers;

Stage 3

Group interview of the Guisborough PLC, comprising 8 magistrates, 2 main grade probation officers, 1 SPO and 1 clerk;

Group interview of the Redcar PLC, comprising 9 magistrates, 4 main grade probation officers, 1 SPO and 1 clerk;

Group interview of the Hartlepool PLC, comprising 7 magistrates, 9 main grade probation officers, 2 SPOs, 1 ACPO, and 1 clerk;

Group interview of the Judges liaison meeting, comprising 4 Judges, 13 main grade probation officers, 2 SPOs and 1 ACPO;

Interview with the clerk to the Teesside Justices;

Interview with the clerk to the Hartlepool Justices;

Interview with the chairman of the Hartlepool PLC;

Interviews with 2 Recorders;

Group interview with the senior management group of the Cleveland probation service, comprising the CPO and 3 ACPOs.

Finally, I think it is helpful to enumerate how many different people were interviewed during the course of this research, both on an individual basis and in groups, as follows:

```
Main grade probation officers = 26
Senior probation officers     =  5
CPO                           =  1
ACPOs                        =  3
Magistrates                  = 23
Judges                       =  4
Recorders                    =  2
Clerks                       =  5
                Total   = 69
```

The results of this research into probation practice, ideology, values and social work methods, are presented in Chapter 7. Next the issue of probation as an alternative to custody is introduced and explored from a probation service perspective in Chapter 8. Finally Chapter 9 presents findings which, in the main, are based on group interviews with magistrates, judges, recorders and clerks on the theme of alternatives to custody. The implications of all these empirical findings for future probation policy and practice are evaluated in Chapter 10 and a number of suggestions are made for the Cleveland probation service to consider.

7 Probation practice, ideology, axiology and methods

Introduction

Earlier chapters touched on various dimensions of the probation order from academic, bureaucratic, professional, and local standpoints. The purpose of this chapter is to present a worms eye view of how 11 probation officers at Redcar and Hartlepool apprehended the meaning of probation work in relation to 53 probation orders. My main concern is to examine how these two teams of officers articulated what they were doing with probationers, their underlying ideologies, which includes a discussion of the care/control issue. Moreover probation practice, ideology and values, will be complemented by considering which social work methods were employed when working with probationers.

Probation Practice

After analysing those social enquiry reports where a probation order was made by the courts, which were later discussed in more detail during interview with the 11 respondents, content analysis of this data revealed that these officers resorted to the following

terminology when describing what they were doing with probationers.
This data has been quantified and presented in rank order in the
following Table.

Table 7.1

The dimensions of probation practice

Providing help, support, advice and guidance	23
Marriage and relationship counselling	16
Assisting with financial/budgeting problems	14
Counselling for alcohol, drugs and gambling problems	14
Dealing with the problem of unemployment	14
Assisting with accommodation problems	11
Helping with emotional problems and stress	8
Alleviating loneliness and depression	6
Examining consequences of offending	6
Providing advice on the use of leisure	5
Improving self esteem	5
Bereavement counselling	2
Obtaining full Benefit entitlements for clients	2
Providing advice on motherhood	1
Providing advice on medical problems	1
Sexual counselling	1
Providing discipline	1
Negotiating with gas and electricity boards	1
Enhancing client maturity	1
Social skills training	1
Helping with probationer's child	1
Enhancing coping abilities	1

It is interesting to observe that practice predominantly consists of
providing a welfare service to offenders who are experiencing a
variety of problems with, for example, accommodation, budgeting,
depression and stress, alcohol and unemployment. Before focusing
specifically on probation cases, at this point the discussion will be
expanded to provide a profile of all 132 offenders selected for this
research. To recapitulate, not all of them were made the subject of a
probation order, but the point here is that nearly all 132 were
considered for probation. By presenting a profile of all these cases
it will be seen quite clearly that numerous problems were coming to
the attention of the Redcar and Hartlepool probation teams, to which
they were attempting to make a response.

Profile of all 132 cases

The Redcar and Hartlepool probation teams provide a service to several criminal courts within Cleveland and in turn receive most of their work from these courts. The 132 cases came from the following Magistrates and Crown courts and it should be observed that as a result of collecting data from Redcar and Hartlepool, cases were predominantly drawn from all the Courts in Cleveland.

Table 7.2

Courts which provided the 132 cases

Court	Frequency
Teesside Magistrates Court	19
Hartlepool Magistrates Court	63
Guisborough Magistrates Court	15
Teesside Crown Court	26
Other Magistrates Courts	05
Other Crown Courts	04
Total	132

There were 107 (81.1%) Males and 25 (18.9%) Females, who fell into the following age group categories when they appeared before the courts:

Table 7.3

Age at sentence by sex

		Sex	
		Male	Female
Age at Sentence	17 to 20	51	7
	21 to 29	39	8
	30+	17	10
	Total	107	25

In an area of the country where unemployment rates are relatively high, it should not be too surprising to discover that a high proportion of these offenders were not working. Furthermore during the period of my own research a survey was commissioned by ACOP into unemployment amongst probation clients in the North East region, an area which covers Cleveland, Durham, Humberside, Northumbria, North,

South and West Yorkshire. This survey discovered that of 13319 clients eligible for or able to work, 9525 (71.5%) were unemployed. To be more specific, when the survey was undertaken on the 30 April, 1987, the total caseload of the Cleveland service was 2062, of which 1320 offenders were eligible for, or able to work (181 females and 1139 males). It was found that, out of 1320, only 107 offenders (8.1%) had a permanent full-time job, whilst 993 (75.2%) were unemployed. The survey unequivocally concluded that 'The results...are quite clear. Unemployment is an overwhelming problem within probation caseloads in the North East' (ACOP, 1987, p5-6).

Returning to my own research, during the period the 132 offenders were selected it was discovered that, at the time they committed their offences, 17 offenders (12.9%) were employed, 96 (72.7%) were unemployed, leaving 19 cases in which data on employment status was not recorded by officers. However by turning to data on whether or not offenders were employed or unemployed when they were sentenced by the courts, rather than at the time they committed their offences, the following data was obtained:

Table 7.4

Employed or unemployed at sentence

	Frequency	Percent
Employed	26	19.7
Unemployed	105	79.5
Unknown	1	.8
	Total 132	100.0

Turning to those 31 offenders who were employed, either at the time they committed their offences, or at the time of sentence, their employment status was as follows:

Table 7.5

Type of employment

	Frequency	Percent
Government Scheme	20	15.2
Full-time permanent job	6	4.5
Part-time permanent job	2	1.5
Casual-temporary work	3	2.3
Unknown	1	.8
Not Applicable	100	75.8
Total	132	100.0

It was also possible to collect some data on the length of time unemployed offenders had been out of work. Albeit the problem of information being missing in 23 cases, the following data begins to show that a number of offenders had been unemployed for a considerable period of time:

Table 7.6

Length of time unemployed offenders had been out of work

	Frequency	Percent
Less than six months	17	12.9
Over six months and under one year	15	11.4
Over one year and under two	12	9.1
Over two and under five	9	6.8
Over five years	20	15.2
Unknown	23	17.4
Not Applicable	36	27.3
Total	132	100.0

There can be little doubt that having such a high percentage of probation clients unemployed creates a dilemma for the service, both in Cleveland and in other parts of the country. Walton has expressed this dilemma by posing the following questions: does the service encourage offenders to pursue and receive whatever skills training they can in the hope that, when the recession is over, they are prepared to re-enter the job market? Or should it accept that many clients will remain unemployed, which implies that the service should be in the business of providing a range of leisure facilities to keep them constructively occupied? (Walton, 1987, p139). According to the above mentioned ACOP survey the practical implications of unemployment for the probation service in the North East are, firstly, to alleviate the worst excesses of poverty through an effective welfare rights strategy; secondly to ensure that MSC schemes are available to clients; thirdly to provide leisure and recreational facilities as a form of 'alternative occupation'. Consequently unemployment and its attendant problems of financial hardship, psychological trauma, marital tension and interpersonal disharmony (Box, 1987, p3) amongst probation clients, is being taken seriously by the service in the North East.

Data was also collected on the educational qualifications of offenders:

Table 7.7

Educational qualifications

	Frequency	Percent
None	80	60.6
CSE	19	14.4
O Levels	3	2.3
Other	2	1.5
Unknown	28	21.2
Total	132	100.0

Furthermore Walton records how NACRO reported in 1984 that 60% of persons joining their employment schemes had no educational qualifications and that 81% of young people undertaking YTS schemes had no qualifications (1987, p145).

During the period this research was undertaken the subjects of race and ethnicity assumed importance within the probation service. In fact, the Home Office set up the Ethnic Monitoring Information Working Party, consisting of representatives from the Home Office, ACOP, NAPO, the Association of Black Probation Officers (ABPO), the CCPC and the Commission for Racial Equality (CRE). The task was to assess whether or not ethnic minorities are receiving equal treatment by the probation service, by undertaking an Ethnic Monitoring Survey in all 56 probation areas on the 31 March, 1987. It was found that out of a total of 2037 who were under the supervision of the Cleveland Service at the end of March, 1987, 1864 (92%) were White. Even though the vast majority of clients are White in Cleveland, it has been argued that the issue of race is problematic for the probation service and wider criminal justice system, which has resulted in one SPO claiming on the basis of his own research in the West Midlands that 'the Probation Service is itself making black people a problem instead of dealing with the problems of black people (Green, 1987, p181).

Whilst acknowledging the importance of this issue for the probation service in the 1980's, race is hardly an issue in this research because all 132 offenders were White.

Next, data was collected on the marital status of offenders and whether or not they had responsibilities for children. What follows in Tables 7.8 and 7.9 are crosstabulations of marital status by sex, which also controls for whether or not clients had children.

Table 7.8

Marital status by sex controlling for offenders who had children

Marital Status	Male	Female	Row Total
	Sex		
Single	10	4	14
Married	8	4	12
Separated	6	1	7
Divorced	3	4	7
Cohabiting	7	3	10
Separated or divorced, but cohabiting	2		2
Widow or widower	1		1
Column Total	37	16	53

Table 7.9

Marital status by sex controlling for offenders who did not have children

| Marital Status | Sex | | |
	Male	Female	Row Total
Single	59	9	68
Married	2		2
Divorced	2		2
Cohabiting	5		5
Column Total	68	9	77

These Tables show that 53 offenders (37 males and 16 females) had children and 77 offenders (68 males and 9 females) did not have children, with such data missing in 2 cases. It should also be acknowledged that 14 offenders who were single (10 male and 4 female), 7 separated (6 male and 1 female) and 7 divorced offenders (3 male and 4 female), had responsibilities for children. This point is mentioned because of the implications for the probation service concerning the personal and social supports these offenders might need when exercising responsibilities for young children.

I also considered it was important to collect data on how many offenders committed offences whilst under the influence of alcohol. This was because probation officers have been aware for some time of the prevalence of alcohol in the commission of some offences. To support this argument, Jeffs and Saunders (1983) after interviewing 1209 people arrested in a south coast resort during a 5 month period in 1979, found that 64% admitted consuming alcohol during the hours preceding an offence for which they were arrested. Other examples are cited in Purser (1987, p157) to support the view that alcohol is a significant factor in criminal behaviour.

Now even though data on drink related offences were missing in 18 cases, in addition to which it is a possibility that probation officers did not faithfully include this information in their reports in a number of other cases, the research discovered the following:

Table 7.10

Were offences drink related?

	Frequency	Percent
Yes some were	7	5.3
Yes all were	29	22.0
No	74	56.1
Other drugs including glue	4	3.0
Unknown	18	13.6
Total	132	100.0

Therefore a total of 40 offenders (30.3%) committed their offences whilst under the influence of alcohol or some other substance.

Consequently, when considering the universe of 132 offenders in relation to a number of selected variables, to present a profile of offenders coming to the attention of the Redcar and Hartlepool probation teams, who were being considered for probation, data presented so far may now be summarised.

Profile summary

The Redcar and Hartlepool probation teams receive work from several criminal courts, and out of a total of 132 offenders 107 were male and 25 female. 105 offenders were relatively young in that they fell within the 17 to 29 age range and the vast majority were unemployed, some not having worked for several years. For those offenders who were working, either at the time their offences were committed or at the time of sentence (N=31), only 6 had a permanent full-time job. A high proportion were single (84 or 63.6%); 53 (40.8%) offenders had responsibilities for children; and 80 offenders (60.6%) had no educational qualifications. Moreover 40 offenders (30.3%) committed their offences whilst under the influence of alcohol or some other substance.

By considering these offenders in relation to a number of variables, one begins to appreciate the characteristics of offenders coming to the attention of the probation teams in question. It is true that, over recent years, the probation service has become increasingly aware of, for example, the employment and educational needs of offenders.

Changes have occurred in society which have adversely affected the clientele of the service, a consequence of the deterioration in socio-economic conditions during the late 1970s and 1980s. This has resulted in the service offering 'tangible responses which seek to ameliorate some of the harsher effects of the recession on the lives of many offenders' (Walton, 1987, p131). Furthermore the ACOP working party report acknowledged that a practical response should be made by the probation service to clients in the current climate when it stated that 'Poverty, the service's role in securing jobs, alternative occupation ie. client access to leisure and education, are all major issues associated with unemployment' (ACOP, 1987, pp5-6).

It is quite clear that the Hartlepool and Redcar probation teams encounter a variety of personal and social problems which are presented by offenders coming to their attention, which in turn has important implications for those who manage the service in terms of its response to such problems, the provision of resources, and appropriate facilities. It also raises the fundamental question concerning what kind of probation service is required in the North East of England in the 1980's, faced as it is with a multiplicity of client problems. This profile adds to the data presented at the beginning of this chapter on the elements of probation practice and highlights the problem areas in which probation officers are attempting to work. But from considering what probation officers are trying to do when faced with such problems, the next section begins to address the issue of underlying ideologies sustaining probation practice. To do so I will return specifically to data on probation orders, rather than all 132 cases.

Sustaining Ideologies

After delineating the dimensions of probation practice, respondents were asked to identify why they were engaging in such practices by considering a prompt card which listed a number of ideologies. I was concerned not only to discover what officers were doing with probationers, but also to understand why, in order to shed light on ideologies underlying practice. Respondent's replies to the prompt card were quantified and the results are presented in rank order in Table 7.11.

Table 7.11
Ideologies underlying and sustaining practice

To advise, assist, befriend, support, care and help	39
To reduce criminal behaviour	39
Enhance offenders self responsibility	38
To meet offenders needs	32
To provide a social work service	29
To prevent crime	25
To provide an alternative to custody	21
Rehabilitation	15
To manage, contain and control offenders	14
Surveillance	10
Conciliate between offender and community	9
Mediation	3
Punishment	2
Pressure group action	2
No clear ideology	1
Reparation	0
Other	0

Even though respondents sometimes confused what they were doing with reasons why, nevertheless the first point to establish is that they were not operating with one ideology when working with probationers, but a combination of ideologies, which means that a somewhat ambivalent and complex picture emerged. For example, one respondent said, in relation to one probationer, that he understood himself to be providing a social work service, advising, assisting and befriending, preventing crime, reducing criminal behaviour, managing, containing and controlling, providing an alternative to custody, rehabilitating the offender, conciliating, enhancing self responsibility and meeting needs. Secondly, as Table 7.11 indicates, some ideologies were mentioned more than others, which will now be explored in more detail. In what follows I refer to myself as **PW** and respondents as **PO**.

All respondents mentioned either advising, assisting and befriending, or providing a social work service, and most included both. One respondent drew a distinction between these two ideologies

134

by saying that:

> PO If you compare providing a social work service with advise, assist and befriend, which is like going round with a cup of tea and sympathy type thing; whereas a social work service is more professional. I feel that is what I trained to be, a social worker working in a court setting. That's how I view myself.

But what does it mean to provide a social work service? To one respondent this meant infusing the criminal justice system with dignity, maintaining social work values, trying to be non-judgmental and encouraging clients to make their own decisions, which is related to the notion of enhancing self-responsibility. Another understood providing a social work service specifically in terms of advise, assist and befriend, but another officer articulated what he meant like this:

> PO As social workers and as a social work agency, we are there to look at the needs of individuals and we relate that to the individual's offending behaviour.
> PW But what does it mean to provide a social work service?
> PO Obviously we are looking at intervention with other agencies and bodies of authority, like negotiating with the DHSS...giving emotional support, support for the drug addict...It covers many things - drink, drugs, solvent abuse and sexual problems - to offer support with whatever problems they have.

Two officers understood a social work service in terms of providing a simultaneous service to both the client and society, which embraces the notion of helping the offender to function better in society. To illustrate this one of these two officers said that:

> PO I think we are working with the offender within the context of society. Therefore, as part of our role we need to bring the two together by offering something to the client, but also have something to offer society by reducing crime and by possibly trying to make the offender see the viewpoint of society...and trying to get society to understand and befriend them. I think it's about offering a service to both the client and society as a whole. It is a matter of trying to bring the client together with society so that you can share the same beliefs as to what good and bad behaviour is about and what is acceptable to the majority.

I continued by asking:

> PW Can you try to explain what you mean by the term 'society'?
> PO The funny thing about society is that it consists of offenders anyway. He is a piece of society and society is a collection of individuals that live on the same planet alongside the offender who is also a member of society.

At first sight it seems that society is predominantly perceived in consensus rather than conflict terms. There was a surprising lack of radicalism during the in-depth interviews amongst all respondents, particularly when probation officers were confronted with numerous problems of a socio-economic nature as the profile above indicated. Rather, the probation officer was mainly concerned with the needs of individuals and not with radically changing society. Moreover these respondents, whilst acting in the best interests of the client, were also concerned with the good of society. However there is a profound dilemma here because the best interests of the client could well be served, for example, by encouraging him to offend for material gain in circumstances where unemployment and living off state benefit create enormous hardship. But there is no indication that these respondents were adopting such a position in their relations with probationers. Instead, they focused on the individual's needs and problems, not on providing a critique of existing social arrangements (However when exploring this issue in more detail with the teams as a group, a different perspective was provided as we shall see later). Respondents focused their attention on the individual offender where advise, assist and befriend was a central ideology as we can see from the following comments by a selection of officers:

> PO I feel that this is the baseline...and befriending is the kind of basis of what we do;
> PO I think if you don't do that you get nothing out of probation orders and I think you become a policeman;
> PO I feel that is what I'm here for;
> PO Well I think that to advise, assist and befriend is implicit in probation orders. If it is not then we are in the wrong job.

Probation practice is therefore sustained by ideologies articulated primarily in terms of providing a social work service, advising, assisting and befriending, which includes the provision of support, care and help. By helping with accommodation, budgeting, alcohol, drugs, and unemployment problems and by providing a counselling service for damaged relationships, marital problems and bereavement, respondents understood themselves to be meeting offenders' needs.

Most of the officers interviewed linked the provision of help with reducing offending and preventing crime which is indicated from the data presented in Table 7.11. In fact all 11 respondents mentioned either reducing or preventing crime and all except two respondents mentioned both.   Here we encounter the dichotomy between what officers consider is desirable and what is achieveable, or between what should be done with what can be done, which is illustrated by the following comment from a probation officer in response to the question:

> PW You have mentioned in your four cases that you are advising, assisting and befriending probationers, in addition to preventing crime and reducing criminal behaviour.   Is this what you are trying to achieve?
> PO We can attempt to achieve it but I don't know whether it should be the main criterion.   It may be a spin-off, but it may not be the ultimate aim...it may be a bonus because I'm not absolutely convinced that we can reduce the amount of offending they may be involved in.

In this case the respondent is saying that advise, assist and befriend is an important aspect of probation work in its own right, irrespective of whether this leads to a reduction in crime. Notwithstanding this comment, all the Redcar and Hartlepool probation officers believe they should be attempting to either reduce or prevent crime.   This logically led to the notion of rehabilitation which was an ideology mentioned by 7 officers and the following explanations were provided:

> PO I think with B, but with other cases too, he was very much on the margin of society prior to his offence and he's a man who has had some status. So really by working with him and addressing his alcohol problem, which he wants to address, I was hoping he could re-establish his dignity and role and position in society;
> PO To me rehabilitation is when someone is in an unsatisfactory situation, with an unsatisfactory home environment, bringing about a change not only in that person but also in their circumstances, to create a better life for the client and to create an environment where they will not feel such a need to offend;
> PO rehabilitation means getting him back into society where he does not offend or feel the need for drugs - very difficult;
> PO ...to get back to the situation as it was before their offending took place.

These examples of what rehabilitation meant to some respondents echoes the dictionary definition which speaks of restoring the delinquent to a useful life and restoring the person to his former rank and priviledges. But again, given the problems facing these offenders, it does seem somewhat unrealistic to talk about rehabilitation. Accordingly such a note of realism was sounded by the following two respondents who, even though they used the language of rehabilitation, said that:

> PO Rehabilitation is re-establishing self respect for the client...I don't necessarily relate rehabilitation to stopping offending, because I feel we do not stop them reoffending - we are a disaster at it.

It was also said that:

> PO I don't think A is ready to change at the moment and the chances are that he will do a prison sentence of over 2½ years and we will not be able to stop him or influence him. I don't know how we in fact rehabilitate people who see us as abnormal because they think why should you work for £200 a week when he can steal this over 3 days. It is difficult to stop people offending when you are not putting anything else in its place.

So even though this officer referred to rehabilitation in one probation case, upon further reflection he acknowledged how difficult this was to achieve in practice. This illustrates that while officers do talk about preventing crime, reducing criminal behaviour and rehabilitation, as desirable objectives for the probation service, some acknowledged the difficulties involved in achieving these objectives.

In addition to providing a social work service, meeting offenders' needs and attempting to reduce criminal behaviour through a process of rehabilitation, respondents also used the language of managing, containing and controlling probationers in the community, surveillance and punishment. However these terms were used much less than social work language so that, for example, only two respondents used the term punishment in relation to two probationers. At first sight there seems to be an inherent contradiction here, which raises the issue of care and control in probation orders, which will now be considered.

Care and Control

A paradox is a seemingly absurd and contradictory statement that may none the less be true, which helps to explain the way in which respondents attempt to make sense of advising, assisting and befriending, with managing, containing and controlling. When I asked them whether they were caring, controlling, or doing both with probationers, they replied that in 14 cases they were caring, in 39 cases they were doing both, which means that in no cases did they see themselves as simply controlling clients. For one respondent who saw advise, assist and befriend as the ideological baseline of probation work, it was also considered that this could be reconciled with the ideology of management and control. I asked:

PW But is it possible to reconcile the two?
PO I think so, but it is difficult though. That's part of our function and sometimes we end up as parole officers so we do have an amount of control. I think that to advise and assist must have a control element because if there is no controlling element people do not know where they stand. The clearer the controls and the more obvious they are, the better for the client.
PW But can you also reconcile social work with punishment, which you mention in one case?
PO It is very difficult...there are people who have specific needs to be punished and they themselves see that there ought to be some element of punishment. It provides validity to the courts and I think that even clients see punishment as valid.
PW But in relation to the two Schedule 11 cases where you mention to manage, contain, control and punish, what does this mean?
PO It means going along 2 days a week for a specified number of hours to attend the Resource Unit, whether he wants to or not and whether he is getting anything out of it. That is the element of punishment as I see it...but caring is control...and when you are caring there is an element of controlling behaviour. I don't think you can have one without the other. It's very difficult to get the balance right, but we keep trying.

Another respondent said that caring is a part of control because he believed that young offenders particularly are looking for controls and that to control is to sometimes care.

PO But it's how it's done, how the control is manifested. I think if you put handcuffs on someone that is blatant and obvious...but if you can teach them to control themselves that's a better form of control. I've never found difficulty reconciling care and control; the most important thing is how control is manifested.

It is accurate to say that, even though reconciling care and control creates more dilemmas for some than for others, the dilemmas do not engender paralysis for probation officers at Redcar and Hartlepool. They feel they can balance and reconcile both approaches, albeit dilemmas, tensions and conflicts, but that there are definite limits to control. In an attempt to articulate what control could mean, one respondent stated that:

PO the main thing is that, initially, I go through with a new probationer what the order means, what it will mean if they breach it and what my role would then be and how I will be made to react if they do not come up to the expectations of the order. That is the baseline from which we start...There are regulations that we both have to adhere to and by keeping them that is a form of control.

Here the officer acknowledges that probation orders contain a number of requirements that must be adhered to by the probationer, which he discusses with the client in an honest and open manner. Consequently if the requirements are breached, the officer will take the appropriate action and return the probationer to court.

Another officer, after affirming that to advise, assist and befriend, was an important ideology in probation work, also said that in two cases he was managing, containing and controlling, on the grounds that probation officers have to accept responsibility for the community. He went on to add:

> PO I think we should work on behalf of the community as well as the client, so in that sense I feel that the element of control is necessary and I find that the response in general is positive from clients when they become aware of an element of control within supervision...I am doing my bit for the community if you like...by virtue of the element of control within the job.

Finally, one respondent said of care and control that:

> PO I think implicit in the conditions of a probation order is the control element. That is what the client accepts when placed on probation. Probation officers give the commitment to advise, assist and befriend, and probationers give a commitment to allow an element of control and to be controlled.

Consequently the reconciliation of social work values, understood in terms of advise, assist and befriend, with the management, containment and control of offenders in the community, whilst bothersome for some academics, is not particularly bothersome or debilitating for these practitioners. They acknowledge the dilemmas, but get on with the job without too much soul searching. They do not emphasise control as the goal of probation; rather, their main concern is to provide support, care and help to clients who are often faced with a multiplicity of long standing problems, which is illustrated in the following observation:

> PO Yes, care and control is a dilemma...but I think we are very much a social work service. I think that if we don't care for clients we are wasting our time. There are other agencies in the community who are responsible for control...We have to care for people and if we don't we might as well pack our bags and go home.

Another respondent did not think it was possible to contain and control probationers, because the officer cannot be with them for 24 hours a day.

To conclude this section it is necessary to briefly mention those remaining ideologies so far not discussed. I do not propose to spend time here discussing the ideology of providing an alternative to custody, because this will be considered in the next chapter. However where conciliating between the offender and the community is concerned, which was mentioned in 9 cases, it may be said that there is nothing grandiose implied by this. One officer said that:

> PO Largely because (client's have) an inability to deal with the community...whether the community turns out to be neighbours, gas board, or landlords...it certainly needs some intervention to smooth the way back there.

Again the emphasis is on reconciling offenders with existing society rather than changing a society which may, to some degree, be conducive to offenders' problems. Moreover mediation was understood in similar terms and not in the sense of mediating between the offender and his victim as a way of dealing with those problems created by offending. Surprisingly no mention is made of reparation, even though this is referred to in SNOP, and only one officer mentioned pressure group action in relation to two of her cases. Both these probationers were made the subject of Schedule 11 probation orders and what she meant by pressure group action was the way in which these offenders would experience group pressure at the Resource Unit which would be applied in an attempt to get them to change their ways. It did not mean groups of offenders putting pressure on the community or wider society to improve the lot of clients considered to be the victims of existing political, economic and social arrangements. Having considerd a number of ideologies underlying practice, let me now turn to how probation officers work with probationers.

Social Work Methods

Earlier chapters focused specifically on the dimensions of probation practice, ideology, care and control, which have now been considered empirically in relation to 53 probation orders. However some attention will now be given to the methods probation officers used when working with these probationers to complete the analysis. The first observation is that as probation officers referred to various

141

ideologies underlying and sustaining practice when working with individual probationers, the same complex phenomenon is encountered when turning to social work methods, where one discovers various methods being used alongside each other. Replies to the prompt card on methods were quantified and Table 7.12 presents this data in rank order.

Table 7.12

Social work methods

Casework	42
Practical help	40
Use of personality	23
Task-centred casework	22
Behaviourist	15
Group work	13
Family therapy	9
Contract work	7
Problem checklist	6
Psychoanalysis	3
Other	3
Pragmatism	2
Community work	2
Heimler scale	1
Transactional analysis	1
Influencing society	0
Don't know	0

One respondent identified 7 different methods with one probationer - casework, group work, practical help, task-centred casework, contract work, family therapy and a problem checklist. He explained that:

> PO I don't think you can identify one method for one particular client. You might use 7 methods. I am not a great lover of family therapy, although I trained in that in 1974. Transactional analysis I think is alright with chips, although it's not a method I would use. I have got to use methods that I feel are comfortable for me and are comfortable for the client...They are all in the drawer and are like a list of cards...you go through them and just don't pick them out at random. You look first at the client.

Further support for this eclectic approach is found in the work of two other probation officers who stated that:

> PO I cannot really identify one particular method that really stands out for me because it should be about what method stands out for the client. If I spot the need in a client to have one

particular method used then I would use that method.

The second officer said that:

> PO Although I obviously know a great deal about methods...I am very reluctant to use one method as such or one particular theory. What I do is, depending on the personality before me and the depth of his problems, use a variety of methods subconsciously most of the time.   It's not until I actually sit down to review the case in the Part B that I am conscious of which methods I have been using.

Therefore several social work methods are being used in combination, rather than one specific method dominating practice.   It is interesting how, within the context of discussing social work training, Parsloe comments that 'Most social work methods teaching starts with a method, which is then applied to case examples. Perhaps we need to take a typical caseload and work from the clients to the methods' (1983, p48), which is what these respondents appear to be doing in most cases.

All except 2 respondents mentioned casework and along with practical help, were the most popular methods when working with probationers. Respondents were asked to say what casework meant for them and their replies included the following:

> PO Casework covers everything on a one-to-one basis really.

Another commented that:

> PO I see casework as just sitting down on a one-to-one basis...I am not pretending that I have any fancy theories behind that...with A I was sorting out loss (bereavement counselling) and with B it's purely a challenge to sort out attitudes which I have failed to do so far..

Yet another officer linked casework with a psychosocial approach, which involved looking at the client in his 'whole situation...in the social environment'.

One respondent who used casework with all his 5 cases linked this approach with using his own personality when he said that:

> PO I think that probation is all about me using myself with clients and casework is the most effective way of using myself with clients...

Consequently a casework approach is being used extensively by all these respondents and the results of this research echo the findings of Boswell when she claimed that 'casework is still the most poplular form of approach to the client, but that it is now combined with other suitable approaches' (1982, p142). Let us now consider some of these other approaches.

It should come as no surprise that practical help was mentioned in 40 cases, given those problems referred to earlier. One respondent felt that providing practical help at the beginning of a probation order was important if she wanted to progress to other problem areas, like emotional or relationship problems. She said:

> PO I think practical help is important. I think it gets the credibility of your client if you can be of practical assistance. Also, it's very difficult to have a relationship with somebody just talking about emotional stuff, but you have to do both. Often practical help is a vehicle, a good way in..

Task-centred casework, mentioned by seven respondents, is a method whereby the probation officer and probationer discuss together the latter's problems, which results in the development of a planned strategy for dealing with those problems (Coulshed, 1988). It involves giving the client certain tasks to perform which will be conducive to building confidence, thereby increasing self-esteem and enhancing self responsibility. As such it is a practical and down to earth way of working and was linked with contract work by four respondents. There was nothing complex about task-centred casework to these officers. It meant that within the context of a one-to-one casework interview, the probation officer explored with the client what the problems were, with a view to setting tasks which would be conducive to surmounting those problems. One respondent was using task-centred casework and contract work together and proceeded to explain that:

> PO I usually incorporate the court's contract with one of my own...during the social enquiry report stage we identified that there were certain problems, so how are we going to address them? Using what the client says we knock together some kind of contract...which is then typed up and signed by me and the client.

Furthermore other methods were being used, such as a problem checklist, to identify problem areas. One officer used the Heimler scale, which attempts to provide help to clients by bringing about changes in their lives. Central to this approach is the Scale of Social Functioning which allows the individual to prioritize those areas of life they wish to develop or change. It has been argued that

'Probation officers are looking for methods of work which will help clients make the best use of their inner resources in being able to cope with life. One such method is Human Social Functioning' (Morley, 1986).

Eight probation officers were conscious of using their own personalities when working with probationers. In fact one respondent, even though he did not refer to this when consulting the prompt card, drew attention to this aspect of his work as he further reflected on his methods of working in the following way:

> PO I did't put that in (the use of personality) because I think we use that almost subconsciously all the time. I think you put a lot of yourself into a case that you couldn't really identify as a social work method.

It was revealed above that probation practice involves some officers in marriage and relationship counselling and within this context family therapy may be used. Family therapy has been defined as 'the psychotherapeutic treatment of a natural social system, the family, using as its medium, conjoint interpersonal interviews' (Walrond-Skinner, 1977, p1). However what academic text books on social work methods mean by the theory and practice of family therapy, is different to how it was understood by the four practitioners who identified this method of working. Instead of using jargon terminology in the way it is defined above, those officers who mentioned this method meant something less esoteric, so that perhaps the correct term should be family work, which was in fact mentioned by one officer. To operate as a family therapist requires specialist training and it transpired that none of these respondents, except one, had received such training (and the one who had received his training as long ago as 1974 claimed that he was not now a great lover of family therapy).

It is also interesting that despite the emphasis on community work in SNOP, it is mentioned by only two officers in two probation cases. And even more surprising, as we have seen already, no officer is working to influence or change society. This reinforces the point that probation work for these two teams is predominantly concerned with the individual offender, rather than creating change within local communities or wider society.

Pragmatism was mentioned by two respondents, which was understood and articulated in terms of a practical and common sense approach to probationers and as such is related to the provision of practical help. Furthermore psychoanalysis, although mentioned as a method with three probationers, was only being used by one probation officer. She explained what she meant by saying:

PO When I say psychoanalysis in the case of A I feel that her offending may be very much about her own life story. As I have come to know her I have come to this conclusion, so it has become more and more urgent to use this type of approach to understand her behaviour to be able to effect change. Until you understand behaviour you cannot achieve any change in many cases.

Even though the term psychoanalysis is used here, this officer was not a trained psychoanalyst, so the term was convenient shorthand for a method which simply encouraged the client to talk about her past to shed some light on present behaviour. In the remaining two cases, one probationer was referred to the County Psychologist with a gambling problem, which involved resorting to a psychoanalytic method; the other probationer was receiving psychoanalysis from a psychiatrist for a sexual problem.

Before completing this excursion into social work methods by considering group work and behaviourism, reference was made to transactional analysis in one case by one probation officer. Transactional analysis has been succinctly described as a technique which

is employed to analyse transactions between people in terms of whether they play parent, adult, or child roles in their responses to what is happening. For example, two adults may foster a parent/child relationship when what is required is an adult/adult relationship. Although it has Freudian connotations, the technique is used to examine and deal with current rather than past behaviour (Boswell, 1982, p160-161).

The officer who referred to psychoanalysis in relation to one probationer, was also the only officer who mentioned transactional analysis in relation to another probationer.

Group work is a method used by the Resource Unit with Schedule 11 probationers and within such a context probationers are confronted with their offending behaviour. Other examples of working with probationers in groups include the Drink Education Group and groups to help with budgeting at the Voluntary Resource Unit. But group work is not a suitable method for all probationers as one officer made clear:

> PO I have some clients who would die in a group. For instance A could not cope with group work (at the Resource Unit) but he had the guts to stand up in court and say he couldn't cope with being videoed and being asked to enact crimes which he said was too painful...So perhaps even using a method like group work with A even though it failed, gave us a lot more insight into the man, but it didn't stop him offending.

Consequently it was acknowledged by the eight officers who resorted to this method that it is not suitable for all probationers, which helps to explain why it was being practised with only 13 out of 53 cases.

Finally, behaviourism (Hudson and Macdonald, 1986) was a method identified by seven respondents with 15 probationers. One said that:

> PO Well the basic philosophy is that all behaviour is learnt. Therefore the behaviourist approach is an attempt to bring about some change in the client to alter the learnt behaviour,

which she thought could be achieved through the Resource Unit package 'Change your ways in 30 days'. To another, behaviourism meant behaviour modification by a system of positive and negative responses to what the probationer says and does. But the worrying feature of this approach, as it was described to me, was that the probation officer has preconceived notions of what is acceptable and unacceptable behaviour, and that he is consequently attempting to impose his values and standards onto probationers. Therefore, it does seem that there are moral problems associated with this method.

Again it was said by another respondent that:

> PO As a behaviourist I help people to understand their behaviour which is causing them to react in a certain kind of way...and try to modify it.

However in the final quotation not only does this officer explain what he means by behaviourism, but he also gives an example of behaviourism in practice.

> PO I am an avid user of the behaviourist approach because I believe it is the one social work method that actually assists improve the self-esteem of our clients if it is used in the way that I use it, which is basically a system of rewarding, encouraging, praising and modelling.
> PW Could you elaborate a little more?
> PO A lot of people, I suspect, offend because they do not have a high opinion of themselves, so if someone does well I praise them to help make the person feel better about himself. The modelling

technique I use is myself or a volunteer. For example, with problem drinkers you can go into a pub with them and show them an alternative mode of behaviour...Most clients are from bad social conditions, mostly unemployed and most have an element of depression in their personality because they don't have a lot going for them. This gives me the opportunity to uplift them and that is a very important aspect in our job. We must lift them out of the doldrums if we can.

It is interesting how this officer refers specifically to modelling, because this is an important feature of the behaviourist method (Howe, 1987, pp89-90). One of the advantages of this method, despite the fact that, like the psychoanalytical method, it focuses primarily on the pathology of the individual, is that 'Behavioural social work demands of its practitioners that they be purposeful and methodical, organised and scientific, concrete and explicit' (Howe, 1987, p82).In other words, it offers a systematic approach to client problems. On this note, let me now try to bring this chapter to a close.

Diverse Practices, Hybrid Ideologies and Eclectic Methods

Content analysis of social enquiry reports where a probation order was imposed, revealed that probation officers at Redcar and Hartlepool are attempting to respond to a multiplicity of problems. Accordingly probation practice is diverse. Furthermore the profile of all 132 cases which had been recommended for probation indicated the scope of these problems by presenting data on a number of variables.

Turning to ideologies underlying and sustaining practice in relation to 53 probationers, it was found that the rationale of probation work was largely dominated by providing a social work service, advice, assistance and friendship, meeting the needs of offenders and enhancing self responsibility. Some respondents saw a connection between engaging in numerous welfare practices and the prevention and reduction of crime, which finds some support in the notion of rehabilitation. These respondents were also closely identified with the 'personalist' school within social work, which is characterised by a client centred approach, respect for persons, the enhancement of self-responsibility, a concern for the welfare of the individual and a concern to help.

To return to an earlier point, even though some respondents when interviewed individually resorted to the language of consensus and rehabilitation, subsequent discussions with the two teams in groups revealed that officers were acutely aware of socio-economic factors adversely affecting offenders, thus revealing a more complex perspective. The left-wing critique of probation articulated by Walker and Beaumont (1981), was challenged by these respondents because while they focused on helping the individual offender, this did not mean they were pressurising them to accept without question prevailing socio-economic arrangements. But in saying that, the teams felt a collective sense of helplessness and hopelessness about constructively changing adverse political, social and economic structures. The teams acknowledged they could not solve the problem of unemployment, for example, which led them to perceive their role in terms of helping offenders cope and survive in an unjust world bedevilled by poverty, inequality, disadvantage and shortage of money. They also wanted to make life more bearable, which echoed the sentiments of Day when he said that 'Social workers face uncertainty in trying to help other people in situations or with problems which are not going to be 'solved' but which care, concern, and understanding might make more bearable..'(1981, p201). Therefore the task was to help clients 'make the best of a bad job', and 'the enhancement of the offender as a person within society as it exists' (McWilliams, 1987, p114).

All respondents believed that a caring and helping approach to individual probationers could be reconciled with control. And whilst tensions, conflicts, paradoxes and dilemmas remain, they said that they could manage these conflicts and strived to achieve a sense of balance and rapprochment between conflicting ideologies. These conflicts between care and control did not debilitate officers from doing the job of supervising probationers. Therefore, although it can be argued that elements of control have expanded over recent years, mainly as a consequence of a greater commitment to law and order since 1979 (Box, 1987, ch 4), the 1982 Criminal Justice Act and SNOP, thus taking on emotive and sinister connotations in some sections of the probation service (see Chapter 2 above), my respondents' approach to probation work was dominated by support and care.

This gives an interesting insight into the relationship between Home Office policy for the probation service at a macro level, compared with what officers are thinking and doing at the micro level of practice and philosophy in two probation teams, where the probation officer engages individual clients. It is as though there are two distinct levels of discourse operating in two different spheres and both having their own language. At one level Home Office civil servants, through SNOP, have created the potential for more control in probation, but at another level these respondents see probation work overwhelmingly in terms of help, support and care. Home Office civil servants and Ministers may have certain views on probation which are increasingly articulated in terms of a tougher attitude towards offenders, but it is clear that individual probation officers also have views, which can result in practice being unaffected by the pronouncements of civil servants or, for that matter, senior managers within the service. Consequently I found that probation practice was dominated by a social work, welfare service to people in need, and not social control, despite the drift towards a more controlling attitude from 'above' throughout the 1980s.

Finally, data was collected on methods of working with probationers to complete the picture of probation work presented in this chapter. As probation officers operated with diverse ideologies, so they had an eclectic, almost pot pourri approach to methods. I did not perceive there was anything profoundly esoteric or theoretically recondite in their approach to methods, which was supported by the officer who stated that 'I am not pretending to have any fancy theories behind (casework)'. Consequently the pretentious terminology of social work methods was shorthand language for approaches to clients which were practical and down to earth. In other words, it was as though the sometimes complex theory of methods found in social work text books during training, became refracted through each respondents pragmatic lens, which resulted in a common sense and practical approach at that point where officers were working with clients.

It can also be argued that this must be the case because, firstly, prospective probation officers during their CQSW training courses receive approximately one terms instruction on a plethora of social work methods. This is hardly sufficient time to acquire expertise. Secondly, probation officers do not have the time to apply social work methods in their 'pure' form with probationers because they have a total of 35 statutory tasks to perform. A perennial complaint of officers is that they do not have sufficient time to work with clients and one respondent rued the fact that

> PO We are getting to be a referring agency really. I seem to be sending a lot of my clients out and I would like to do some of that work myself.

Thirdly, very little in-service training is provided on social work methods once trainees have been appointed to the Cleveland service. Finally, it seems that the development of new methods of working with offenders have occurred with no obvious conceptual basis, particularly in the sense that methods are not selected on the basis of their efficacy at reducing or preventing crime, but rather on the basis of what is most comfortable for officers and clients. Even though a multiplicity of methods are being used with probationers, no research is being done to monitor which approaches have potential, which does seem to be a deficiency. In other words, the Cleveland probation service does not have objective criteria to help officers assess which methods could be the most effective with different types of offenders. For as this research indicates, individual probation officers resort, on the whole, to the same methods with all probationers. It may be argued that probation officers should be attempting to match client with methods of working more systematically than they are doing at the present time and also measuring the effectiveness of their intervention, which is a point I'll return to in the final chapter. Consequently there are weaknesses in the area of methods of working, which is surprising for an agency claiming professionalism.

Having said that, it is questionable whether all probation officers need training in those methods discussed above. Because this research has indicated that probation practice is dominated by providing a welfare service to offenders experiencing a variety of problems relating to accommodation,budgeting, stress, alcohol and unemployment, it would seem that officers primarily require the counselling skills to identify and clarify such problems and also to have the practical knowledge to constructively provide assistance. Accordingly I would argue that the vast majority of officers should have the knowledge to give practical advice on, for example, welfare rights and Benefit entitlements. This would help to demystify much of the professional language which currently accompanies discussions on social work methods. However should some offenders require more specialised and skilled help for emotional or psychological problems, a case can be made for referring them either to probation officers who have been specifically trained in, for example, family therapy or transactional analysis, or to specialists from other disciplines drawn from social work, medicine, psychology and psychiatry. It would seem that greater inter-agency cooperation is required at this point.

In essence, whilst probation officers are engaged in a diverse range of practices, which are sustained, at times, by conflicting ideologies and with an eclectic approach to methods, the unifying thread weaving its way through all the paradoxes and dilemmas is a commitment to a personalist philosophy concerned with the meeting of human need. Probation work for these respondents is primarily about a social work service to the disadvantaged and not about social control or social action. With this in mind, the next chapter turns to consider other dimensions of probation work mentioned in earlier chapters, particularly the theme of using probation orders as an alternative to custody.

8 Probation and alternatives to custody: views from probation officers

Introduction

This chapter looks at other features of the data which involves further considertion of all 132 cases. However, for reasons already explained, even though the discussion in the previous chapter was based on 53 probation orders, from time to time in this chapter I will consider all 63 probation orders.

Types of offences

When the 132 offenders appeared before the courts during the first six months of 1987, they were charged with a variety of offences. A total of 237 offences were recorded against these offenders (excluding offences taken into considertation-tics) which have been allocated to three main categories - property offences, offences against the person and other offences. Table 8.1 reveals how 166 (70%) involved either stealing or causing damage to property, while Table 8.2 and 8.3 show that 16 (6.8%) were against the person and 55 (23.2%) were neither property or offences committed against the person.

Table 8.1 Property offences

Other thefts	37
Other burglary	31
Burglary DH	22
Shoplifting	17
Deception	17
Attempted burglary	11
Handling/Receiving	8
Criminal damage	8
Going equipped	7
Fraud/Forgery	4
Attempted theft	2
Attempted deception	1
Arson	1

Total 166

Table 8.2 Against the person

Section 47 AOABH	7
Indecent assault on F	3
Threatening behaviour	2
Robbery	2
GBH	1
Offensive weapon	1
Total	16

Table 8.3 Other offences

Breach of current order	25
Other RTA	15
Drive whilst disqual.	7
TWOC	4
Drugs	3
Firearms	1

Total 55

Finer distinctions may be made within the universe of these 132 cases and the first is between the 63 probation orders, 35 custody cases and the remaining 34 cases which include the following subcategories of non-custodial sentences:

a) 2 Conditional Discharge, 1 Fine, and 1 Attendance Centre Order;

b) 1 Probation Order to continue + CD, 4 PO to continue + Fine, and 1 PO to continue + Community Service Order;

c) 13 CSO's

d) 10 Suspended Sentences, and 1 Suspended Sentence Supervision Order.

Table 8.4 presents details of offences committed by each of the three categories. It will be seen that the 63 probation cases committed 73.7% property offences, 4.5% offences against the person and 21.8% Other; the custody cases committed 72.2% property offences, 7.6% against the person and 20.2% Other; finally, the remaining category of 34 cases committed 58.3% property offences, 10.4% against the person and 31.3% Other offences.

154

Table 8.4

Offences by probation, custody and remaining cases

	Probation	Custody	Remaining
Burglary DH	5	14	3
Other burglary	10	13	8
Attempted burglary	5	5	1
Shoplifiting	13	1	3
Other thefts	20	10	7
Attempted theft	1	1	0
Handling/Receiving	3	3	2
Going equipped	2	3	2
Deception	12	4	1
Attempted deception	1	0	0
Arson	1	0	0
Criminal damage	4	3	1
Fraud/Forgery	4	0	0
Indecent assault on F	1	1	1
GBH	0	0	1
S47 AOABH	2	2	3
Offensive weapon	1	0	0
Threatening behaviour	1	1	0
Robbery	0	2	0
TWOC	2	2	0
Drive whilst disqual.	2	2	3
Other RTA	6	5	4
Drugs	3	0	0
Breach of current order	10	7	8
Firearms	1	0	0
Total	110	79	48

Charges, tic's and previous court appearances

In addition to presenting information on types of offences concerning these three case categories, it is also necessary to introduce comparative data on the number of charges and tics and number of previous court appearances, to discover if there are discernible differences between them. I begin with comparative data on probation and custody cases.

It is interesting to observe that the 63 probationers were charged, on average, with 3.5 charges and tics, compared with 4.5 for the custody group. In other words, those who received a custodial sentence were charged, on average, with more offences and tics than probationers, which is perhaps not surprising. Next the custody cases had, on average, previously appeared before the courts on more occasions than probationers, 5.8 compared with 3.7 times. Even though

155

there are discernible differences between the probation and custody groups when considering measures of central tendency (the mean) in relation to charges/tics and number of previous court appearances, prior to either probation or custody being imposed, there are slight differences when turning to measures of variability or spread.

The midspread measure (dq) for probationers in relation to charges and tics is 4 and the standard deviation (sd) is 3.1; for the custody cases the dq is 4 and the sd is 3.8. When considering previous court appearances for probationers the dq is 6 and sd 3; for the custody cases the dq is 5 and sd 2.7. Therefore, the dq and sd measures for charges/tics and previous court appearances, for both probationers and those who received a custodial sentence, indicates that data are relatively widely spread out from the mean.

From the remaining 34 cases who received non-custodial sentences, the average number of charges and tics for the a) 4 CD, Fine and ACO cases was 2.3; b) 6 probation to continue cases was 1.7; c) 13 CSO's was 1.5; d) 11 Suspended Sentence and SSSO cases was 1.4. The average number of previous court appearances for these four subcategories was 2.8, 6.7, 4.1 and 5.6 respectively. Consequently there are some differences between the three categories of probation, custody and remaining non-custodial cases, in relation to number of charges and tics and number of previous court appearances. But to complete the presentation of this background information which contextualises the discussion to follow, the focus will be narrowed even further by looking at the 63 probation orders.

Male and female probationers

Using the method of presentation adopted in the previous section, I begin by comparing male and female probationers in relation to number of charges and tics, and number of previous court appearances. Interestingly male probationers, on average, had fewer charges and tics than females, 3 compared with 4.5. Where types of offences are concerned, the principal or single most serious offence committed by male and female probationers, according to the scale of seriousness devised by Bale (1987) may be adjudged to be the following:

Table 8.5

Single most serious offence committed by male probationers

	Frequency
Dwelling house burglary	5
Other burglary, including attempted burglary	12
Shoplifting	3
Theft and Deception, including attempts	10
Fraud and Forgery	1
Drugs offences	1
Indecent assault on Female	1
Threatening behaviour	1
TWOC/Road Traffic Offences	3
Going Equipped	1
Handling/Receiving	1
Firearms offences	1
S.47 Assault	1
Total	**41**

Table 8.6

Single most serious offence committed by female probationers

	Frequency
Shoplifting	8
Theft and Deception	9
Criminal Damage	1
Fraud and Forgery	1
Other Burglary	1
Arson	1
Drug offences	1
Total	**22**

One of the most significant features is the way in which 5 male offenders were placed on probation after committing dwelling house burglary, an offence considered serious by the courts and warranting almost immediate custody. In fact, in a speech to ACOP in 1986, one senior Judge stated that:

> Offences like house burglary should always attract custodial sentences, involving as it does the violation of a home, the infliction of fear and distress and the fact that it is a crime very close to personal assault (Gower, p6).

Moreover many other offences committed by both male and female probationers involved property, which reiterates an earlier point that the vast majority of these offences involve property of one form or another, rather than serious offences of violence against the person.

157

When turning to previous court appearances male probationers, on average, had previously appeared before the courts more often than females, 4.3 times compared to 2.6. Moreover the range of charges and tics for females is more spread out than for males. For females the dq is 7 and sd is 3.9; for males the dq is 2 and sd 2.5. When considering previous court appearances the dq for females is 3 and sd 2.6; for males the dq is 6 and sd 3. Therefore, on average, male probationers had fewer charges/tics than females, but more previous court appearances.

Furthermore, only 2 males and 5 females were appearing at court for the first time when probation was imposed, which means that 56 out of 63 probationers (88.9%) had previously appeared before the courts. 27 out of 63 probationers (20 males and 7 females) had previously appeared more than 3 times, which again suggests that Redcar and Hartlepool probation officers are attempting to have probation orders imposed on offenders with relatively long criminal records, thus consistent with both SNOP and Cleveland probation policy in relation to the use of community supervision.

It should also be re-emphasised that probation officers had recommended probation orders for a group of 35 offenders who received custodial sentences. Probation officers are being encouraged by the Home Office in SNOP and the Cleveland Future Directions Document, to supervise as many offenders as possible in the community, especially in cases where custodial sentences would otherwise be imposed. However the problem is that even though probation officers were seemingly trying to do this in these 35 cases, the courts were unwilling to make probation orders.

To summarise, the first section of this chapter has presented data on all 132 cases in relation to property offences, offences against the person and other offences. Data has also been presented on number of charges and tics, including previous court appearances, and a distinction was made between 63 probation orders, 35 custody cases and 34 remaining non-custodial cases, where the data was analysed by comparing measures of central tendency and spread. I also distinguished between male and female probationers. Therefore, against this background, the remainder of this chapter will examine, from a probation perspective, a number of important issues introduced in earlier chapters, specifically the theme of alternatives to custody which is prominent in both SNOP and the Cleveland Future Directions Document. This discussion will be informed and enriched by interviews undertaken with Hartlepool and Redcar probation officers. But first, and by way of introduction, a note on the contemporary crisis within the prison system.

Crisis in the prisons

During the autumn of 1987 the Observer newspaper published an article called 'The Crisis In Our Prisons' (Lustig, 11.10.87), and it is not too difficult to understand why such an article appeared at this time. Table 8.7 shows how the prison population has been steadily rising for serveral decades, reaching an all-time high of 50,969 during July, 1987, when this research was in progress. This occurred when the certified normal accommodation, which is the number of prisoners the system can officially contain without overcrowding, was 41,655 at the end of April, 1987 (NACRO, 1987b).

Table 8.7

Prison population in England and Wales 1908-1987

1908	22,029
1918	9,196
1928	11,109
1938	11,086
1948	19,765
1958	25,379
1968	32,461
1978	41,796
1980	43,936
1981	44,436
1982	44,000
1983	43,326
1984	44,433
1985	47,582
1986	46,635
1987	50,073

To put this another way, in 1985 just over 96,000 offenders came into custody under sentence and approximately 52,000 were serving sentences of under 18 months, and 13,000 3 months or less. About 30% of the total prison population are imprisoned for petty offences and in 1985 just over 20,000 were sent to prison for non-payment of fine. And since 1980 the number of untried and unsentenced prisoners has increased, despite the 1976 Bail Act. The average number of untried and convicted unsentenced prisoners in 1975 was 5,609, but in 1985 this had escalated to 9,697, making 14% and 21% respectively of the average prison population (Stern, 1987, p30).

Looking further afield there is evidence to show that the United Kingdom imprisons more people than other major Western European countries, both in absolute numbers and in proportion to its population. In 1984 the UK imprisoned 193,976 offenders. Second in the league table was Turkey at 117,833 and last was Portugal with 10,817. When comparing the number imprisoned per 100,000 population the UK was at the top of the league table with 344.7, Turkey was second with 312.9 and last was Portugal with 109.8 (NACRO, 1986). To make matters worse, the Home Office has estimated that the prison population by 1995 could reach somewhere between 54,400 and 59,400, which led NACRO to comment that if recent trends continue these projections will have to be revised upwards (NACRO, 1987b, p3).

Because the prison population has been rising over recent years, the theme of 'alternatives to custody' has been on the political agenda since the mid-1960s (Bottoms, 1987). In 1968 the prison population stood at 32,500, which was nearly a 3-fold increase since 1938 when it was 11,100. Bottoms argues that, assuming that the crime rate would continue to increase, policy makers in the 1960's faced the choice of either accepting the prison population would continue to rise, or seek alternatives to custody: 'They chose the latter option, and have continued to do so at intervals ever since; though in the 1980's they have also seemed at times to be planning for an ever-increasing prison population' (p181). However despite alternatives to custody which have been introduced over the last 20 years, such as the Suspended Sentence, Community Service Orders, the Bail Act and Parole, including, more recently, Probation Orders with extra conditions, the custody rate has continued to increase and there is some evidence to show that so-called alternatives to custody have instead been used as alternatives to other non-custodial disposals. This led Bottoms to conclude with the rather pessimistic comment that:

> While the government also remains of the view that non-custodial measures should be used whenever possible, few outside observers see in present government policy any real likelihood of improving the recent dismal track record of attempts to limit prison use in England (1987, p199).

Notwithstanding this pessimistic outlook and the fact that alternatives to custody have often proved not to be alternatives at all, it continues to have thematic importance.

The previous Chapter suggested that probation officers at Redcar and Hartlepool may be located within the personalist, rather than the radical or managerial schools of contemporary probation work. Even though each of the three schools have their own particular and unique characteristics, McWilliams argues that 'each of the schools of thought shares the opinion that the probation officer's task in court is to offer realistic disposals with a view to reducing custodial sentences' (1987, p97).

It may also be recalled how SNOP stated that the probation service should put into effect probation orders, particularly in cases where custodial sentences would otherwise be imposed, which finds support in the first objective of the Cleveland probation service where it is stated that the service should promote community supervision programmes as direct alternatives to custody through probation orders. Therefore, are probation officers at Redcar and Hartlepool attempting to do this?

Probation as an alternative to custody

To recapitulate, my original intention at the beginning of 1987, clarified in Chapter 6, was to interview a total of 14 main grade probation officers at Redcar and Hartlepool. Because of circumstances beyond my control, 3 officers left Cleveland before they could be interviewed. I was therefore left with 11 probation officers which meant that it was only possible to cover, in depth, 53 out of 63 probation order cases, and 32 out of the 35 custody cases.

Having reminded the reader of this caveat, the 11 probation officers interviewed stated they were not surprised at the imposition of a custodial sentence in all except 2 out of 32 cases, even though

161

probation had been recommended to the court.   In these two cases, one officer had mentioned a probation order in a total of 14 social enquiry reports during the first six months of 1987 and the courts subsequently imposed 9 custodial sentences. He explained that:

> PO I expected 8 custodial sentences...I think that the 8 custodial sentences were almost inevitable...I expected them all except A where I really felt there was definitely more than an even chance that the lad could be made the subject of a probation order.

In the second case where surprise was expressed a female offender was committed to prison, which resulted in a rather animated probation officer fulminating that 'I thought it was disgraceful'.

It is not too difficult to understand why, in all except two cases, probation officers expressed little surprise at these custodial sentences.   It has already been stated when considering the quantitative data presented above that, on average, custody cases were charged with 4.5 offences/tics, in addition to which they had previously appeared before the courts, on average, 5.8 times. Moreover the single most serious offence which culminated in custody for all 35 custody cases was as follows (therefore including the 3 cases for which 3 officers could not be interviewed):

Table 8.8

Single most serious offence which resulted in custody

Offence	Frequency
Burglary Dwelling House	15
Other Burglary	11
Theft/Deception	2
Robbery	2
TWOC	1
Indecent Assault	1
Handling/Receiving	1
Driving whilst Disqual.	1
Abstracting electricity	1

Total 35

One officer considered that one of her cases was borderline custody, 'but it was a dwelling house burglary', thus making custody comprehensible. Another officer acknowledged that there was a strong possibility that one of his clients would receive a Detention Centre sentence, 'mainly based on the fact that it was a dwelling house burglary'. Yet another officer expressed surprise that there were only 5 custodial sentences out of 15 cases in which he had written reports, explaining that these 5 custodial sentences were inevitable.

Therefore, because of the offences committed, particularly dwelling house and other burglary; the previous record of the offender and the number of previous court appearances; the fact that several officers mentioned that some offenders had committed offences which involved a considerable amount of money - one officer mentioned between £1000/2000 for one offender; and because in 7 out of 35 cases the offender was in breach of either a probation order or suspended sentence, little surprise was expressed at these custodial sentences, even though probation supervision had been mentioned to the court as the disposal for consideration. Consequently probation officers were attempting to have probation orders made in cases where custody was a realistic possibility.

In addition to considering the expectations and perceptions of probation officers, I applied the Risk of Custody scale developed by Bale in the Cambridge probation service, which introduced a more objective assessment of the custody cases under discussion. This instrument, which takes into account ten items of information - gravity of principal offence, number of additional offences, whether subject to a suspended sentence, whether a community service order was imposed during the last 12 months, number of previous convictions, number of convictions during the last two years, number of previous custodies, court, sex and whether remanded in custody or on bail - has been designed to assess which offenders are at risk of a custodial sentence. In Cambridge it has been found that 79% of non-custodial disposals score between 0 and 50 on the scale, while 83% of immediate custodial sentences score over 50. Consequently using the data collected by the Recording Schedule, I discovered that 30 out of 32 custody cases scored over 60 on the scale, which helps to confirm why probation officers expressed little surprise at the vast majority of these custodial sentences. But in the two cases where surprise was expressed are concerned, the first offender scored 70 which indicates a risk of custody, but the second who was a female scored only 30,

163

which explains why the probation officer was so angry. Even though the scale may not exactly suit the practices of the Cleveland Courts, because it is based on the sentencing decisions of Cambridge Magistrates and Judges between December 1985 and June 1986, nevertheless the results are interesting when considering those offenders who received a custodial sentence. It has also been used sucessfully in other probation areas (Bale, 1988).

The research also found that 26 out of 35 custody cases (74.3%) had previously not had a probation order. Even though 11 of these 26 had previously had a Supervision Order (available to those aged between 10 and 16) it is surprising that so many had not had the benefit of adult supervision provided by a probation order prior to receiving custody. More disturbing still is that 13 out of 35 offenders who received custody had previously not had either a SO or PO; and 13 out of the 15 (86.7%) who received a Youth Custody Order, as opposed to DC or Prison, had not had a probation order. One may therefore begin to ask why the courts do not allow offenders a period of community supervision before imposing a custodial sentence. There may well be a case for the probation service taking the initiative in making the Courts its target for change, rather than offenders, which would involve persuading Magistrates and Judges to seriously consider making probation orders, for example, in cases where a custodial sentence is a possibility but where the offender has previously not had the benefit of adult community supervision. However as the next Chapter indicates, there are sometimes good reasons why sentencers will not consider community supervision, especially for the more serious offender.

When I asked respondents if they were trying to have probation orders imposed by the courts in cases where offenders were facing a custodial sentence, eight probation officers gave an unqualified 'yes' in answer to this question. However one said:

> PO Yes, if I feel that a probation order would work, I would ask for one where an offender would normally receive a custodial sentence...if they are a suitable candidate for probation for various reasons and could be contained and be prepared to discuss things, and there's a possibility of changing their behaviour, I can't see why it shouldn't be used.

Another respondent commented that:

> PO I don't always. I like to have something to work on. I feel we must have something to work on if a probation order is imposed. But if there is nothing else I will attempt to put up some form of package as an alternative to custody.

These two qualified responses are included here because they contain enormous difficulties and illuminate a dissonance between the findings of empirical research and the realities of practice. One officer apparently decided on probation by how she 'feels' about an offender, whether or not the offender is a 'suitable candidate' and whether or not such an order would 'work', which in itself provides an interesting insight concerning how this officer selects offenders for probation. However it has already been discussed in Chapter 1 how the justification for using probation is not its rehabilitative efficacy, or that it 'works' in preventing recidivism. Moreover Fielding, within the context of discussing probation officers perceptions of the aetiology of crime states that

> officers draw no clear implications from 'theory' to practice. Their needs are not dispassionate, but committed. They must construct a report to make sense of the case before the Court and, if they recommend probation, through which efforts at change can proceed. Analysis is to point up the potential for change in the offender, that the Court may be convinced and that probation workers may see the case as appropriate for work. However research has drawn pessimistic conclusions about the ability of social workers to accurately perceive potential for change (1984, p13).

Consequently if probation officers only recommended a probation order in cases where it was supposedly considered to 'work', where offenders were 'suitable candidates' and where there was a possibility of 'changing their behaviour', very few offenders would be recommended for probation, even if probation officers knew exactly in the first place which offenders conformed to these criteria.

It should be recalled that probation officers have more reliable guides than 'feelings' when deciding whether or not probation will be successful. They could, for example, use the criteria established by Philpotts and Lancucki, where it is claimed that when probation is used for men convicted for the first time and after many previous convictions, the results are not encouraging in terms of reconviction. But when probation and fines are used with men with a few previous convictions, the results may be more positive. (Incidentally this research found that 7 offenders were selected for probation on their first court appearance and 15 after they had previously appeared 8 times). Consequently what one probation officer seems to be indicating here is that selecting offenders for probation hardly complies with a rigorously scientific, or academic assessment procedure, nor are the findings of research considered; rather, selection is determined more by feeling and emotive responses to individual offenders during interview. In other words, she is not engaged in a dispassionate or detached scientific enterprise, nor does she seem concerned with research results. Rather, she is engaged in an art form where gut feeling, human emotion and guessology predominates when determining which offenders should be recommended for probation.

One may also question whether it is imperative for officers always to 'have something to work on' within the context of a probation order, particularly when an offender is facing custody. It may be argued that probation can be a more humane response to offending than custody; that is has the potential to be a more positive and constructive experience than custody; and that it is no more and certainly no less effective in preventing further criminal behaviour, than custody. It is also less costly, a factor which should not be overlooked in the post-SNOP climate which is concerned to obtain value for money. This may be the reductionist position, but there are occasions when probation officers could argue that there is a case for offering a probation order as an alternative to custody irrespective of whether there is something to work on, or that it 'works'. This may simply involve the offender reporting to the probation office, in the way illustrated by Bryant et al. Even though this kind of approach to probation supervision may find some acceptance within the probation service, the courts may be unsympathetic on the grounds that something more is required.

Notwithstanding the problems associated with how some officers select probationers, the utility of probation and the questionable point of whether it is always necessary to have something to work on, 8 out of 11 officers were trying to have probation orders imposed in

166

cases where offenders were facing a custodial sentence. But, to be more specific, in how many cases where a probation order was imposed, was probation considered to be an alternative to custody?

The 11 respondents had written reports in which 53 probation orders were made, which means that the 3 officers not available for interview had the ten remaining probation orders between them, making a total of 63. Accordingly these 11 officers said that probation was used as an alternative to custody in 26 out of 53 cases. In fact, all 26 offenders adjudged to have received a probation order as an alternative to custody had appeared before the courts previously. When applying the Risk of Custody scale it was found that 20 out of these 26 cases scored over 60, which tends to confirm the views of respondents that these orders were imposed in circumstances where there was a risk of custody.

It is interesting to note that 19 out of 63 probation orders (30.2%) were made in cases where a probation order had previously been imposed on these offenders. In other words, 19 were receiving probation for a second time. Even more interesting is that 26 out of 63 probationers (41.3%), had previously received a custodial sentence prior to probation in 1987.

It may be argued that these respondents are trying to have probation orders made where offenders are in danger of receiving a custodial sentence. They were unsuccessful in achieving this in the 35 custody cases mentioned earlier, but they perceived that 26 out of 53 probation orders were made as an alternative to custody. Therefore, some attempt is being made to comply with the central policy objectives of both SNOP and the Cleveland Future Directions Document. This was neatly illustrated by one respondent who said that:

> I've always worked on the premise over the last few years that we always offer the courts alternatives to custody...so I always do even though the people are going to prison anyway. I offer the courts alternatives because you only get, as in my case, 1 out of 14 right...But the difficulty is that with high risk offenders it is very difficult to divert Magistrates away from a further period of custody.

Probation and its place on the tariff

The courts can make a probation order instead of imposing a sentence, in cases where it is considered expedient to do so, having regard to the circumstances and nature of the offence, and the character of the offender. Sometimes probation may be used as an alternative to custody for serious or high tariff offenders. Sometimes it is imposed because offenders have certain needs, rather than because of their deeds, in what may be described as low tariff cases. But how did my respondents make sense of the issue of using probation for high and low tariff offenders?

Ten officers believed that the probation service should be targetting high tariff offenders for probation. However one of these officers expressed caution when she commented that

> PO Yes, I think you can if you word the social enquiry report properly...and there are obvious grounds for such an order. Where you run into problems is if the grounds are not clear cut...unless there are specific problems you can latch on to, then just asking for a probation order in a blanket sort of way leaves little chance.

The implication here is that if probation officers construct a well argued report in which they delineate in detail what they propose to do with the more serious offender, rather than a throw away line at the end of the report that probation is a good idea, then they may be successful in targetting the serious offender for probation.

This begins to suggest that probation officers know and understand what the courts are looking for in reports which could be efficacious in persuading them to take a chance by putting a serious offender on probation, which is an issue to return to later. However if the criminal justice system is going to reduce the number of offenders currently entering custody, Magistrates will have to be diverted away from imposing custodial sentences and diverted towards imposing probation orders instead. To achieve this a quantum leap will be necessary in the way Magistrates currently exercise their sentencing powers, in order for them to use probation orders much more than they do at present.

Finally there was one respondent who said that the service should not necessarily target high tariff offenders for probation. He said that:

> PO I don't think it depends on the sentence facing the individual; it depends on the suitability of the individual to probation. I

think we are making the mistake of putting probation into the tariff system, whereas it is outside the tariff system...it can be used anywhere.

A very important point is being raised here which logically leads on to the issue of low tariff cases.

Opinion was divided on the question of whether or not probation should be used in low tariff, less serious cases. First of all, 3 officers justified probation orders in low tariff cases on the basis of it being a preventative measure. One explained it like this:

> PO Yes, on the basis of preventative work which is one of my special interests. I should like to do more preventative work and more work on a voluntary basis with the people on the periphery of offending. I think it is a neglected area of probation.

Secondly, another probation officer saw a place for probation in less serious cases if the offender had a 'social work problem', or had needs. But the same officer went on to explain that these probation orders were necessary 'to balance out your caseload'. The point being made here is that a probation officer's caseload comprised solely of high risk, serious cases, would create considerable stress for the officer. Consequently some less serious cases are necessary on the grounds of occupational survival. This is an important point, sometimes overlooked by probation officers who are evangelically concerned to reduce the prison population. In other words, whilst much fine rhetoric is articulated and a great deal of passion generated concerning the provision of alternatives to custody by the probation service in more serious cases, particularly by NAPO, there would be a high price to pay if such rhetoric was translated into reality. There is no doubt that probation officers would find themselves under considerable pressure to successfully contain serious offenders in the community, which is why one officer indicates that some low tariff cases are necessary in order to cope and survive in the job.

Thirdly, the complexity of the issue under discussion here and the ambivalent responses it generated, is illuminated by the following respondent. During our discussion I asked:

> PW If a person if appearing for the first time, let's say, whose offences are not serious, but who you feel has problems which could be ameliorated by being under supervision, would that be a legitimate use of probation?

169

PO That would depend very much on the case because a first time offender could be pushed too far up the tariff. You would have to think very carefully about that. You would look at voluntary supervision and support first, rather than a probation order straight away. If you get into that (using a probation order early on) its straight up the tariff and where do you go from there? Having said that, there are the odd cases where the first time offender comes up, where the offence would not merit probation, but such an order would be appropriate. But be careful about pushing up the tariff.

The interesting point to note here is that a probation order is perceived, by this probation officer, as having a particular place on the tariff of court disposals.

Finally, yet another probation officer, whilst acknowledging that the tariff is in operation in the Hartlepool courts said:

I do not see probation as fitting in any one place on the tariff and I think it can fit where it needs to be. I prefer to see it nearer the top, but there will be times when I think it will be found lower down.

On the whole these respondents believed that probation orders should be available for a wide range of offenders, including both serious and less serious offenders, not just one specific group.

Probation and extra conditions

When respondents were asked to consider what the Cleveland probation service could do to get more probation orders imposed in cases where custody is a possibility, they made the following responses. First of all, officers must be specific in their court reports when recommending probation, by delineating what they propose to do with offenders. Secondly, the service must have appropriate resources and facilities to offer clients, such as alcohol groups, drug users groups and groups for single mothers. Thirdly, Magistrates should be given a periodic progress report on probationers, particularly in high risk cases. Fourthly, and crucially, the probation order must appear credible to the courts and one way of achieving this is for officers to accompany offenders to court where they could address the Bench in support of their recommendation for probation. For as one officer said:

PO Until we get the confidence of the Magistrates we are not going to move up the tariff and we are not going to get the more complex or risky cases.

Finally it was considered that more probation orders could be made in cases where custody is a possibility if the service develops its use of extra conditions. Because the issue of extra conditions is important for the probation service, especially since the 1982 Criminal Justice Act, it will now be considered more carefully.

Even though 8 respondents said that extra conditions should be developed to make probation a more credible alternative to custody, most of them felt they had to qualify their answers. As one remarked:

> PO I think that it is one way of possibly putting pressure on Judges and Magistrates to give such an order, but I think we have to be careful not to get too tied up in these conditions because what we are doing, to some extent, is making the probation order less flexible than it otherwise might have been...But sometimes, in cases where you are so close to a custodial sentence, then possibly conditions would give more credibilty to probation.

Another respondent added to this by saying that extra conditions may well be necessary for the heavy end offender. However

> PO I'm not really in favour of a lot of extra conditions because I think they are inviting trouble. As a service we have conditions in (normal probation) orders and we have not been very good at following them through.

Yet another officer said that extra conditions are legitimate so long as the client knows exactly what he is letting himself in for, which echoes the criteria for the use of such conditions adumbrated by Raynor (1985) earlier.

Another probation officer made a telling comment when he said that:

> PO I think that probation is a credible alternative to custody without any (extra) conditions...We have to be careful not to go too far down the road of presenting highly structured conditions where you actually have a prison in the community. We must have some checks, but let's not go too far.

But the problem with this comment is that, even though this officer may be articulating a view which would be echoed by many probation officers, it may well be that courts require the probation service, not necessarily to create 'prisons' in the community, but most certainly to develop and expand the use of extra conditions before a significant impact could be made on the proportionate use of custody. In another interview one officer said:

PO Nothing can ever be an alternative to custody. If a person is going to be sent to prison, they are going to be sent to prison, end of story. There is no such thing as an alternative to custody.

PW Surely there are some cases where offenders may be facing custody, but where Magistrates adjourn the case for the probation officer to explore alternatives, either a probation order or a community service order?

PO Yes, in those cases, yes. But I don't think that conditions are necessary though. I think conditions are a red herring. If conditions are necessary it tends to imply an unwillingness on the part of the client, or the probation officer to deal with the case. If a client needs conditions to make him comply then I would question the validity of the probation order.

PW But could extra conditions make Magistrates more disposed to a probation order?

PO Are we trying to make Magistrates happy or are we dealing with clients? I'm not in the job of making Magistrates happy. I'm in the job of having successful probation orders and if having a condition attached makes it less likely for me to be successful with a case then I don't want that condition, whatever the Magistrates want...The Magistrates confidence in the probation service has perhaps been lost because the probation service is larger...we have centralised courts and therefore Magistrates don't know individual probation officers.

From the discussion of professional concerns in Chapter 4 it is clear that the issue of extra conditions within probation orders touches a raw nerve in some officers and most of my respondents revealed a degree of ambivalence about this subject. Because the issue of conditions in probation orders will remain important for the probation service in future, I want to pursue this further by returning to the quantitative data which sheds more light on how probation orders with extra requirements were used at Redcar and Hartlepool, compared with normal probation orders.

A probation order with an extra condition was mentioned in 20 out of 132 reports at Redcar and Hartlepool. In 18 reports the probation officer solely recommended a probation order with a condition, but in a further two cases a probation order with a condition was mentioned in combination with a CSO. 9 offenders received a probation order with a condition, 6 received YC, 5 were sent to prison and 1 offender ended up with a normal probation order. (In 1 case out of the 9 where a probation order with a condition was made, it followed the social enquiry report recommending a psychiatric report).

Of the 9 who received a probation order with an extra condition, 5 received a Specified Activities Order (Schedule 11 4 A (1)(b)), 1 to receive mental treatment, 1 to live where directed by the probation officer and the remaining 2 were instructed to attend the Drink Education Group at the Woodlands Road Day Centre in Middlesbrough. There were 8 males and 1 female.

When comparing the 9 probation orders with extra conditions with the 54 normal probation orders, it may first of all be noted that the group of 9 offenders who received an extra condition were charged, on average, with 2.4 charges and tics. The 54 normal probationers were charged, on average, with 3.7 charges and tics. Interestingly those who received an extra condition had, on average, fewer charges and tics. It is also revealing to consider in detail the type of offences these 9 probationers had committed.

The first was charged with two road traffic offences;
the second with one offence of going equipped to steal and one of breaching an existing court order;
the third with one offence of handling/receiving stolen goods;
the fourth offender was charged with road traffic offences, other thefts and breaching an existing court order;
the next offender with one offence of burglary (not a dwelling house), shoplifting and other thefts;
the sixth offender was charged with one offence of burglary (not a dwelling house);
the seventh offender with road traffic offences, a non-dwelling house burglary and drive whilst disqualified;
the next offender with drug offences;
and the final offender (the only female to receive an extra condition) was charged with arson.

None of these 9 offenders had committed a dwelling house burglary offence. And even though, on average, they were charged with 2.4 charges and tics, 3 were charged with only one offence, 2 with two charges and tics, 3 with three and 1 with six offences. When considering how many times these 9 had previously appeared before the courts, 1 had appeared once, 3 two times, 1 four times and 4 eight times, an average of 4.8.

Turning to the 54 normal probation orders, it is worth reiterating that, on average, they were charged with 3.7 charges and tics. 13 out of 54 offenders had 6 or more charges and tics, as opposed to just one offender with 6 who received an extra condition. Even though the normal probation group had, on average, previously attended court on fewer occasions compared with the extra condition group - 3.6 times compared with 4.8 - one should observe that 22 out of 54 normal probation orders were made in cases where offenders had previously appeared at court on 4 or more occasions.

Consequently the data reveals that the courts were making probation orders without extra conditions in cases where a number of offenders were facing several charges and tics; where 5 offenders had committed a dwelling house burglary; and where 22 out of 54 probationers (40.7%) had previously appeared before the courts on 4 or more occasions. Therefore, the question must be asked, notwithstanding that there are only 9 probation orders with extra conditions to analyse compared with 54 normal orders: If normal probation orders are being made in the circumstances just described, why does the probation service need to resort to extra conditions to make probation a credible alternative to custody? It appears that the officer who said that 'I think probation is a credible alternative to custody without any conditions', has a point.

Alternatively, having established earlier that in all except 2 out of 32 custodial sentences were officers surprised at the outcome and that, as we have just seen, 8 out of 11 officers think that extra conditions could make probation a credible alternative to custody, why did these probation officers only mention a probation order with an extra condition in 11 out of the 35 custody cases? Surely, if they considered such conditions would add credibility to their recommendation for probation, they would have been mentioned more frequently? Finally, when applying the Risk of Custody scale to this data it was found that, first of all, in the total of 20 cases where an extra condition was recommended, only 12 scored over 60. Secondly, only 3 out of 9 cases where a probation order was made with an extra condition, scored over 60. This reinforces an earlier point that extra conditions are not being used in every case in circumstances

174

where an offender is at risk of custody and thus reveals a rather complex and ambivalent situation.

The future of the Probation Order

I considered it was important to conclude the interviews with these 11 main grade probation officers by giving them the opportunity to express their ideas concerning the development of probation supervision in Cleveland. They all had something to say on this matter and at one or two points their answers overlapped. For example, six of the officers said that probation packages provided by the Resource Unit, through which the Schedule 11 extra conditions are operated, were a good idea and a move in the right direction. One of these six respondents went on to say that Schedule 11 conditions should be expanded, but another felt that the development of Schedule 11 should now be consolidated before anything else is introduced or the current packages expanded.

Several officers also wanted to see the development of more resources and facilities to offer clients within the context of a probation order, such as a parenting skills group and a budgeting group. One respondent said that, in addition to the probation service itself providing a range of resources, officers should look to the wider community to tap resources which could be of benefit to clients:

> PO I have always been using them (community resources) and encouraging clients to take them up...let's use all facilities available.

One officer returned to the theme of wanting probation orders to have clear and specific goals and another wanted to see more client involvement when the service is deciding what kind of resources should be provided for them. However the comments of the next officer, whilst beginning on a negative note, end up as a positive and constructive suggestion which should be considered seriously by both the service and the courts:

> PO I really don't have any thoughts on future developments. I just implement what I am told to implement.
> PW By whom?
> PO By management or whoever. I don't really have any strong views about making policy. Certainly for people who you are thinking of

sentencing to less than six months imprisonment...I think the court could take a calculated risk by saying that 'we were going to sentence you to six months imprisonment, but as an alternative we are going to impose a 12 month probation order'. In short sentences, say anything under six months, a non-custodial sentence could be tried and that would certainly alleviate some of the problems they have in the prisons and it would give the person a further opportunity.

The crucial factor mentioned here is the role of the courts in undertaking to put into practice such a policy.

One officer rued the fact that she did not have sufficient time or space to work with clients, which is a perennial complaint of probation officers, and felt that some clients had a better deal than others. Another officer expressed the view that:

PO It may well be that we have to accept that we do not argue strongly, eloquently enough, or support our recommendations. So may be we have to develop our skill in asking for probation orders. I still maintain that my main success has been where I have been to court and stood up and said something.

To summarise, these were the ideas of probation officers concerning how they would like to see probation orders developed in Cleveland: to maintain Schedule 11 conditions; to develop more resources to benefit clients; point clients in the direction of community resources and involve them more in determining what these resources should be; probation orders should have clear goals; impose a probation order instead of a short prison sentence; provide officers with more space and time to work with clients; and develop the skill in asking for probation orders at court.

Finally an alternative perspective articulated by one respondent should be considered:

PO I don't see there is any need to develop the probation order. There is nothing wrong with the probation order as such, it is how people operate them. There are plenty of powers under a normal probation order...their scope is wide enough...What I would like to see, now that main grade officers are being asked to take more complex cases and deal with them in more complex ways, is the time to operate such cases. Fair enough, ten years ago when life was much easier, we were not asked to do as many things with cases. Nowadays, things are alot more complex. We are asked to do alot more and we have no time to think or plan. That time is not forthcoming. I think that is a management problem and I wish they could start getting to grips with that, instead of looking at the flavour of the month.

176

Nevertheless this perspective may have to be questioned because those recommendations for probation failed to prevent a custodial sentence from being imposed in 35 cases. Perhaps the probation order needs to be developed in some way after all.

Conclusion

The first part of this chapter considered data based on all 132 cases as a backcloth to the discussion which followed on the theme of probation as an alternative to custody. From various perspectives, which included looking at custody cases where probation had been recommended to the courts, the place of probation on the tariff and the use of extra conditions, probation as an alternative to custody was considered. However in the conclusion to this chapter I must return to probation supervision in relation to both SNOP and the Cleveland Future Directions Document.

Both the quantitative and qualitative data presented in this chapter would strongly suggest that, in a number of cases, probation officers at Redcar and Hartlepool were attempting to achieve these national and local policy objectives by having probation orders made in cases where custody was a strong possibility, if not inevitable. To reiterate, the research found that even though the respondents were not surprised at custodial sentences in all except 2 out of 32 custody cases, probation had nevertheless been recommended as an alternative. Moreover, 8 out of 11 respondents said they were trying to have probation orders made in cases where offenders were facing custody and that 26 (or 20 if Bale's Scale is applied) out of 53 probation orders were imposed as an alternative to custody.

Even though I have concentrated on the probation order in this research, it should also be acknowledged that amongst the 34 remaining non-custodial sentences referred to earlier, is a group of 24 cases comprising 13 CSO's, 10 Suspended Sentences and 1 SSSO. These disposals are also used as alternatives to custody by the courts and it is reasonable to suggest that this is how they were used in some of these cases when one considers the offences committed: 3 offenders committed dwelling house burglaries, 5 other burglary, 3 Section 47 AOABH, 1 Indecent assault, 1 GBH, 1 Drive whilst disqualified, 4

177

breach of existing court orders, 4 theft and 2 going equipped to steal. In fact, when applying the Risk of Custody scale to these 24 cases, it was found that 10 - 7 CSOs, 2 SSs, 1 SSSO - scored over 60, which indicates that these 10 were given non-custodial disposals when a custodial sentence was a possibility.

Notwithstanding the way in which this research indicates that, at a micro level, probation officers were successful in a number of cases at diverting offenders from custodial sentences, it should nevertheless be emphasised that 35 offenders received a custodial sentence, and from a macro perspective the prison population continues to rise. Box would argue that one must understand contemporary penal policy within the context of changing social relationships, deepening economic crisis, recession, unemployment and income inequality, which creates a problem for government concerning what to do with those who are adversely affected by the contemporary socio-economic climate. Unemployment, argues Box, creates havoc, despair and disillusionment, and because there is an increasing number of economically marginalised people, particularly within the inner cities, a serious problem for government exists. Therefore 'successive British and American governments have actively striven to defuse this situation, not by pursuing policies of 'full employment', but by screwing down the lid of social control' (Box, 1987, p131).

Consequently there are more police, magistrates and judges, more probation officers and prison officers, who can be used and depended upon to play their part in the control of the most threatening section of the surplus population. Thus Box argues that the scenario is for more prisons at the 'hard' end of the criminal justice system and more social control at the 'soft' end by probation officers, to deal with the effects of the recession. Prison is therefore an important tool in the war against crime within the current socio-economic climate and if there is an element of truth in Box's thesis, it is difficult to see how pursuing alternatives to custody can be a resounding success. There is also a problem for the probation service when, although pursuing a policy of alternatives to custody, a number of probation officers continue to recommend custodial sentences. In other words, the theme of alternatives to custody, which remains of thematic importance in the 1980s, is sometimes more rhetoric than reality, more a case of what is desirable than achievable and more a case of central government through the Home Office saying one thing to the probation service, but doing something else as it continues to expand the prison estate. There is no doubt, therefore, that the analyses of both Box and Bottoms (1987) make it difficult to see how one could expect probation orders to make a significant impact on the custody rate.

However this research, despite having to take cognizance of the analyses of Bottoms and Box, suggests that at a micro level it may well be possible to make modest inroads into the numbers currently being sent into custody, despite those 35 custodial sentences. Furthermore, there is some evidence from the juvenile criminal justice system to suggest that changes can be achieved at the local level if local areas have developed clear policies and strategies for change. For example, Tutt and Giller have argued as a result of their extensive involvement with numerous local authorities 'that a department with a clear policy, and committed staff, can bring about major changes in local juvenile justice systems unaffected by national legislation and structures' (1985, p27).

To do something similar with adult offenders and to specifically develop probation as a direct alternative to custody, depends on the probation service establishing a policy to achieve this which has the support of the local criminal justice system, particularly magistrates, clerks and judges. Therefore if this chapter has presented a probation perspective on alternatives to custody and heard from probation officers concerning their ideas for the development of probation to divert more offenders from custody, the next chapter presents the perspective of the decision makers.

9 Probation and alternatives to custody: views from sentencers

Introduction

In the third and final stage of the research my approach in the group interviews with magistrates, judges, probation officers and clerks, in addition to the remaining individual interviews with recorders and other clerks to the justices, was the same. I commenced the interviews by briefly explaining the findings of the quantitative research, drawing particular attention to those 35 cases in which a custodial sentence had been imposed, notwithstanding that probation had been recommended to the courts in the probation officer's report. Even though one of the judges said that

> You should not worry about the figures you produced; they are not unreasonable and you should not think that the judge can comply with your recommendations in one hundred percent of cases,

nevertheless the Home Office, as we have already seen in Chapter 3, has made it clear to the probation service that its mandate is to deal with the more serious offender in the community. After sketching some of the more important features of these 35 custody cases, the question posed at the beginning of all the interviews was: 'Are there any further provisions the Cleveland probation service can develop to make the probation order a more credible and effective alternative to custody for the more serious offender?'

Before presenting the answers given to this question, the first section will consider ways in which respondents articulated their perceptions of the probation order during the first few months of 1988 which, in itself, provides some useful insights for the Cleveland probation service to take cognizance of when planning future policy.

Perceptions of the Probation Order

It should first of all be recalled that 15 out of 35 offenders sent into custody were charged with dwelling house burglary offences and a further 11 offenders were charged with other burglary offences. This led one magistrate at the Guisborough Probation Liaison Committee (PLC) to comment that

> M These 35 cases where they had been before the courts about 5.8 times previously and graduated through the system and probation, in their context a probation order does not seem relevant, it seems like a let off for them.

I reminded the magistrate who made this comment that a large proportion of those given a custodial sentence had not had adult supervision in the community prior to receiving custody. I specifically pointed out to all eight magistrates at Guisborough that

> PW 26 out of these 35 custody cases had previously not had a probation order. Does that affect your response when sentencing? Or are you as magistrates saying that because of the nature of the offence and the number of times offenders have appeared at court in the past, these factors would exclude you from putting a dwelling house burglar, for example, on probation?

Another Guisborough magistrate replied

> M Yes, especially where the emphasis is on dwelling house burglary. The public feeling is that a probation order is not required or appropriate, because they want offenders to get prison. The public feel that the punishment does not fit the crime in such cases.

Throughout all the group interviews with magistrates and judges there was a high level of agreement between them that, for the more serious offender, probation was a 'let off' and a relatively 'soft option'. This perspective was captured well by the magistrate at the Redcar PLC who, and with some confidence, seemed to speak on behalf of all his

181

colleagues when he said that

> M In the public's eyes probation is a cop out because they are not getting punished... As magistrates we have to consider the views of the community, as well as our own views, and then take each case individually. In certain circumstances you have to consider the background to the case and in some cases probation does not seem the right thing to do. For example, when an old lady is burgled and is in the house when it happens, that can be a bad situation... For dwelling house burglary, the sentence is punishment. Probation does not appear to be punishment.

The problem concerning which offenders are suitable for probation was taken up by the Assistant Chief Probation Officer who, because of his senior management responsibility for the court team in Middlesbrough, was present at the judges liaison meeting. He said that

> ACPO The service acknowledges that probation is viable for some offenders but not for others. But we have difficulties with the grey areas, so can you give us guidance on what influences you in these grey areas? Not just dwelling house burglary, but theft, violence and other offences.

In reply one of the judges said

> J I am prepared to take a risk with a petty offender because I do not feel prison is effective. But the violent man is a problem... It may be possible to deal with a Section 47 assault in the community, but with the Section 18 and Section 20 there is more likelihood of imprisonment. A Section 18 offence will almost always result in custody and a Section 20 is likely to. In a wounding with intent or GBH the offender is not likely to get a non-custodial sentence.

This judge is referring to three violent offences from the 1861 Offences Against Persons Act. It is interesting that Thomas in his well received book on the Principles of Sentencing confirms that for a Section 18 offence the sentence is usually imprisonment. However a Section 20 differs from a Section 18 because of the notion of 'intent'. This means that under Section 18 it has to be proved there was an intention to inflict grievous bodily harm, whereas under Section 20 the intention is not established. Section 47 is a less serious charge than either Section 18 or 20 and applies to that category of violent offences where only a moderate degree of injury has been caused (Thomas, 1979, p99).

After clarifying that probation will not seriously be considered for certain types of violence, the same judge who made these comments

182

returned to the offence of dwelling house burglary. He began by saying that

> J The Home Office is telling you one thing and someone is telling us something else and we are not receiving the same message. We get directives that dwelling house burglars should receive prison, so there is conflict between what the Home Office wants us to do and what it wants you to do. Also the public's viewpoint may not coincide with the Home Office view. Your figures for the custody cases are interesting, in that 15 out of 35 offenders had committed dwelling house burglary and a further 11 with other burglary offences. Moreover, the bulk of the 35 were repeat offenders. The time might come when that kind of individual has to get prison for a period of time... In such cases if you talk about non-custodial sentences then we are looking at something more than a simple probation order. For people under stress a probation order might be helpful, but for a repeat criminal then it is difficult.

It must be said that the other three judges who attended this meeting concurred with these sentiments by their non-verbal nods of approval, one of whom went on to add that

> J In particular cases we send offenders to prison because there is not a lot left to do. All we can do is remember that it is desirable not to send people to prison if possible, but dwelling house burglary is the wrong side of the fence.

The feeling which emerged from the group interviews with magistrates and judges, and particularly on the basis of their perception of what the public feels about certain types of offences and the sentences which correspond to these offences, is that they have reservations about probation orders in cases where offending is relatively serious, for example, dwelling house burglary and particular types of violence, and where the offender is a recidivist. Taking up the notion of the 'public' and exploring it further, one of the judges expanded on this theme by saying that

> J The problem really is the feeling of the public. Since becoming a judge I have become rapidly aware of the views of what we call the public. Probation is still a soft option for the public. I do not think that if the offender is serious or if he is a risk to the public, they will be satisfied if he is placed on probation.

These views and perceptions begin to question, challenge and undermine the mandate of the Home Office contained in SNOP to the service which affirms that probation should be increasingly used for the more serious offender as an alternative to custody. For if the probation order, from a probation service perspective, was considered in the last chapter to be a viable alternative to custody for many of these 35 offenders, it is clear that from the perspective of these sentencers probation lacks credibility. In other words there remains a fundamental dissonance between what is considered desirable by the probation service on the one hand and what is considered possible and achievable according to sentencers, on the other. Consequently this led me to ask the magistrates at Guisborough the following question, which resulted in the following exchange:

PW Are you saying, therefore, that if the court is faced with having to deal with a dwelling house burglar, then no matter how much the probation service tries to persuade you otherwise and irrespective of the alternatives on offer, the offender will be given a custodial sentence?

One magistrate replied:

M That is a fair assessment, but not always the case. It depends on the individual circumstances of the case. You are talking about probation being used as an alternative to custody. But in the minds of many magistrates, community service orders are often used as an alternative. If magistrates are considering custody, then they think about a CSO as an alternative.
PW Are you saying that when considering an alternative to custody, a CSO is perceived to be more credible than probation? Could this be because you perceive that probation orders are more appropriate for less serious offenders?

The same magistrate answered:

M Not necessarily more credible, but we are looking at probation orders being used before offenders get to the average of 5.8 previous court appearances. My experience is that a CSO is second, in terms of gravity, to a prison sentence and that a probation order is for those appearing for the second or third time.
PW But the probation service is under pressure from the Home Office to deal with the more serious offender in the community and those who have committed serious offences and who have long criminal histories, by using probation orders.

Then, as though confidently speaking for his 7 colleagues, the same magistrate replied:

M But we make probation orders on those we think might benefit from probation, not so much as a punishment but because the probation service might be able to do something before they slip further into crime. By the time it is their fifth time in court, it is a bit late.

Moreover the deputy clerk to the justices who was present at the Guisborough PLC contributed further to what this magistrate had said by stating that:

> C It seems to me that there is a certain clientele that you are able to help. If more is required, then that does not come within the remit of the service.

After exploring this with the meeting in more detail I eventually asked

> PW So are you saying that the probation service largely exists to provide a social work service to relatively minor offenders, to help and support those in need; but that another and separate organisation is required to provide community punishments for the more serious offender who could be feasibly dealt with in the community?

One of the magistrates replied:

> M Magistrates perceive the probation service as providing help and support rather than punishment.

It is again interesting that the remaining 7 magistrates who were present did not express disagreement at this comment. Moreover this is an important insight , particularly at a time when the probation service is being challenged to provide punishment in the community as an alternative to custody.

It should be acknowledged at this point of the discussion that when the magistrate just quoted considered that by the time an offender arrives at his fifth court appearance it is a little late to receive probation help, there is some empirical research to support this view. According to Brody (who more or less supported the findings of Phillpotts and Lancucki considered towards the end of Chapter 1),

> the usefulness of probationary sentences, in particular, seems to be dependent to some extent on whether the offender has a record of previous convictions or not... The strongest evidence seems to indicate that an intermediate group of offenders, who are neither first offenders not yet confirmed recidivists, are possibly the best targets for experimental measures (1976).

It is therefore worth pointing out that, in the light of Brody's findings, it seems illogical for the Home Office to be targetting the more serious offender and recidivist for supervision because this must reduce the success rate.

Despite the fact that some probation orders are made in cases of relatively serious offending, because my own investigation reveals that probation orders are sometimes made in cases where offences of dwelling house burglary have been committed (and other local research

185

which I have done supports this; Whitehead, 1988), nevertheless it may be argued that the way magistrates and judges perceive probation as a let off, soft option and a vehicle for providing help rather than punishment, suggests that probation is not well suited or an obvious choice as a disposal to achieve those objectives articulated by the Home Office in SNOP. It does seem to lack credibility in the minds of those sentencers I interviewed, who also perceived that the public will not stand for probation being used for the more serious offender. There is further support for this argument in the following comments made by one of the magistrates. This not only touches on the theme of how magistrates perceive probation in the late 1980s, but also says more about what they perceive to be the wishes of the public. After reminding the magistrates again at Guisborough about the Home Office mandate it was said by one of them that

> M In thinking about allowing the serious offender back into the community, I do not think the community would trust the offender too much.

In reply the senior probation officer said

> SPO We recently had the SPO of the Resource Unit here to talk to the PLC about the Schedule 11 'Change your ways in 30 days' scheme.
> PW Is not this a useful development and something to think about for the more serious offender?

The deputy clerk replied

> C How can you really change anyone's ways in 30 days? I have my doubts and you will not change the opinion of the public.

This was added to by a magistrate who said

> M What could a probation officer write in his probation report to offset the immediate prejudice against a dwelling house burglar going into custody? This is what the public want... If such an offender is to be dealt with in the community then we have got to find a way through the initial prejudice concerning house burglary.

Before turning to consider ways in which probation could begin to break through this 'initial prejudice' where more serious offences are concerned, by making probation into something more credible and effective, this section, on how sentencers perceive probation and the current state of the art on the subject of alternatives to custody, may be concluded by the views of one magistrate from the Hartlepool PLC who seemed to speak for her other six colleagues when she said

186

with some animation that

> M As a magistrate of some years, the same offenders keep on coming
> back year after year and we look at what has happened to them.
> These people have had everything from us, yet they still offend
> and we think we have failed. At the end of the day we haven't got
> much choice as to how we deal with them. We have had CSOs, CAYP
> and Change Your Ways... Some things work and some don't. I know
> the Home Office pressurises the service to work with offenders in
> the community, but we are told to imprison them and then not to
> imprison them because there is no room. It's a vicious circle.
> We try to approach the subject with fresh heart every day, but we
> come across cases where there are no other alternatives to prison.
> It is a minefield for us and for you.

Consequently because of the way these magistrates and judges perceived
probation as a let-off and as a soft option; because of how they
perceived the wishes of the public concerning how they should deal
with the more serious offences of dwelling house burglary and
violence, it may be argued that there are problems with the probation
order as an alternative to custody for these magistrates and judges in
Cleveland, notwithstanding the pressures being exerted on the service
and courts by the Home Office and the way in which some relatively
serious offenders continue to be placed on probation. This may sound
contradictory, but it must be said that even though some probation
orders will continue to be imposed, almost inexplicably, in cases
where offenders are at risk of losing their liberty, to begin to make
a significant impact on the custody rate, both locally and nationally,
the probation service must find ways of making inroads into the batch
of 35 custody cases by diverting more of them from prison and youth
custody towards supervision in the community. In these cases the
courts said no to probation.

After constantly bringing the respondents back to the central
question posed at the beginning of the interviews, some of the
comments made in response to this question begin to provide clues
concerning how the probation order as it operates within the
Cleveland probation service could be developed into a more credible
disposal for the offender who is at risk of receiving a custodial
sentence. Some of these ideas may be nothing more than straws in the
wind, but they do begin to suggest ways in which policy and practice
can be developed to achieve the central objective of both SNOP and the

Cleveland Future Directions Document. It should also be noted that from time to time the discussion below strays beyond the probation order to touch on other disposals which were referred to by some respondents. With this caveat in mind, how can the probation order be developed into something more credible?

Making the Probation Order more credible and effective

Throughout the interviews with magistrates, recorders and judges, a number of ideas emerged for making the probation order a more credible alternative to custody. Notwithstanding those problems and reservations concerning how sentencers currently perceive probation, it is nevertheless important to make the point that it may be possible to change the current situation and the perceptions of sentencers, by reconstituting the elements of probation supervision. This depends on the probation service being sensitive to the views, ideas and requirements of sentencers, and this part of the research was undertaken to contribute to the process of dialogue with the courts, the importance of which must not be underestimated if change is to be effected within the local criminal justice system.

First of all it must be acknowledged that the myth still prevails that if only probation could be demonstrated to be successful at keeping offenders out of further trouble, then courts would be more disposed to use probation in future. This theme permeated, to some degree as we saw in the previous chapter, my interviews with probation officers and it also surfaced in the group interviews in the third stage of the research. To illustrate this the clerk at the Redcar PLC asked, when it emerged during the discussion that 26 out of 35 offenders who received a custodial sentence had not previously had supervision in the community:

> C Of those 9 who had previously been on probation, had they reoffended during the period of supervision? If not, you have a strong argument with the magistrates for another order.

Furthermore, one of the recorders, who argued that probation could be a suitable disposal even for dwelling house burglary, went on to expand by saying that

> R The argument for probation, even in the more serious cases, is that it is effective in changing a person's criminal tendencies.

188

> So if you take that as the starting point then a probation order
> is appropriate whatever the offence. So a probation order should
> not be excluded in cases where the offence is a dwelling house
> burglary. The probation officer should focus his mind on whether
> or not he feels the offender can be changed by a period of
> probation.

It must be said that this is a good example of the mythological and idealistic view of probation, which continues to have a strong appeal in the 1980s for some who work within the criminal justice system. The problem is that such a view is contradicted by a substantial amount of empirical research. Because this whole issue has been discussed in some detail at the end of Chapter 1, the arguments do not need to be repeated here. The fact remains that for many of my respondents the findings of empirical research into the effectiveness of probation has simply not got through. It is interesting that on this point Garland reminds us that the contemporary penal complex does not prevent crime, any more than the criminal justice system over the last two hundred years has prevented crime. Rather

> The 'success' of the penal-welfare strategy - a success which has
> allowed its persistence for nearly a century - is not, then, the
> reform of offenders or the prevention of crime. It is its ability
> to administer and manage criminality in an efficient and extensive
> manner, while portraying that process in terms which make it
> acceptable to the public and penal agents alike (1985, p260).

Even though the service may not be naturally disposed to this interpretation of its role, it is now becoming critical that it should seriously consider reconceptualising the rationale of supervision, particularly when faced with having to deal with the more serious offender.

But let me return at this point to the views of respondents on how to make probation a more credible alternative to custody by quoting the magistrate at the Redcar PLC who said:

> M In the example given of those 35 who received custody, to deter
> me from giving a custodial sentence I would like it spelt out in
> the report why I should consider a probation order; I want to know
> how it would operate and what the officer would do with the
> offender. I want this in black and white. I don't want a soft
> option. I want it spelling out how the service would work with
> the offender to stop him reoffending in future. As magistrates we
> would have to have a good deal of detail to persuade us to make a
> probation order in such circumstances. Sometimes reading the
> reports you get the impression that people get off lightly.

Here the themes of probation being seen as a soft option for serious offenders and the need for demonstrated efficacy are referred to again. However this magistrate says there is a need for well argued probation reports, a suggestion from which his colleagues did not demur. So even though it was argued earlier that there are problems in getting the courts to make probation orders on serious offenders, according to the magistrate just quoted the probation report has an important part to play in persuading the courts to impose probation in such cases. It is worth speculating that if social enquiry reports were improved by officers supporting their recommendations for probation by presenting cogent arguments, the courts could be persuaded to take a risk with more offenders in the community.

Let us stay with probation reports for the moment, because this is perhaps the most important and crucial way in which probation officers can affect the court's attitudes and thinking. One of the recorders stated that

> R   A person may commit a burglary because he is short of money and because of various debts. It is important that the officer in his report explores the reasons for these debts in some detail and spell out how he would constructively help the offender. I would certainly have more confidence in a report from the probation service on that basis than I would in the case of a report where it simply said 'He's got debts'. That is worse than useless, for it seems to me you have got to go further.

He went on to say on the basis of over 30 years local experience that:

> R   in my experience, where you get an experienced probation officer who understands what he's doing and making recommendations; and if the court knows the officer and trusts him, then the court is much more likely to follow his recommendation.

Furthermore in my discussions with the Clerk to the Teesside justices, he was convinced that there was room for improvement in some reports prepared on offenders who were at risk of a custodial sentence. If fact he was critical of some reports he had read in court for being 'weak' and went on to say that social enquiry reports should be well argued, and that probation officers should articulate a clear planned programme of work, which he felt would help to persuade courts of the merits of probation.

Continuing this theme, but also introducing the additional and related dimension of officers attending court when their report is being presented, one of the magistrates at Redcar stated that

> M Before we give custody a great deal of thought is given. Custody is not imposed lightly. Therefore, you should explain what you feel, but in the end the decision is made by the bench.

A probation officer responded to this by asking

> PO Do you think that you are influenced by an officer's attendance at court if he has something to say? It is important that we know this and as to how we can influence you.

The same magistrate replied

> M Yes, some reports are good, but some are awful. If you feel strongly about a case, come to court and tell us. And if the officer cannot attend personally, please put forward your views to the court officer who can pass them on to us.

It was also felt quite strongly by two magistrates at the Hartlepool PLC that, in cases where an offender was in danger of custody, but had nevertheless been placed on probation, the commitment to provide a periodic assessment on an offender to the court could dispose sentencers to take a risk by making a probation order. One of these two magistrates reminded the meeting that

> M In years past the probation case committee received information on clients under supervision. In future, could we have feedback on clients so that we have more faith in the system?

The other added

> M Yes that's a very good point, for it would increase the credibility of the service.

Unfortunately this suggestion is fraught with problems, because if more and more serious offenders were placed on probation, the chances are that the courts would be made aware of more and more failures. We know this because Home Office report 34/86 on probation orders found that those who were placed on probation with no previous convictions had a lower reconviction rate compared with those who had. In fact, for offenders who had already experienced custody before receiving probation it was found that two-thirds were reconvicted within 2 years. Consequently even though such a suggestion has, at first sight, a certain appeal, it could nevertheless be counterproductive in the long run and actually result in fewer probation orders being made once courts realised how many probationers were reoffending. Something of this problem is captured in the following ambiguous and confusing exchange between a probation officer and the deputy clerk at the Guisborough PLC:

C To do that (submit a report on probationers) would mean extra work for probation officers.
PO That does not matter.
C I suppose you could make a verbal report to the court.
PO But we have to write quarterly assessments on our cases anyway.
C This would mean that you would have to bring back to court those offenders who were not complying. But it seems that many are not brought back, so are you being too soft?
PO Well it is usually further offending which brings offenders back to court, rather than breach of requirements. However if this did happen you would only be seeing the failures here and not the successes. If we are taking a risk with an offender and the risk has been successful, that would be an encouragement to try again.
C I do not feel this is the case. There are several factors to weigh up here and at the present time one must not forget that dwelling house burglary creates prejudice. Even though there may be a case for the probation service reporting back on a probation order made in a case on a dwelling house burglar, the fact is that imprisonment is the right and just punishment for these offences.

Therefore it hardly seems that offering to submit reports on cases where sentencers have taken a risk is sufficient in itself to convince courts that this could make probation a more attractive proposition and credible alternative to custody.

There is little doubt what the vast majority of 23 magistrates and 4 judges, 2 recorders and 5 clerks, require from probation if it is to be developed into a more credible alternative to custody. To illustrate this one of the clerks stated that

C If you are dealing with a person on probation, then that person should work with the officer and not waste time. But if you are asking courts to give you more serious offenders on probation orders then we want to do more with them. What can we do? Report more often? More discipline? Why not get them involved in something like the Territorial Army and get them doing something useful. It is nice to have probation if they do as they are told, but for the more serious offender you need to offer more. You need discipline in it.

A Guisborough magistrate added to this by saying

M A lot of people see probation as a soft option and if serious offenders are to be dealt with in the community then they want offenders to be given something nasty to do, like a short, sharp, shock. Give them something to do that is punishment.

The views of the judiciary were summed up by one judge who stated that

J Any alternative to custody has to be perceived by the public as being a hard option and for burglary it must be something the public will perceive as punishment... possibly something might be acceptable which involves compulsory hard physical work. That might be acceptable, but if you are not sending someone to prison there has to be punishment. I find it difficult to visualise what this might be, but that is what occurs to me.

Therefore the elements of discipline and punishment are considered important if probation, or any other alternative to custody come to that, is to have credibility with courts and the public. Even though the judge just cited had difficulty visualising what these elements might mean in practice, other respondents had no shortage of ideas. First of all, let me consider in more detail what the probation service can do within the present legislative framework to begin to satisfy the requirements of judges and magistrates for a more credible alternative to custody. In other words, to explore what the local service can do now. Secondly, I'll discuss suggestions which are more innovative and which would require legislative changes to bring them into effect, if it was considered desirable to do so.

What can the Cleveland probation service do now?

To recapitulate, it has already been suggested that cogently argued probation reports, which includes providing a detailed plan of action to be undertaken by the prospective probationer during the supervision period, in addition to the probation officer attending court in support of his recommendation for probation, could make a difference when courts are being asked by the service to put a serious offender on probation. Furthermore the courts want probation in such cases to have an element of discipline, punishment and hard work, in order to assuage the perceived feelings of the wider public. Consequently it does seem possible for the Cleveland probation service to develop existing practices and innovate new ones, within the existing legislative framework. Let us consider what this could mean in practice.

I have already referred to the 'Change Your Ways in 30 Days' scheme, which has been developed in Cleveland under Schedule 11 of the 1982 Criminal Justice Act. To most of the magistrates at the Hartlepool PLC this scheme had both appeal and potential. But one of the judges, within the context of discussing extra requirements attached to probation orders, asked: 'Is there a Day Centre'? I explained that Cleveland did not have Day Centre provision under Schedule 11 4B of the 1982 Criminal Justice Act, which led to the following exchange between one of the judges and the ACPO.

> J What stops you from setting this up?
> ACPO The Change Your Ways regime requires people to attend during two sessions per week.
> J But on a Day Centre requirement I could order 60 days. I would like to see this in a probation order if the criminal is not presenting a risk to the public. Someone who perhaps needs social training and putting back into the work system, certainly that would be a useful thing to have.
> ACPO The Schedule 11 programme is now up and running, but there is no particular reason why there is no Day Centre.
> J You closed Centres down at one point didn't you?
> ACPO We had to make attendance non-compulsory.
> J But it can be done now and it is a good idea...Why not look towards the setting up of a Day Centre which compels a man to do actual physical work for a period of up to 60 days, which would be a start and more than we have at the moment.

Notwithstanding the judge's comments on Day Centres being suitable for offenders 'not presenting a risk to the public' and for the socially inadequate, it is possible to speculate that if a Day Centre required the attendance of the more serious offender for 5 days per week, this could be a useful development in persuading courts to use such a provision as an alternative to custody. Such a facility could have even greater appeal if the following suggestion by a judge was taken seriously. For the more serious offender he said that

> J I agree that something else needs to go with the (probation) order, perhaps attendance at a local Day Centre doing manual work... But straightforward probation will not be favoured by the public.

Concerning the issue of requirements attached to probation orders, one of the Recorders said

> R If probation had built within it conditions or requirements which required positive things to be done, that it in some way interferes with the convenience of the probationer, that he has to attend a course, for example on drugs or alcohol or education, then probation would be more than simple reporting. If the probation officer had the authority to require an offender to attend some course or facility in the community, then it could have more meaning than it currently has. And if the probation officer could only spell out in his report that for the first 6 months of the order this will happen and for the second 6 months

this will happen, then the judge knows what is going to happen. If fact, it is not a bad idea to have a clearly worked out contract where the terms of the order are set out. If this could be done then the judge knows what is going to happen and probation could look a realistic option. Probation must be made to appear not as a soft option but require real input from the offender...This would be a marked contrast to what appears to happen in some cases now.

These constructive comments from the recorder, especially on the need for the service to be clear about what it proposes to do with an offender on probation, are reinforced by the magistrate at Redcar who responded to the suggestion from a probation officer who felt that tracking could be introduced which would make a difference to the way probation is perceived. The magistrate said

M Well if you come along offering alternatives to custody you have to show that something will he done with that person, like 'Change Your Ways in 30 Days', where the offender will learn something from it. There should be something more than just a probation order, for I see the probation order as just simply giving the client a talking to about the offence.
PW Then what else can the service do to make the probation order a more effective and credible alternative to custody?
M Discipline has to come in to it and, for example, curfews. Make them do something positive, like community service, where offenders are seen to be helping the community.

One or two points should be expanded upon here. First of all tracking was mentioned by a probation officer, which was a scheme developed in Massachusetts, USA, as an alternative to custody for juvenile offenders and imported to this country towards the end of the 1970s. As it developed in the USA, tracking provided care, support and a high degree of surveillance which offered protection to the community from serious offenders. Not only did the tracker know where the youth was at all times, but he also provided support to the young person through the family. In this country a handful of tracking schemes have emerged for young offenders in the 1980s, as part of an Intermediate Treatment requirement within a Supervision Order. One scheme, run by the probation service in Leeds, was clear that tracking had a clear control component. The Leeds scheme also boldly claimed that tracking had reduced the numbers of juveniles going into custody and that it had a lower reconviction rate compared with custody. Therefore it may be possible to consider such a scheme for adults, operated within the context of a probation order, which may meet the requirements of magistrates and judges for alternatives to custody to have elements of discipline, punishment and control. In their assessment of a number of tracking schemes, Brockington and Shaw stated that

> Although its current use here is not widespread, as a form of intensive surveillance which aims at providing protection for the community from more serious offenders, while retaining elements of both coercion and treatment, it represents an important innovation (1986, p37).

Secondly was the suggestion from one magistrate for curfew, which was also mentioned by one of the judges in conjunction with electronic tagging. During the third stage of the research the government was seriously considering a range of measures which could eventually be introduced as alternatives to custody during the lifetime of this parliament (which began in 1987), such as house arrest or curfew, tagging or electronic surveillance, direct compensation through the offender's earnings to the victim and tough and demanding community service at the weekend. In fact these ideas were made public in July 1988 in a Green Paper, which will be discussed in more detail in the last chapter.

Where tagging is concerned this measure, like tracking, originated in the USA and by 1988 was operating in 10 American states. It appears that it is being used mainly with the petty, rather than the more serious offender. It operates by having an electronic tag fitted to the offender's leg, neck, or wrist, and is controlled by a computer which rings the offender at home at random intervals. Once the telephone rings the offender has only a few seconds to insert the tag into a receiver which is fitted to the telephone. This process verifies his identity to the computer and confirms that he is either complying or not complying with the requirements of his sentence.

At its annual conference in October 1987 the National Association of Probation Officers decided not to cooperate with tagging on the grounds that it would move the service away from its role of advising, assisting and befriending, to one of surveillance. It has also been criticised by the Police Federation in the Today Newspaper (10.02.88). Notwithstanding these objections Mr John Patten, Minister of State at the Home Office, is reported to have said that

> We want to try to find ways of punishing people in such a way as makes it possible for them to get that one last chance before they go to jail because all the evidence is that, once they get in, they are likely to reoffend time and time again (The Times, 09.02.88).

At the time of writing the government had not made a decision concerning the introduction of tagging, but when interviewing one of the recorders during the early part of 1988 he said that

> R I heard the other day that there is a possibility that tagging could be introduced in future, although I also read that the probation service came out against the idea. I would have thought tagging was a good idea and that if supervision could be accompanied by tagging, then this is far better than locking him up for 23 hours a day... If courts could make a probation order with a rap over the knuckles, I think that would be more acceptable and lead to the making of more probation orders.

The same recorder also mentioned mediation and reparation schemes, in addition to an important role for the defence solicitor who should stress the negative effects of custody and the positive features of supervision when mitigating. I should add that during the 1980s a good deal of interest has been shown in reparation and mediation schemes. A survey undertaken during 1983-84 discovered that out of 42 police force areas, only 6 did not have a reparation-mediation scheme in existence or being planned (Marshall, 1984). Within the context of the criminal justice system the concept of mediation has the twin components of aid to the victims of crime and the rehabilitation of offenders. And both of these are encapsulated in the concept of reparation, which is a process through which offenders make restitution to victims by means of compensation or services. Such an approach is meant to induce a sense of responsibility in offenders and encourage their reformation. It is also intended that, if used instead of imprisonment, it would bring offenders into a practical and more meaningful relationship to the local community from which they may well feel alienated. Even though such schemes should be taken seriously and if used within the context of a deferred sentence could, for example, result in an offender eventually avoiding a custodial sentence, one must question whether such an approach would satisfy the demands of the sentencers interviewed in this research for credible alternatives to custody to have elements of punishment and discipline.   Is there not a danger that   reparation and mediation schemes could also be perceived as a 'soft option'?   Notwithstanding this danger, the Index of Probation Projects mentions several mediation-reparation schemes, either operating or being planned by the probation service (1986-87, pp26-27).

Moving on, one of the recorders had something interesting to say on the Suspended Sentence Supervision Order (SSSO). After touching on a theme we have come across several times already he said

> R There is no doubt that the fraternity (legal profession) considers that a probation order, for a relatively serious offence, is a case of an offender getting away with it... This is why counsel in such circumstances will not go for a probation order but for a SSSO.
> PW Is this because it is perceived that a SSSO has more teeth than a probation order?
> R That's right. The judge may conclude that the sentence is 9 months, but then suspend it, but in so doing the offence has been marked. So instead of submitting that an offender should be put on probation, it is submitted that probation is this case is not appropriate because the offence is serious. Therefore, a SSSO is mentioned because it marks the offence, but it also offers help to the offender. The advantage of this sentence is that it seems to meet both public and private needs.

A court on passing a sentence of imprisonment of more than 6 months and suspending it, may impose an order placing the offender under the supervision of a probation officer. The limitation of a SSSO to sentences of more than 6 months means that the Magistrates Court will only rarely impose such an order. Weston (1987) says that the object of this limitation is to enable the possibility of extra work falling on the probation service to be controlled. However under the Powers of Criminal Courts Act 1973, Section 26 (2), there is the power to alter this provision. It should also be acknowledged that a SSSO is less flexible than a probation order and less adaptable to the needs of individual offenders. But even though the consent of an offender to the making of a SSSO is not required, the only requirements are that the offender should keep in touch with the officer and notify any change of address.   There is no power to add any further requirements. Consequently the SSSO has limitations at the present time to make a substantial difference to the alternatives to custody debate and is used relatively little.

It was also suggested by the clerk to the Teesside justices that, at a senior level, the probation inspectorate could perhaps do more to persuade senior figures at the Home Office, both ministers and civil servants, to take the initiative on community disposals and alternatives to custody. He also felt that better use could be made of the Probation Liaison Committee, through which the probation service could present itself better than it appears to do at present. However one must remember that PLCs are attended by magistrates who are pro-probation anyway, which means that ways must be found to communicate with those sentencers who do not come into direct contact with the probation service and who are not disposed to what the probation service can offer courts, when considering the appropriate sentence for the more serious offender. Consequently, at various levels, it does seem important for the probation service to find ways of communicating its message to the wider local criminal justice system and to improve the way in which it presents itself.

Finally, one of the judges liked the idea of the probation hostel being used for relatively serious offenders. In fact, this was a timely reminder because a report prepared by the Home Office on hostels pointed out that there continues to be a decline in the use of approved hostels for persons on probation with a condition of residence. The proportion of probationers fell from 48.7% of the approved number of places on the 31 January 1984, to 36.5% on the 30 June 1987. During the same period the number of bail cases increased from 15.3% of approved places to 28.5% (Home Office, 1987). Therefore, it seems worth considering how the probation hostel, of which there is one in Middlesbrough, could be developed to divert offenders from custody.

It is clear that there are a number of suggestions which the Cleveland service can consider which, according to this research, could make some difference to the way offenders are sentenced using existing disposals. However other suggestions were made by magistrates, judges and recorders, for dealing with the more serious offender which will require new legislation. To these ideas I now turn in the final section of this chapter.

Potential future developments

Firstly, one magistrate suggested that when a probation order is made there should be included a sentence of imprisonment, which would be suspended, but which would be activated in circumstances where the probation order was not complied with. For non-compliance this magistrate felt that custody should be automatic.

Secondly, the most interesting ideas came from the judges and recorders. Acknowledging that sentencers consider that punishment is a prerequisite if serious offenders are to be dealt with in the community, and bearing in mind their concern to protect the public, led one judge to comment that

> J One must consider something that is beyond, higher up, than either a probation order and a community service order, and it must have a recognised punishment element.
> PW So does this mean that to deal with the dwelling house burglar in the community, for example, then a new disposal is required?
> J I would like to see a situation where an offender could commence his sentence by having two or three weeks in prison, then proceed to community service doing physical work, then finally a period with a probation officer talking with the offender about what can be done. Or perhaps you could have a period in prison with the rest subject to supervision on completion of an Order in the community. If we get something with bite in it at the beginning and let the probation service have the client after that, then that might be better from the public's point of view.

Therefore, the suggestion from this judge was for a new sentence with a tripartite structure.

Thirdly, the Senior Probation Officer of the court team, within the context of the judges liaison meeting, introduced other ideas she had been presented with by judges not present at the liaison meeting. The most important was the suggestion for developing the SSSO to include certain extra requirements. As we have already seen, this order combines only two conditions at the present time but, like probation, is a disposal with the potential for further development. It is worth saying a little more about the SSSO by including the comments of one judge who said that

> J I think a SSSO should have bite in the supervision part of the sentence, but it does not. As judges we do make suggestions to the Home Office. For example, I have suggested that a SS should be available for those under 21 as well as those over 21. But they say that this would increase the prison population.

Of course, this seems to be one of the dangers inherent within other suggestions made above.

Fourthly, both recorders advocated that if probation could be combined with a CSO or ACO, it would enhance the credibility of the order to the courts in more serious cases. Moreover, the clerk to the Teesside Justices reinforced this suggestion by saying that:

> C I feel that a probation order has more chance of being accepted in more serious cases, if a probation order could be made with a CSO or ACO and if the probation officer had the power to ensure that an offender went to an attendance centre.

Finally, it was suggested that the officer should have additional powers which could ensure, for example, that the offender reported more often to the probation officer.

Consequently a number of suggestions were made to make probation a more credible alternative to custody, in addition to the development of other disposals, like the SSSO. Some of these could be developed within existing legislative arrangements, but other suggestions would require the provision of new legislation if they were thought viable.

Summary and conclusion

Because a plethora of ideas and suggestions concerning the future development of the probation order emerged during the third stage of this research which interviewed magistrates, judges, recorders and clerks, in addition to suggestions for the creation and development of disposals which would require new legislation, it is appropriate to conclude this chapter by summarising what these are.

Firstly, what can the probation service do now?
Improve the presentation of social enquiry reports to ensure that if probation is recommended for an offender at risk of a custodial sentence, the arguments are cogently presented. Officers must explain to the court exactly what is going to happen to the prospective probationer and the tasks to be undertaken during the supervision period. To this end it could be helpful to establish a contract between the officer, probationer and the court;

The officer should attend court in support of his report and be prepared to address the court, in cases where probation is recommended for a relatively serious offender;

Periodic assessments to the court which imposed the probation order in contentious cases, to keep them in touch with the progress of the probationer. However this suggestion is fraught with problems as was pointed out earlier.

Supervision in the community must have elements of discipline and punishment. Offenders must do something useful whilst on probation and not waste time. For serious offenders something nasty, like a short, sharp, shock is required, which means that probation should be a hard option and involve, for example, compulsory hard physical work. To be a credible alternative to custody, probation must interfere with the convenience of the probationer;

The development of extra requirements under Schedule 11 4 A (1)(a) and 4 A (1)(b) of the 1982 Criminal Justice Act;

The setting up of a Day Centre in Cleveland which could incorporate the experience of physical work;

The offender should be able to attend a range of courses as part of the probation order to assist with various problems such as drug and alcohol abuse. Moreover, probationers should be able to receive educational help and have the opportunity to acquire social skills. This will require positive input by the offender;

Tracking;

The development of mediation and reparation schemes;

To improve the services provided by the defence solicitor in cases where the offender faces a possible custodial sentence;

To improve the dialogue, at a senior level, between the probation Inspectorate, civil servants and Ministers at the Home Office, in order to encourage the use of probation as an alternative to custody;

To make better use of the probation liaison committee, through which the probation service could argue its case for the supervision of more serious offenders in the commmunity;

To explore the probation hostel as a vehicle for diverting some offenders from custody.

Secondly, what suggestions would require further legislation?

The introduction of curfew and tagging;

202

The development of the suspended sentence supervision order to include additional requirements. Also make the SSSO available for those under 21 in both the crown and magistrates courts;

To develop the probation order so that it has the power of a suspended sentence. Consequently if the offender breached the requirements of supervision he would automatically receive a custodial sentence;

The creation of a new tripartite sentence which would incorporate an initial period spent in custody, followed by community service and finally a period spent with the probation officer discussing what can be done in future;

Combine a probation order with either an Attendance Centre Order or a Community Service Order, to improve its credibility;

Provide probation officers with additional powers.

The last three chapters have presented from quantitative and qualitative standpoints, the findings of empirical research into various aspects of the probation order within the Cleveland probation service. Data has been collected from probation officers and from a number of sentencers. It cannot be argued that these findings are representative of the Cleveland probation service as a whole, or the probation service nationally. The claim that it is representative, or that it has external validity, is nowhere made. What I do claim, however, is that this research provides a number of useful insights into practice, ideology and perceptions of probation supervision which can contribute to the development of probation policy, particularly if the perceptions of magistrates and judges, recorders and clerks, are taken seriously. This research also touches on a number of issues which are important for the future of the service, such as the development of credible alternatives to custody, an issue which is constantly being debated within the Home Office. Consequently the task of the final chapter is to conclude this book by exploring these issues further.

10 Community supervision for offenders at risk of custody

Introduction

The first part of this final chapter returns to those models of probation discussed earlier which, it should be recalled, emerged during the 1970s in response to the decline of the rehabilitative ideal.   Next, the main findings of the empirical research will be reviewed.   Accordingly these findings have implications for the context of probation work within which the Cleveland probation service particularly will attempt to manage the more serious offender in the community.   Finally, the last section will begin to reflect on possible ways forward in Cleveland, which has implications for other area services.

Models of Probation

Even though the work of the 56 area probation services has burgeoned, diversified and become more complex over the last two decades, some features of probation work remain more or less the same.   This may be illustrated by returning to Chapter 1 where it was noted how the police court missionaries, long before the creation of the probation system in 1907, were involved in working with inebriates. They were also involved in matrimonial disputes, prison after-care work, finding employment for offenders, disputes between neighbours, working with difficult children and dealing with problems arising from poverty. These practices were supported by an ideology articulated in the theological language of saving offender's souls. But even though the ideological context of probation work has changed since then as Chapter 1 explained, nevertheless probation officers continue to be involved in similar practices.

When turning to the supervision of offenders subjected to probation orders those models considered in Chapter 2, with the exception of the control model, basically understood probation practice as a social work service to offenders with numerous problems. And even though Harris's model is divorced from statutory penal disposals, nevertheless he concurs that probation is about social work and the provision of welfare services. In fact, and again with the exception of the control model, the concept of 'helping' clients is important within these models.

Ideologically Harris articulated the rationale of welfare and also emphasised the provision of a caring service to all those in need as an end in itself; Walker and Beaumont stressed the need for socialist probation officers to mitigate the harsh effects of a capitalist criminal justice system on working class offenders; Bottoms and McWilliams were concerned with the values of hope for the future and respect for persons, as was Raynor. Furthermore Raynor articulated that probation practice based on the principles of help, negotiation, participation, shared assessment, respect for offenders and a reduction of coercion, would contribute to improving the criminal justice system by helping to set matters right and by helping all those adversely affected by crime to live more satisfactorily with its consequences. Finally Bryant et al believed that their model of probation practice would increase the confidence of the courts in the probation order.

Axiologically at one extreme of the care-control continuum Harris stressed care, whilst Walker and Beaumont emphasised minimal control by endorsing the principle of voluntarism. Bottoms and McWilliams, and Raynor, attempted to balance the concepts of care and control, with Bryant et al veering towards the control end of the continuum. Finally, at the opposite extreme of the continuum to Harris the control model saw probation as providing punishment, control and surveillance.

Even though there are some subtle and not so subtle differences between all 6 models in relation to the dimensions of probation practice, ideology and values, nevertheless one may accurately claim that all the models, with the exception of Harris, perceive that probation may be imposed as an alternative to custody. As such they continue a long tradition which can be traced back to the creation of the probation system itself, which saw the probation order as a vehicle for saving some offenders from prison. In fact Downes asserts that between 1918-1939 probation was used as an alternative to custody (Downes, 1988, p6). Whilst the target population for this measure is now different to what it was in earlier years, because today the emphasis is on diverting from custody the more serious offender rather than the relatively minor and/or first offender, and even though ideological features are largely discontinuous with the past, nevertheless the theme of using probation as an alternative to custody is continuous with its use during the early years of this century. This is a view firmly endorsed by the Home Office in its Statement of National Objectives and Priorities considered in Chapter 3.

When turning to the SNOP model it was made clear that in addition to managing resources more economically, efficiently and effectively, the central theme is the supervision of as many offenders as possible in the community, especially in those cases where custodial sentences would otherwise be imposed. This means developing the probation order to manage the more serious offender in the community, particularly by the development of extra conditions under Schedule 11 of the 1982 Criminal Justice Act. However there remain the vestiges of a social work service articulated as advice and guidance to offenders, even though the dimensions of control and discipline are being emphasised much more than social work.

Next, Chapter 4 saw how the NAPO model articulated its understanding of probation supervision in the language of advise, assist and

206

befriend, and the provision of help, guidance and support through a one-to-one relationship between officer and probationer. Probation work is primarily social work and the model prefers voluntarism and minimal control rather than extra conditions and compulsion. Moreover even though the model affirms that probation can be offered at all stages of an offender's criminal career, NAPO emphasises its use as an alternative to custody for the more seriously convicted offender.

Finally in Chapter 5 I turned to the views on probation of the Cleveland probation service. Like many of the other models it wants to provide constructive social work help to probationers, in addition to diverting offenders from custody mainly by the development of extra conditions. But it also hopes that the 'normal' probation order will achieve this objective. However it is clear that within a framework of extra conditions and therefore increased social control, the needs of individual offenders will continue to be assessed in order to provide a social work service which will be beneficial to them.

These are the main points of those models of probation discussed in the earlier chapters of this book, a summary of which may be found in Tables 2.1, 3.1, 4.1 and 5.1. They have emerged during the last few years as an attempt to reconceptualise the nature of probation work in a situation where probation could no longer be simply understood as a vehicle to save souls or rehabilitate offenders. Today the central role for probation is largely understood as a vehicle to prevent more serious offenders being dispatched into custodial institutions and to reduce offending during the period of supervision. Even though nearly all the models considered in Chapters 2 to 5 would, to varying degrees, endorse this view of probation, one must seriously question whether they have the cachet to achieve these objectives, particularly the diversion of the more serious offender from custody within the Cleveland probation service particularly. In order to explore this further it is important to recapitulate the main findings of the empirical research presented in Chapters 7 to 9.

Empirical Findings

In Chapter 7 probation practice, according to 11 probation officers at Redcar and Hartlepool, was mainly articulated by the language of providing help, support, advice and guidance with problems concerning marriage and relationships, budgeting, alcohol, drugs and gambling, unemployment, accommodation, emotional problems and stress, alleviating loneliness and depression. In other words probation practice for my respondents was mainly concerned with providing a welfare orientated service to offenders with numerous personal, emotional and social problems.

When turning to ideologies underlying and sustaining practice (Table 7.11) all respondents used the language of advise, assist and befriend and/or the provision of a social work service to explain the rationale of their activities. These probation officers were also concerned to meet the needs of individual offenders. In so doing they were more closely identified with the 'ideal type' personalist school, rather than the managerial or radical schools within the contemporary probation service identified by McWilliams (1987).

However all respondents were also concerned to either reduce criminal behaviour or prevent crime and several resorted to the language of rehabilitation, despite the research which has questioned the rehabilitative efficacy of treatment within the criminal justice system.   Nevertheless one or two officers were not convinced they could prevent reoffending or rehabilitate offenders. It is true that these respondents have high occupational ideals and aspirations, like the prevention and reduction of crime, whilst sometimes recognising that these are difficult objectives to achieve. Consequently one should conceptually distinguish between what is desirable and what is achievable when supervising offenders in the community. The reality seems to be that the two are often conflated and therefore confused.

When respondents were interviewed as individuals the notion of society was largely conceptualised in consensus terms, which meant they did not engage in a radical critique of the political, economic and social structure of the North East of England, which is surprising given those problems of a socio-economic nature identified in Chapter 7 which impinge on the lives of offenders. However when this subject was explored in more detail with respondents as groups within their teams, they did acknowledge the adverse effects of social factors on offenders but felt helpless to do anything constructive about them.

Furthermore some probation officers resorted to the language of management, containment and control, surveillance and punishment when articulating the rationale of probation work. However this language was used much less than the social work language of meeting the needs of individual offenders. In other words, the language of care was unquestionably more important than punishment, surveillance, or control.

When exploring the subject of axiology, in 14 out of 53 probation orders respondents said they were caring for probationers and in the remaining 39 cases they said they were both caring and controlling. Notwithstanding the dilemmas involved in balancing care and control these respondents believed this could be achieved. It may be pragmatically argued that control is an ineluctable element of probation supervision, a point acknowledged by these respondents. However as one officer said, the most important point is the way in which control is manifested. Moreover, control is of secondary importance compared with support and care and these probation officers mainly want to help offenders, not to police them. This is important within the contemporary context of debate because the emphasis is more and more on punishment in the community (Home Office, 1988).

Turning to the empirical findings on social work methods, it was found that a variety of approaches were being used with probationers. However it may be argued that this research has, albeit to a limited extent, demythologised the recondite language of social work methods and approaches heard on social work training courses because the approach of respondents was practical and down to earth.

Furthermore, I consider there is room for improvement in this area of probation work. If these respondents could more systematically identify client problem areas, specifically by allowing clients to determine what these are themselves, then this could result in a more intelligent approach to and selection of methods of working. For example the Mooney Checklist, which allows clients to identify their own problem areas, could help in the assessment process which, in turn, could lead to more appropriate and focused intervention by probation officers. Moreover if the same checklist was administered to the same clients at a later stage in the supervisory process, it could begin to provide a means whereby middle and senior managers could assess the impact of service delivery. Subsequently, if it could be suggested that the intervention of probation officers was helping to reduce the personal and social problems of clients, this information could be related back to both magistrates and judges in their respective meetings with the local service as evidence of constructive work with offenders (see Raynor, 1988, p113f). Such an approach would also go beyond the obsession with reoffending rates by directing attention towards other aspects of probation work, like reducing personal problems.

Moreover those methods used more than others were casework, practical help, the use of personality, task-centred casework and behaviourism (Table 7.12). In other words these social work methods are predominantly directed towards individual offenders, which is consistent with those practices and ideologies of probation work articulated in terms of a personalist, rehabilitative, consensus approach, rather than an approach which is radical and directed towards social action. Surprisingly even though there is some interest in mediation, reparation (Davis et al, 1988) and community work (Broad, 1988) within the wider probation service, these were approaches hardly ever mentioned by these respondents. Consequently the inherent danger within this is that from a left-wing perspective, offenders continue to be depoliticised whereby problems related to the socio-economic structure are translated into problems of personal pathology and inadequacy.

Therefore there seem to be elements of confusion and ambivalence in probation work with offenders who are the subject of probation orders according to these respondents. Summaries hardly ever capture the minutiae, subtleties, complexity and diversity of probation work, but it may be said how this research has found that officers at Redcar and Hartlepool were faced with a multiplicity of problems by offenders, to which they were attempting to make a constructive and meaningful response. Diverse practices, a response to diverse problems, were being sustained by diverse and sometimes conflicting ideologies. Care and support were valued more highly than control, but the language of management, containment, surveillance and punishment was sometimes heard; rehabilitation and crime prevention remain desirable goals albeit a recognition that these goals are difficult to achieve; the focus, both ideologically and methodologically is the individual offender, despite the climate of adverse social and economic factors.

Moreover, and this is a crucial issue towards the end of the 1980s, the dimensions of probation supervision discovered in this research provides the context within which these respondents were attempting to pursue a policy of supervision in the community as an alternative to custody for a number of offenders, which must now be considered further.

Data on all 132 cases were explored in the first section of Chapter 8 on type of offences, number of charges and previous court appearances, for the three categories comprising 63 probationers, 35 custody cases and 34 remaining non-custodial cases. However the theme of alternatives to custody was central to this chapter. Consequently some of the main findings may be summarised as follows.

Even though 8 out of 11 respondents said they were attempting to have probation orders imposed where offenders were 'at risk' of custody and that 26 out of 53 probation orders were adjudged to have been imposed as an alternative to custody (or 20 if Bale's Risk of Custody scale is applied), nevertheless a further 35 offenders were given custodial sentences after being recommended for probation. 10 respondents believed that the probation service should be targetting the more serious offender for probation, but interestingly 26 out of 35 custody cases had not previously been on probation.

It has already been argued that some attempt is being made by these probation officers to achieve the policy objectives of both SNOP and the Cleveland Future Directions Document concerning working with as many offenders as possible in the community. Furthermore it should be recalled that probation is not simply a disposal for the high tariff offender, even though the service is being encouraged to target this group, because it continues to be used for all types of offender, both high and low tariff. In fact it is the disposal par excellence through which probation officers seek to help a wide range of offenders with various needs and problems and varying levels of criminality.

However it may also be considered that in trying to cater for such a diverse range of offenders the probation order is trying to achieve too much, with the implication that for the more serious offender it suffers from a lack of credibility. Consequently perhaps it should be used less for minor offenders and more for relatively serious offenders, but this has profound managerial implications in terms of staffing levels, increased stress on officers, further decline in success rates, and the additional demands this would engender within the organisation, which are issues sometimes overlooked.

Nevertheless let me turn again at this point to the group of 35 offenders who received a custodial sentence after being recommended for probation. Even though respondents stated that all except 2 of these custodial sentences were expected, the important point is that probation was the disposal mentioned to the courts for consideration. I have already discussed this group in some detail but it is appropriate to say a little more about these 35 cases in comparison with those 20 probation orders selected by using the Bale Risk of Custody Scale, who were placed on probation as an alternative to custody.

First of all 17 out of 35 custody cases (48.6%) were aged 17 to 20; 13 out of 35 (37.1%) were aged 21 to 29; which leaves 5 (14.3%) offenders who were aged over 30. Or to put this another way, 30 out of 35 custody cases (85.7%) were aged between 17 and 29 years. Thus one is talking about relatively young people.

Secondly where the 20 probation cases are concerned it was found that:

The average number of charges was 2.9
The average number of previous court appearances was 5.9
6 out of 20 (30%) had previously been on probation
15 out of 20 (75%) had previously been in custody

Where the 35 custody cases are concerned it was found that:

The average number of charges was 4.5
The average number of previous court appearances was 5.8
9 out of 35 (25.7%) had previously been on probation
24 out of 35 (68.6%) had previously been in custody

Therefore whilst both the probation and custody groups had, on average, a similar number of previous court appearances, the custody group was charged, on average, with more offences (4.5 compared with 2.9).

Moreover the custody group was charged with proportionately more serious offences than probationers - 42% dwelling house burglary offences compared with 25%. Consequently there are discernible differences between these two groups which helps to explain why these 35 offenders received a custodial sentence compared to the group of 20 cases where probation was imposed. For the group of 20, probation was considered appropriate by the courts as an alternative to custody, but not for the group of 35.

If the Cleveland probation service wants to make a significant impact on the use of custody in the 3 petty sessional divisions of Hartlepool, Teesside and Langbaurgh (which includes Redcar) from which the vast majority of cases were drawn in this research, then it must begin to make inroads into this group of 35 cases by diverting them from custody. Of course these respondents had some suggestions for making the probation order a more credible proposition to the courts for the more serious offender - such as cogently argued SERs, more resources to offer clients, periodic progress reports to courts on probationers, attendance at court by the officer when advocating probation to add credibility to the recommendation and the development of extra conditions. Importantly as one officer remarked:

> Until we get the confidence of the Magistrates we are not going to move up the tariff and we are not going to get the more complex or risky cases.

If the more serious offender is to be supervised by the Cleveland probation service in the community rather than languish in custody, then sentencers have to be convinced that the service has a credible alternative to offer. From interviewing a number of sentencers it became clear that they wanted something 'more' to what was presently being offered in those 35 cases which received a custodial sentence,

213

particularly if the offence is dwelling house burglary, before they could be convinced that an alternative to custody was a viable proposition. Therefore the question which had to be put to magistrates, judges, recorders and clerks was: 'Are there any further provisions the Cleveland probation service can develop to make the probation order a more credible and effective alternative to custody for the more serious offender'?

In Chapter 9 the question which sentencers were asked to consider had these 35 custody cases specifically in mind. It transpired that magistrates, judges and recorders perceived that a probation order was a 'let off', 'soft option', 'cop out' and a case of 'getting away with it' particularly where the offender had committed dwelling house burglary. Accordingly this helps to explain why recommendations for probation were not taken seriously by the courts in these 35 cases.

Consequently if probation is to be perceived as a credible alternative to custody it was felt that supervision in the community must incorporate something more to what was currently on offer. Specifically, probation orders had to incorporate elements of discipline, punishment and hard work in addition to interfering with the convenience of the offender. However, and this is a problem for the probation order, one of the sentencers commented:

> For dwelling house burglary the sentence is punishment. Probation does not appear to be punishment.

It was also felt by some that probation is a disposal which should benefit, help and support, rather than punish offenders. Consequently if probation continues to be offered as an alternative to custody in the way it has been for offenders with the characteristics of these 35 custody cases, then the Cleveland probation service could continue to have difficulties persuading the courts to impose supervision in the community.

During February 1988 a senior civil servant at the Home Office made a speech at a conference at Hull University on the theme of alternatives to custody and the probation service. He prefaced his remarks by saying that even though what he had to say reflected his own interpretation of the current situation, nevertheless he was

214

attempting to present the preoccupations within Whitehall. He spoke of their being a window of opportunity for the probation service concerning the provision of alternatives to custody, but went on to say how there was a credibility gap between the probation service and sentencers on this issue. He also commented, and it is worth quoting him in full, that

> The perception of many sentencers is that, despite all that has happened over the last ten years or so, there is a sense in which the existing pattern and practice of non custodial disposals simply does not mesh with the need for certain offenders to expiate their affront to the community, to make reparation to their victims and, frankly, to suffer some inconvenience comparable in scale, if not in nature, to that of their victims. This comes across strongly from discussions with the judiciary at every level and it is not surprising if it is reflected in Minister's own perceptions. Ministers are simply reflecting this mood when they argue that a more effective way of dealing with even these restricted categories of offenders in the community may lie in a combination of strict discipline and support, and requirements which are demanding and challenging (Head, 1988, p12).

It has already been considered in Chapter 9 how a number of sentencers at Redcar, Guisborough and Hartlepool magistrates' courts and a group of Teesside crown court judges, including two recorders, made a number of suggestions which they felt would enhance the credibility of the service when attempting to divert serious offenders from custody. In fact it may be added that probation officers would have little difficulty endorsing the suggestions for improvements within social enquiry reports, attending court, extra conditions which included Day Centre provision, the development of Hostels, mediation and reparation schemes.

However the achilles heel for the probation service over the last decade, but accentuated throughout the 1980s, concerns the elements of discipline, control and punishment within the process of supervising offenders in the community. The problem was highlighted with the Younger Report in the mid-1970s (Home Office, 1974) whose proposals were successfully rejected by the probation service. But one may speculate that the service will not be able to resist those pressures for the enhanced social control of certain offenders towards the end of the 1980s as it did in the 1970s. For if the probation service wants to provide credible alternatives to custody for relatively serious offenders then it must provide what the courts require, or make way for other organisations which will provide punishment in the community in the way that both sentencers and the Home Office now consider appropriate.

One of the problems, highlighted by Chapters 7 to 9, is that there is some dissonance between the outlook of the probation service and the courts in Cleveland. There can be little doubt as this research suggests that depending on your role and function within the criminal justice system different values, perceptions, languages, concerns and priorities, are associated with different organisations. To illustrate this the context of probation work within which the alternatives to custody debate is articulated by probation officers is determined predominantly by the language of help, care, support, advise, assist and befriend, guidance, meeting needs, welfare and social work. Alternatively the language emphasised by sentencers is that of control, discipline and punishment. Of course the reality of what probation officers and sentencers think and do is much more complex, subtle and ambivalent than this as we have already seen. However it may be said that the two agencies have different concerns expressed through different perceptions and languages, particularly where the more serious offender is concerned.

Therefore there is a real problem here, because if the probation service is serious about offering the courts realistic alternatives to custody for cases similar to those 35 discussed earlier then, it may be argued, it must take the views of sentencers seriously by offering 'more' than is currently being provided. Consequently I would argue that this research has elicited a number of important insights provided by magistrates and judges on the subject of supervision in the community as an alternative to custody which will assist senior managers to shape and develop future policy and practice. The question, of course, is to what degree managers respond to these insights and, if they do, whether main grade probation officers will assimilate the more punitive elements of community supervision the courts seem to require. But if they don't then one may assume that the future of the probation service could be in doubt. Moreover as a consequence of the Home Office discussion document on 'Punishment, Custody and The Community' (1988) and NAPOs response in anticipation of this document (1988a), conflict within the service seems likely to increase rather than decrease. It is difficult to see how the probation service could, without opposition, take on board some of the new proposals which means that the future is acutely uncertain. It is also difficult to see how there can be a rapproachment between the practice and philosophy of probation articulated by these probation officers in Cleveland and the requirements of sentencers on the issue of probation as an alternative to custody for dwelling house burglary offences. The implications of this will now be considered.

Ways forward

The main challenge facing the Cleveland probation service and other area services in England and Wales, is to assimilate the views of both sentencers and the Home Office for more intensive forms of community supervision which will appear tough enough to divert more offenders from custody, whilst retaining social work values. The service is being challenged to demonstrate to magistrates, judges and the wider public that it can provide discipline and punishment in the community for the more serious and more heavily convicted offender, whilst remaining faithful to a basic core of humanitarian values and ethical principles. According to my respondents and after listening to the views of the local service articulated in Chapter 5, it appears that probation officers have managed to balance the conflicting demands of care and control in the past. However it would be wrong to glibly assume that officers will continue to successfully perform this high wire balancing act, particularly when aspects of control and punishment are in the process of being accentuated.

At a time when local probation services are being encouraged to adopt a more controlling posture, it may be argued that if the Cleveland service reaffirms its commitment to a position of ideological and axiological purity by emphasising welfare, help, care and support, rather than social control, discipline and punishment, particularly when advocating alternatives to custody for serious offenders, then it is possible that more and more offenders will

217

continue to enter prison and youth custody centres. Is this what the Cleveland probation service, NAPO and the service as a whole wants? If not and should the Cleveland service wish to remain an integral part of the local criminal justice system and continue to have a voice in the decision making process of sentencing, then it must be realigned to adapt to new and changing circumstances by becoming a part of the new realism. In other words it has to shed some of its ideological purity by assuming a more pragmatic approach to the supervision and control of offenders and its place within the local criminal justice system. Unless it does so it may not be possible to help those offenders it is now recommending for community supervision, because they will continue to be committed to custody.

It could, of course, reject this line of argument which seems to advocate yet another classic pragmatic compromise and seek a solution in the direction of the Harris model. By arguing that enough is enough, that its values and social work principles have been eroded over recent years, that it has compromised itself too much by getting involved in the prison system in the 1960s and community service in the 1970s; therefore, it could not possibly consider becoming even more controlling and punitive, which means restating its position as a caring and welfare orientated service which primarily exists to meet the needs of individuals in an increasingly harsh penal and social climate. In fact my own knowledge and experience of probation work since 1979 has led me to conclude that the vast majority of probation officers would like nothing better than to be left alone to practice social work. However to do so would run the risk of the probation service becoming a second rate organisation with increasingly less influence, thus handing over the statutory supervision of offenders to another organisation. Is this what the service wants? I have little doubt that, on the basis of the empirical research presented above and because of the arguments of NAPO and others within the service presented in Chapter 4, a strong case could be made for a solution along the lines of the 'pure' social work model. But the price the service may have to pay could well be its own dissolution.

Alternatively one could argue that if the probation service has the will and capacity to exercise its collective imagination which will be required if it is to accommodate the new ideas, language and approaches emanating from Queen Anne's Gate, particularly those contained in the 1988 Green Paper concerning punishment in the community, then it may well have an important role to perform in future years. But to do so its practices, ideology, values and methods will have to be reformulated to varying degrees, to achieve the goal of providing credible alternatives to custody for more serious offenders which have the support of sentencers. What this could mean in practice will now be explored.

Going beyond the Probation Order?

It may be argued that the probation order has an image problem in Cleveland because it was difficult for probation officers to sell this disposal as an alternative to custody for that group of 35 offenders who received a custodial sentence after being considered for probation. Therefore it is possible to conclude that the probation service must seriously consider advocating a new disposal, for a new and rapidly changing situation, in which the service has been entrusted with the mandate of supervising as many offenders as possible in the community. It does not appear that the standard probation order has the right image and properties to provide the kind of alternative to custody which appeals to courts. Consequently one could argue that a new disposal is necessary for the new era in which the service is having to justify its existence. Such a solution has been proposed by both ACOP and the Home Office whose views will now be considered in turn.

ACOPs proposals for a Community Restitution Order

In a discussion paper entitled 'More Demanding Than Prison' (ACOP, 1988) prepared by a group of senior managers from the Probation Practice and Court Work Committee of ACOP, the introduction states that

> The aim is to facilitate a marked shift in sentencing away from the use of custody, by the introduction of a new form of community based sentence. The proposals seek to capitalise on the best aspects of probation practice over the years, reformulated in a radically different way (p2).

Accordingly the paper proposes a new sentence which is intended to replace those custodial sentences of up to 30 months which are currently being imposed in the crown court, which will mark offending behaviour with denunciation and deterrence. Even though it is proposed that this new sentence will be tough and demanding and thus appropriate for offenders convicted of dwelling house burglary and certain types of violence, the emphasis will be on restitution. Therefore the proposed new sentence has been called the 'Community Restitution Order' of which there are four major components.

Firstly, the offender would be required to make restitution for the damage or loss incurred by the offence. This could involve participation in those schemes currently in operation through the community service department of each local probation service. The level of restitution would be set according to the length of custodial sentence the court would have imposed for the offence under consideration. For example, 6 to 12 months imprisonment would attract 60 to 120 hours restitution.

Secondly, social training, which is intended to confront the offender with his offending behaviour.

Thirdly, problem solving. This aspect of the new sentence would involve the probation officer and offender working together to deal with a number of problem areas and exploring the best ways of solving them. However it may well be the case that some other specialist agency in the community, rather than the probation service itself, would provide the kind of assistance required by the offender.

Finally, the fourth component concerns living arrangements. The court may well be content for the offender to remain in his own home. Alternatively, it may be necessary to place the offender in approved lodgings or a probation hostel. It is envisaged that specific arrangements for accommodation would be negotiated with the court in each individual case.

The Community Restitution Order would make significant demands on offenders, particularly during the early stages of the sentence, which implies regular contact and close supervision. Therefore it is proposed that at the highest level restitution would be worked during one full day at the weekend for a total of 40 weeks; social training and problem solving would be undertaken one evening per week each, giving a total over 40 weeks of 560 hours. Moreover the offender would have to consent to the new sentence, which would involve establishing a contract between the court and offender as the basis of the new sentence. Consequently it seems that the court would have to carefully assess the demands which should be made on the offender so that the sentence would not only reflect the seriousness of the offence, but also satisfy the demands of the court and public for a credible alternative to custody.

A major innovation in ACOPs proposals is the 'Community Restitution Board' comprising a crown court judge and representatives from community agencies. It seems that its role would facilitate greater involvement by the community in the management of crime, complement the work of the sentencing court and generally oversee the operation of the new sentence. It would also consider breaches of the order, suggestions for amendments to the original contract and refer breaches back to the court where appropriate.

There can be little doubt that ACOP acknowledges the necessity for a new sentence, which is intended to persuade the courts that the probation service has a credible alternative to custody for dwelling house burglary and certain types of violence. However in making this new sentence 'more demanding than prison' a number of offenders could, contrary to expectations, gladly embrace the security of prison. I say this because it is fallacious to assume that all offenders will do anything to avoid custody because probation officers know only too well from first hand experience that some offenders would, for example, rather go to prison than pay fines imposed by the court. Moreover for those offenders who did consent to the new sentence there is little doubt that it would be extremely demanding and would require a considerable commitment over a number of months. Consequently it seems that probation officers who supervised the order would require consummate skill in helping offenders to successfully complete the new sentence without being returned to court for breaching its stringent requirements.

It should also be added that the proposals for the Community Restitution Order are unclear concerning the future of the probation order. At one point it seems the probation order will be abolished, which means that if the court decides an offender required help, then this would be provided by simply invoking the 'problem solving' element of the Community Restitution Order. However should the probation order remain a disposal to be considered by the court in cases where offenders required help with various problems, in the way the order continues to be used at present, it would be necessary to clearly differentiate between those cases in which probation orders are appropriate, rather than the Community Restitution Order. This is necessary to avoid pushing offenders up the tariff too quickly and to avoid using the new disposal as an alternative to other non-custodial disposals rather than prison, which has been the fate of so-called alternatives to custody in recent years.

Punishment in the Community

Several weeks after ACOPs attempt to get ahead of the game, the Home Office declared its hand in a Green Paper entitled 'Punishment, Custody and The Community' (1988). This document explains how the Home Office is particularly concerned that in 1987 99,700 17 to 20 year old young men and 12,300 young women were sentenced by the courts. Of these over 20,000 young men and 600 young women were given a custodial sentence. This is the custodial problem the government wants to tackle by creating a new form of punishment in the community with components which embody three main elements:

 punishment by some deprivation of liberty;
 action to reduce the risk of reoffending;
 recompense to the victim and public.

This new sentence would enable courts to make requirements which might include one or more of the following:

 compensation to the victims of crime;
 reparation and mediation;
 community service;
 hostel and other approved accommodation;
 relevant activities through the local probation day centre;
 tracking;
 electronic tagging to enforce curfew/house arrest;
 requirements not to visit certain locations;
 education and training for misuse of alcohol and drugs.

This new sentence should be credible enough to convince courts that it will be used as an alternative to custody but positive elements, such as the provision of appropriate help, are not precluded. It seems that, like the ACOP proposal, certain elements from the above menu could be selected to suit different offenders. Moreover it is envisaged there would be some judicial oversight with the power to both relax and increase requirements, depending on the progress or otherwise of the offender. Now even though the fine details of these proposals have still to be worked out throughout 1989 and beyond, the important point to make is that the possiblity of a new sentence is on the penal policy agenda.

In December 1988 NAPO published its response to the Green Paper (NAPO, 1988b) in which it stated that it did not accept that reducing custody would be achieved by punishment in the community. NAPO argued that the Green Paper provides only a limited analysis of current penal problems because, among other things:

it ignores the causes of crime;
it overlooks that the public are less punitive than one assumes;
it does not consider restricting the powers of the courts to achieve its stated aim of reducing custody;
it fails to consider the evidence of the failure of recent alternatives to custody.

NAPO categorically rejects proposals for a new sentence, but it does acknowledge that better use could be made of existing disposals like probation and community service. In fact NAPO echoes the response of ACOP (1989) to the Green Paper at that point where ACOP states that the Home Office should monitor the effects of strengthening existing community disposals before experimenting with a new sentence. (During the early weeks of 1989 area probation services were busy working out their response to Part 2 of the Green Paper which has become known as 'Tackling Offending-An Action Plan').

It does seem sensible to proceed on the basis advocated by ACOP when it suggests that the results of strengthening existing disposals, which will be developed during 1989, should be evaluated first. Consequently within the context of existing legislation it would be useful to sketch the lineaments of a realigned model of probation supervision, which uses the format adopted in earlier chapters. Because it would be unacceptable to the Home Office for the probation service to operate solely as a self-employed welfare agency, and anathema to the probation service to operate solely as a controlling agency, the model which follows is a pragmatic compromise in the best tradition of probation work over the last few years.

The elements of community supervision for more serious offenders
Practice
Probation officers should continue to engage in those practices delineated in the first section of Chapter 7. This is because offenders will continue to experience problems associated with unemployment, limited education, lack of social skills, poor accommodation, relationship, marriage and family problems. Accordingly probation officers should provide help in these areas of difficulty which implies that local probation management teams will have to provide appropriate resources and facilities to both officers and clients. In other words, I envisage that probation officers will continue to provide what has been described as a social work, caring, supportive and welfare oriented service to offenders.

Ideology
Probation officers should engage in these various practices not because, as in the past, by doing so they will save souls or rehabilitate offenders, but primarily because an organisation is needed within each local criminal justice system which can respond to the problems of offenders in a humane, supportive and caring way. Offenders, if they so choose, should be helped to resolve their problems simply because they have problems which are adversely affecting their lives, as an end in itself. In other words an organisation is needed which can unequivocally take a moral and humanitarian position at a time when the emphasis within the criminal justice system is increasingly on tougher attitudes, discipline, punishment and control. The moral argument that offenders can and should be helped should not be overlooked when the probation service is being reshaped to manage more serious offenders in the community.

Axiology

I have no doubt that probation officers will continue to care and that it is morally right they should support offenders as much as possible. However - and this is the sphere of probation work which needs to be realigned most of all, notwithstanding the tensions and dilemmas incurred - the social work task will have to be performed within a new framework whose parameters are determined by the language of control, discipline and punishment. Moreover the probation service must learn how to use this new and sometimes foreign language and thus become part of the new realism, if it is to convince the courts that it can supervise the more serious offender.

Having made such a statement it must be said that the concepts of punishment, discipline and control, do not have to evoke images of 19th century chain gangs, transportation, or the reintroduction of the birch. Rather the new language which the service will have to adopt can be defined, for example, in terms of establishing much clearer contracts with the court to ensure that offenders do certain things on a regular basis and at stated times during the period of supervision. To unpack this further, more demanding and tougher supervision could be interpreted to mean offenders having to attend probation facilities two or more nights per week, in addition to undertaking some weekend work to the benefit of the community. Accordingly such measures would introduce more 'control' than is present under existing types of probation supervision which can mean nothing more than an offender visiting the probation officer one day per week for half an hour. Furthermore if it is desirable for offenders to be in contact with the probation service on three separate occasions each week for two to three hours per session, could it not be argued that such measures are demanding and that they interfere with the convenience of offenders? And by making more demands on offenders in terms of time and commitment, could not the probation service argue that this is a form of both discipline and punishment in the community?

It is important for the service to unpack, clarify and define what it means by community punishment, discipline and control, and then to negotiate its new approach with the Home Office, representatives of the local criminal justice system and NAPO. Consequently not only could such a supervisory structure which resorted to the language of punishment, rather than emphasising care and support, help to convince courts that the probation service has a credible alternative to custody, but it would also ensure that probation officers would still be able to help offenders as much, if not more, than they do now because of increased contact.

This change of linguistic style has important implications for the way in which probation officers compose social enquiry reports, which are their shop window to the courts. This research has already established that reports could be more effective if they contained cogent arguments for community supervision. It may also be argued that they could be improved even further if arguments for supervision were presented in the language the courts want to hear, thus enhancing their appeal and credibility.

By adopting this realigned approach it may well be the case that conflict between care and control would indubitably remain and perhaps be exacerbated, but the new language could be defined and interpreted in such a way to allow the service to undertake constructive work with offenders. The important innovation required from the probation service is to submit itself to a form of cosmetic surgery which will have the effect of changing its appearance to courts without radically altering the substance of its social work approach to offenders. It must talk tough whilst acting in meaningful and constructive ways once courts have made offenders the subject of community supervision orders. In other words, it is a case of changing surface images, languages and structures to satisfy courts, whilst retaining the best elements of probation practice to satisfy probation officers' occupational need to engage in social work. For even though the Home Office has more or less fixed future policy for the service, there remains discretion at that point where policies are implemented.

Methods
Finally, as now, the probation service should continue to use a variety of social work methods. However this research has indicated

that probation officers need to improve their assessment procedures and techniques which allows offenders to determine their own problems so that methods of intervention are selected more appropriately. Officers also need to be more focused and skillfull in the way they intervene. Therefore, the Cleveland probation service should consider using some kind of check list which could subsequently be used as an instrument to measure the effectiveness of their intervention, not necessarily in terms of reduced offending, but in terms of a diminution of client problems. But a diminution of client perceived problems may well be followed by a reduction in crime (Raynor, 1985).

Conclusion

From other research undertaken concurrently with the research documented in this book it has been reinforced how, in a majority of cases, dwelling house burglary offences continue to attract custodial sentences in cases where even probation with an extra condition was recommended to the courts by officers (Whitehead, 1988). Moreover I have found that 178 (46.6%) out of 382 17-20 year olds received a custodial sentence for various types of burglary during 1988 in Cleveland. Consequently if dwelling house burglary offenders became the target group for a realigned model of probation which was more successful than existing probation orders at diverting them from custody, it is possible that the Cleveland probation service could begin to make a significant impact on the proportionate use of custody, particularly for the 17-20 year old age group, which has been consistently higher than the proportionate use of custody in England and Wales over recent years (Between 1983 and 1986 the proportionate use of custody in Cleveland for 17-20 year old males was 17.6%, 15.7%, 17.2% and 14.5%, compared with 14.7%, 13.2%, 13.8% and 12.3%, for England and Wales).

It is against this background that I have argued for a new model of community supervision, within existing legislation, through which the probation service can provide credible alternatives to custody for more serious offenders. Its practices and methods of working can continue the best traditions of probation work articulated in those

227

models encountered in earlier chapters and its ideology should be
orientated more towards help for its own sake rather than, in a
utilitarian sense, solving the problem of crime. However a quantum
leap is required in the axiological sphere which would move the
service more towards the control end of the care-control continuum to
achieve its central goal. In so doing the service would conform to
the latest criminal justice 'fashion' emerging from within the Home
Office which, in the course of time, may well be replaced by some
other 'fashion' which could be more acceptable to the service. But in
the mean time cooperation rather than confrontation with the Home
Office will ensure the survival of the organisation at a time of
crisis. Even though this research allows me to argue for a realigned
model, a number of problems and counter-arguments should be seriously
considered in this conclusion.

First is the problem of a catch 22 dilemma where the alternatives
debate is concerned. On the one hand it is clear that the Home
Office, ACOP and a number of sentencers want a form of community
supervision which is both onerous and hard in order to appear
credible. It must also be demanding, tough and, according to ACOP,
even more demanding that prison. Only then will an alternative to
custody be acceptable.

On the other hand what is acceptable to sentencers could well be
unacceptable to offenders, so that its appeal to the former could be
cancelled out by its rejection by the latter. What I mean by this is
that in creating what is considered to be a 'genuine' alternative
could be perceived by offenders as something worse than prison.
Therefore in making an alternative more demanding than prison, it
could be rejected by offenders for this very reason. Furthermore for
the high risk, recidivist, serious offender, it may well be that
custody holds little fear and so, on finding the new model too hard
and tough, will take the easy way out by refusing to comply with its
requirements, thus eventually being committed to custody after being
breached. This is the problem of unintended consequences because,
inadvertently and unwittingly, the proposed solution of a new model
could result in even more custodial sentences.

Second is the counter-argument which states that all this talk about alternatives to custody is nothing but humbug, because the reality is that more and more prisons are being built to accommodate more and more offenders. One explanation for this phenomenon can be found in the arguments of Mathiesen (1974), Fitzgerald and Sim (1979), Sim (1987) and Box (1987) where, within the context of discussing the politics of imprisonment, prisons are seen to play an important role in the containment of working class people who are surplus to requirements under contemporary socio-economic conditions. During recession when young people particularly are unable to find work and are therefore not under the discipline of the work place, prisons are required to discipline those groups within society who constitute a threat to social order. Consequently the alternatives debate, it is argued, should be understood within a context where prison is perceived as a functional and continuing necessity for a capitalist society. Because of this there will not be a significant shift to community disposals.

Third is the counter-argument which states that the tenets of the Green Paper and the corollary of redefining the work of the probation service and wider criminal justice system to deal with crime by a new model, completely misses the point. It misses the point because the emphasis remains on changing individual offenders instead of changing those social conditions which are associated with offending.

Since 1979 British society has become progressively more unequal and divided (CPAG 1988; Bottomore 1987, p134). It is therefore argued (and this is an unpopular argument to the Home Office) that the causes of crime must be located in material conditions (Box 1987, p196). This implies that the only way crime will be successfully combated and custody eventually reduced, is by creating a more just and fair society by redistributing wealth and power more equitably. Some support for this position is found in Braithwaite (1979) who argues that 'gross' economic measures designed to reduce the gap between rich and poor, rather than targetting specific groups with the aim of lifting them out of poverty, will reduce crime. He states that 'A strong prima facie case has been made in this study for the proposition that reducing inequality of wealth and power will reduce

229

crime' (1979, p236).

The point can be made that the criminal justice system, which includes the probation service, is only of marginal significance to the problem of crime. According to this analysis what is happening towards the end of the 1980s is best described by Scull when he says that 'tinkering around with the criminal justice system in a radically unjust society is unlikely to advance us very far toward justice, equity or, come to that, efficacy' (1983, p165).

Finally, it may be argued that if the Home Office was genuinely concerned about reducing the custodial population, it would abandon the Green Paper in favour of the following proposals:

exercise the power of executive release;

curb the powers of sentencers to incarcerate offenders;

impose a ceiling on the number of offenders in custody;

pursue reductionist rather than expansionist custodial policies (Rutherford 1984);

social action to deal with the causes of crime.

Needless to say these proposals are not on the Home Office agenda towards the end of the 1980s. Consequently it is unlikely that the Green Paper and even my own attempt at a pragmatic compromise sketched in the realigned model of community supervision, will solve current penal problems. This may be a pessimistic note on which to finish but I am afraid we are living in rather pessimistic times.

Bibliography

ACOP (1983) Minutes from meeting of the Committee of Regional
Representatives on the 8th September.

ACOP (1985) The Probation Liaison Committee, January 1985.

ACOP (1986) The Development of Financial Management Information
Systems in the Probation Service, Deloitte, Haskins and Sells,
September 1986.

ACOP (1987) Unemployment in the North East. A Probation Perspective,
Cleveland Probation Service.

ACOP (1988) More Demanding than Prison, a draft discussion paper,
24th May 1988.

ACOP (1989) 'The Community And Crime:A Strategy for Criminal
Justice'. ACOPs response to the Green Paper Cm 424.

Bailey, R. (1980) 'Social Workers:pawns, police or agitators?',
in: M. Brake and R. Bailey (eds), Radical Social Work and
Practice, London:Edward Arnold.

Bale, D. (1986) The Cambridge Risk of Custody Scale, Version 2,
Cambridge Probation Service.

Bale, D. (1988) 'Summing up for the Defence', Probation Journal,

35, 1.

Barr, H. (1966) Probation Research. A Survey of Group Work in the
Probation Service, HMSO.

Beaumont, B. (1984a) 'Probation Work - The Potential for Progressive
Development', in: Probation; Direction, Innovation and Change in
the 1980s, York Conference, 11-13 July, NAPO.

Beaumont, B. (1984b) '1984 and Ahead:Prospects for the Penal
System', Probation Journal, 31, 1.

Beaumont, B. (1976) 'A Supportive Role', Probation Journal, 23, 3.

Beaumont, B. (1986) Annual Report for 1985-1986, NAPO.

Beaumont, B. (1988) 'A tough heart and a muddled mind',
SWT, 23 June 1988.

Betteridge, R.A. (1984) 'Making the most of the Probation Order',
unpublished paper.

Biestek, F.P. (1961) The Casework Relationship, O.U.Press.

Bochel, D. (1976) Probation and After-Care, Scottish Academic Press.

Boswell, G.R. (1982) Goals in the Probation Service, unpublished
PhD Thesis, University of Liverpool.

Bottomore, T. (1987) Sociology, A Guide to Problems and Literature,
Allen and Unwin.

Bottoms, A.E. (1987) 'Limiting Prison Use:Experience in England
and Wales', The Howard Journal, 26, 3.

Bottoms, A.E. and McWilliams, W. (1979) 'A non-treatment paradigm
for probation practice', BJSW, 9, 2.

Bottoms, A.E. and Preston, R.H. (1980) The Coming Penal Crisis,
Scottish Academic Press.

Box, S. (1987) Recession, Crime and Punishment, Macmillan.

Braithwaite, J. (1979) Inequality, Crime and Public Policy,
Routledge and Kegan Paul.

Brittan, L. (1984a) Interview with the Editor of the Probation
Journal, 31, 1.

Brittan, L. (1984b) Speech to an ACOP conference, 20 September.

Broad, B. (ed)(1988) Enquiries into Community Probation Work,
Cranfield Press.

Brockington, N. and Shaw, M. (1986) 'Tracking the Trackers',
Research Bulletin 22, Home Office Research and Planning Unit.

Brody, S.R. (1976) The Effectiveness of Sentencing, HMSO.

Brody, S.R. (1978) 'Research into the Aims and Effectiveness of Sentencing', The Howard Journal, 17, 3.

Bryant, M., Coker, J., Estlea, B., Himmel, S. and Knapp, T. (1978) 'Sentenced To Social Work?', Probation Journal, 25, 4.

Bryman, A. (1988) Quantity and Quality in Social Research, Unwin Hyman.

Burgess, R. (ed)(1982) Field Research:A Sourcebook and Field Manual, George Allen and Unwin.

Burnham, D. (1981) 'The new orthodoxy', Probation Journal, 28, 1.

Butler, S. (1872) Erewhon, in: Everyman Library Edition, 1932, Dent:London

Butler, T. (1983) 'The Financial Management Initiative', in: Future Direction of the Probation Service, Bournemouth Residential Conference, 12-13 May 1983.

Carter, R.M. and Wilkins, L.T. (eds)(1976) Probation, Parole, and Community Corrections, Second Edition, John Wiley and Sons.

Chapman, J. (1977) 'Defining the vital tasks', Probation Journal, 24, 1.

Christie, N. (1982) Limits to Pain, Martin Robertson.

Clarke, R.V.G. and Cornish, D.B. (eds)(1983) Crime Control in Britain. A Review of Policy Research, State University of New York Press, Albany.

Clarke, R.V.G. and Sinclair, I. (1974) 'Towards more effective treatment evaluation', in: European Committee on Crime Problems, Collected Studies in Criminological Research, Vol XII, Strasbourg, Council of Europe.

Cleveland Probation Service (1984) Consultative Document Regarding Organisational Changes.

Cleveland Probation Service (1985a) Letter by CPO to Probation staff.

Cleveland Probation Service (1985b) Future Directions Discussion Papers.

Cleveland Probation Service (1985c) Interim Report to staff.

Cleveland Probation Service (1985d) Working Party on Organisational Changes, Statement by NAPO.

Cleveland Probation Service (1985e) Further Consultative Document.

Cleveland Probation Service (1986) Future Directions Document.

Cohen, S. (1985) Visions of Social Control, Polity Press.

Coker, J. (1984) 'Sentenced To Social Work?:The Revival of Choice', Probation Journal, 31, 4.

Coulshed, V. (1988) Social Work Practice. An Introduction, Macmillan.

CPAG (1987) The Growing Divide, A Social Audit 1979–1987.

Creedon, M. (1984) 'Sense of Purpose?', Personal Account, Probation Journal, 31, 1.

Croft, J. (1978) Research in Criminal Justice, HMSO.

Cullen, F.T. and Gilbert, K.E. (1982) Reaffirming Rehabilitation, Anderson Publishing Company.

Davies, M. (1969) Probationers in their Social Environment, HMSO.

Davies, M. (1972) 'The Objectives of the Probation Service', BJSW, 2, 3.

Davies, M. (1982) 'Community-based alternatives to custody:the right place for the probation service', unpublished address to a conference of chief probation officers.

Davis, G., Boucherat, J. and Watson, D. (1988) 'Reparation in the Service of Diversion:The Subordination of a Good Idea', The Howard Journal, 27, 2.

Dawtry, F. (1958) 'Whither Probation', BJ Delinquency, 8, 3.

Day, M. (1987) 'The politics of probation', in: J. Harding (ed) Probation and the Community, Tavistock.

Day, P.R. (1981) Social Work and Social Control, Tavistock.

Despicht, K. (1987) Specificity in Probation Practice, Social Work Monograph 56, University of East Anglia.

Downes, D. (1988) Contrasts in Tolerance:Post-war Penal Policy in the Netherlands and England and Wales, Oxford.

Downie, R.S. and Telfer, E. (1980) Caring and Curing:A Philosophy of Medicine and Social Work, Methuen.

Drakeford, M. (1983) 'Probation:containment or liberty?', Probation Journal, 30, 1.

Faulkner, D. (1983) Speech at the Bournemouth Residential Conference, 12–13 May.

Faulkner, D. (1984) 'The Future of the Probation Service', in:
Probation; Direction, Innovation and Change in the 1980s,
York Conference, 11-13 July, NAPO.

Faulkner, D. (1986) Personal correspondence with the author in
June, subsequent to visiting Home Office.

Fielding, N. (1984) Probation Practice. Client Support under Social
Control, Gower.

Fitzgerald, M. and Sim, J. (1979) British Prisons, Basil Blackwell.

Folkard, S., Lyon, K., Carver, M.M. and O'Leary, E. (1966)
Probation Research, A Preliminary Report, HMSO.

Folkard, S., Fowles, A.J., McWilliams, B.C., Mcwilliams, W.,
Smith, D.D., Smith, D.E. and Walmsley, G.R. (1974) IMPACT Vol 1,
The design of the probation experiment and an interim
evaluation, HMSO.

Folkard, S., Smith, D.E. and Smith, D.D. (1976) IMPACT Vol 2,
The Results of the Experiment, HMSO.

Fullwood, C. (1984) FMI and the Probation Service, ACOP.

Fullwood, C. (1987) 'The Probation Service:From Moral Optimism
Through Penological Pessimism Into The Future', Justice of the
Peace, November 1987.

Garland, D. (1985a) Punishment and Welfare, Gower.

Garland, D. (1985b) 'The Criminal and his Science', BJC, 25, 2.

Glover, E.R. (1949) Probation and Re-education, Routledge
and Kegan Paul.

Gower Judge, (1986) in a Speech to ACOP in: Social Order, Social
Justice and the Law, Residential Conference Papers, ACOP.

Green, R. (1987) 'Racism and the Offender:a probation response',
in: J. Harding (ed) Probation and the Community, Tavistock.

Griffiths, W.A. (1982a) 'A New Probation Service',
Probation Journal, 29, 3.

Griffiths, W.A. (1982b) 'Supervision in the Community', Justice of
the Peace, 21 August.

Grimsey, E.J. (1987) Efficiency Scrutiny of HM Probation
Inspectorate, Home Office.

Hakim, C. (1987) Research Design. Strategies and Choices in the
Design of Social Research, Allen and Unwin.

Hammond, W.H. (1969) 'The Results of Evaluative Research', in: Home Office, The Sentence of the Court, HMSO.

Harris, R. (1977) 'The Probation Officer as Social Worker', BJSW, 7, 4.

Harris, R. (1980) 'A Changing Service:The Case for Separating 'Care' and 'Control' in Probation Practice', BJSW, 10, 2.

Harris, R. and Webb, D. (1987) Welfare, Power and Juvenile Justice, Tavistock.

Harris, R. (1988) 'Taming the Whitehall Machine', The Observer, 21 February.

Haxby, D. (1978) Probation:A Changing Service, Constable.

Head, M.E. (1988) 'Alternatives to Custody:Implications for Policy and Priorities in the Probation Service', Day Conference at Hull University, February 1988.

Heasman, K. (1962) Evangelicals in Action:An Appraisal of their Social Work in the Victorian Era, London:Geoffrey Bless.

Hedges, A. (1985) 'Group Interviewing', in: R. Walker, Applied Qualitative Research, Gower.

Hil, R. (1986) 'Centre 81:Clients' and Officers' Views on the Southampton Day Centre', in: J. Pointing (ed) Alternatives To Custody, Basil Blackwell.

Hollis, F. (1964) Casework A Psychosocial Therapy, Second Edition, Random House, New York.

Home Office (1909) Report of the Departmental Committee On the Probation Of Offenders Act, 1907, CMND 5001, HMSO.

Home Office (1922) Report of the Departmental Committee On the Training, Appointment and Payment of Probation Officers, CMND 1601, HMSO.

Home Office (1936) Report of the Departmental Committee on the Social Services in Courts of Summary Jurisdiction, CMND 5122, HMSO.

Home Office (1959) Penal Practice in a Changing Society, CMND 645, HMSO.

Home Office (1962) Report of the Departmental Committee on the Probation Service, CMND 1650, HMSO.

Home Office (1974) Young Adult Offenders, HMSO.

Home Office (1977) A Review of Criminal Justice Policy 1976, HMSO.

Home Office (1983a) Probation Service in England and Wales.
Statement of National Purpose and Objectives, Draft.

Home Office (1983b) Future Direction of the Probation Service,
Draft, June.

Home Office (1984a) Probation Service in England and Wales.
Statement of National Objectives and Priorities.

Home Office (1984b) Criminal Justice. A Working Paper, HMSO.

Home Office (1986) The Sentence of the Court, Fourth Edition, HMSO.

Home Office (1987) Approved Probation Hostels and Bail Hostels,
Statistical Digest 1986-87.

Home Office (1988) Punishment, Custody and the Community,
CM 424, HMSO.

Hood, R. and Sparks, R. (1970) Key Issues In Criminology,
Weidenfeld and Nicholson.

Howe, D. (1987) An Introduction To Social Work Theory, Wildwood
House Limited.

Hudson, B. (1987) Justice Through Punishment, Macmillan.

Hudson, B.L. and Macdonald, G.M. (1986) Behavioural Social Work:An
Introduction, London:Macmillan.

Hugman, B. (1977) Act Natural, London:Bedford Square Press.

Hugman, B. (1980) 'Radical Practice in Probation', in: M. Brake
and R. Bailey (eds) Radical Social Work and Practice,
Edward Arnold.

Hunt, A.W. (1964) 'Enforcement in Probation Casework', BJC, 4,
pp239-252.

Hurd, D. (1986a) Speech to the 26th AGM of the Central Council
of Probation Committees, 20 May.

Hurd, D. (1986b) Speech to ACOP Conference, September.

Index of Probation Projects (1986-87) National Probation Research
and Information Exchange.

James, A. (1979) 'Sentenced to Surveillance', Probation Journal,
26, 1.

Jarvis, F.V. (1972) Advise, Assist and Befriend. A History of the
Probation and After-Care Service, NAPO.

Jeffs, D. and Saunders, W. (1983) 'Minimising Alcohol Related

Offences by Enforcement of the Existing Licensing Legislation', British Journal of Addiction, 78, 1.

Jones, S. (1985) 'Depth Interviewing', in: R. Walker, Applied Qualitative Research, Gower.

Jordan, W. (1971) 'The Probation Service in the Sixties', Journal of Social and Economic Administration, 5, pp125-138.

Jordan, W. (1983) 'Criminal Justice and Probation in the 1980s', Probation Journal, 30, 3.

Kidder, L.H. and Judd, C.M. (1986) Research Methods in Social Relations, Fifth Edition, CBS College Publishing.

King, J.F.S. (ed)(1958) The Probation Service, First Edition, Butterworths.

King, J.F.S. (ed)(1964) The Probation Service, Second Edition, Butterworths.

King, J.F.S. (ed)(1969) The Probation and After-Care Service, Third Edition, Butterworths.

Leeson, C. (1914) The Probation System, London, P and S King and Son.

Le Mesurier, L. (ed)(1935) A Handbook of Probation, NAPO.

Lloyd, C. (1986) Response To SNOP, University of Cambridge, Institute of Criminology.

Lustig, R. (1987) 'The Crisis In Our Prisons', The Observer, 11 October.

Marshall, T. (1984) Reparation, conciliation and mediation, Research and Planning Unit Paper 27, Home Office.

Martinson, R. (1974) 'What Works?-questions and answers about prison reform', The Public Interest, Spring 1974, pp25-54.

McCord, J. (1978) 'A Thirty-year follow-up of treatment effects', American Psychologist, 33, pp284-289.

Mathiesen, T. (1974) The Politics of Abolition, Martin Robertson.

McWilliams, W. (1983) 'The Mission to the English Police Courts 1876-1936', The Howard Journal, 22, pp129-147.

McWilliams, W. 1985) 'The Mission Transformed : Professionalisation of Probation Between the Wars', The Howard Journal, 24, 4.

McWilliams, W. (1986) 'The English Probation System and the Diagnostic Ideal', The Howard Journal, 25, 4.

McWilliams, W. (1987) 'Probation, Pragmatism and Policy', The
Howard Journal, 26, 2.

Millard, D. (1979) 'Broader approaches to probation practice', in:
J.F.S. King (ed) Pressures and Change in the Probation Service,
Cropwood Conference series No 11, Cambridge Institute of
Criminology, University of Cambridge.

Monger, M. (1964) Casework in Probation, London, Butterworths.

Morgan, R. (1979) Formulating Penal Policy:The Future of the
Advisory Council on the Penal System, NACRO.

Morley, H. (1986) 'Heimler's Human Social Functioning', Probation
Journal, 33, 4.

Morrison, A. (1984) 'National Objectives and Service Values',
Probation Journal, 31, 3.

Moser, C. and Kalton, G. (1985) Survey Methods in Social
Investigation, Second Edition, Gower.

NACRO (1986) News Briefing, Imprisonment in the 1980s:Some Facts
and Figures, August 1986.

NACRO (1987a) News Briefing, Non-Custodial Sentences, April 1987.

NACRO (1987b) News Briefing, The Prison Population-Recent
Developments, 10 July 1987.

NAPO (1982) The Use of the Probation Order and the Provision
of Alternatives To Custody, Policy Paper Approved at the 1982 AGM.

NAPO (1983a) NAPO Response to the Home Office Draft. Statement of
National Purpose and Objectives, 18 November 1983.

NAPO (1983b) Draft Policy Document-Conditions in Probation Orders,
Practice Guidelines, 12 April 1983.

NAPO (1983c) Opposition To Night Restriction and Negative
Requirements, PD1/83.

NAPO (1984) Home Office Statement on the Probation Service-NAPOs
Response, June 1984.

NAPO (1985) Criminal Justice-An Alternative Strategy, May 1985.

NAPO (1988a) Punishment in the Community, NAPO News, No1, July 1988.

NAPO (1988b) 'Punishment, Custody and the Community', The Response
of The National Association of Probation Officers.

Parry-Khan, L. (1988) Management By Objectives in the Probation
Service, Monograph 63, University of East Anglia.

Parsloe, P. (1967) The Work of the Probation and After-Care Officer, Routledge and Kegan Paul.

Parsloe, P. (1983) 'The Transfer of Skills from Learning to Practice', in: Research in Practice Teaching, CCETSW Study 6.

Pease, K. (1985) 'The Future of Research and Information in the Probation Service', in: E. Sainsbury (ed) Research and Information in the Probation Service, University of Sheffield Conference, 7-11 January 1985.

Pitts, J. (1988) The Politics of Juvenile Crime, Sage.

Probation Journal (1974) Special Edition on the Younger Report, 21, 4.

Probation Rules (1984) Home Office.

Probation, The Next Five Years (1987) Joint Statement by the CCPC, ACOP, NAPO.

Purser, R. (1987) 'Responding to the drink/drug-using offender', in: J. Harding (ed) Probation and the Community, Tavistock.

Radzinowicz, L. (1958) The Results of Probation, Macmillan.

Raynor, P. (1984) 'National Purpose and Objectives' : A Comment, Probation Journal, 31, 2.

Raynor, P. (1985) Social Work, Justice and Control, Blackwell.

Raynor, P. (1988) Probation as an Alternative to Custody, Avebury:Aldershot.

Reid, W.J. and Smith, A.D. (1981) Research in Social Work, Columbia University Press.

Roberts, J. (1984) 'Management, Innovation and Probation Practice', in: Probation; Direction, Innovation and Change in the 1980s, York Conference, 11-13 July, NAPO.

Roberts, R.W. and Nee, R.H. (1970) Theories of Social Casework, The University of Chicago Press.

Rutherford, A. (1984) Prisons and the Process of Justice:The Reductionist Challenge, Heinemann.

Ryan, M. (1983) The Politics of Penal Reform, Longman.

Satyamurti, C. (1979) 'Care and Control in Local Authority Social Work', in: N. Parry, M. Rustia, and C, Satyamurti, Social Work, Welfare and the State, Edward Arnold.

Scull, A. (1983) 'Community Corrections:Panacea, Progress or

Pretence' in: D.Garland and P. Young (eds), The Power To Punish,
Heinemann.

Simm, J. (1987) 'Working for the Clampdown : Prisons and Politics
in England and Wales', in: P. Scraton (ed), Law, Order and the
Authoritarian State, O U Press.

Simon, F.H. (1971) Prediction Methods in Criminology, Home Office
Research Study No7, HMSO.

Sinclair, I. (1971) Hostels for Probationers, Home Office Research
Study No6, HMSO.

Smykla, J. (1984) Probation and Parole:Crime Control in the
Community, London:Macmillan.

Spencer, N. and Edwards, P. (1986) 'The Rise and Fall of the Kent
Control Unit:A Local Perspective', Probation Journal, 33, 3.

Stelman, A. (1980) 'Social Work Relationships:an exploration',
Probation Journal, 27, 2.

Stern, V. (1987) Bricks of Shame, Penguin.

Stone, N. (1988) Probation Law Social Work File Part 3, University
of East Anglia.

Thomas, C. (1978) 'Supervision in the Community', The Howard
Journal, 17, 1.

Thomas, D.A. (1979) Principles of Sentencing, Second Edition,
Heinemann.

Timms, N. (1964) Social Casework, Routledge and Kegan Paul.

Tutt, N. and Giller, H. (1985) 'Doing Justice To Great
Expectations', Community Care, 17 January 1985.

Walker, H. and Beaumont, B. (1981) Probation Work, Basil Blackwell.

Walker, H. and Beaumont, B. (eds)(1985) Working With Offenders,
Macmillan.

Walker, N. (1983) 'The Effectiveness of Probation', Probation
Journal, 30, 3.

Walker, N. (1987) Crime and Criminology, Oxford.

Walker, R. (1985) Applied Qualitative Research, Gower.

Walrond-Skinner, S. (1977) Family Therapy-The Treatment of Natural
Systems, Routledge and Kegan Paul.

Walton, D. (1987) 'The residential, employment, and educational
needs of offenders', in: J. Harding (ed) Probation and the

241

Community, Tavistock.

Weston, W.R. (1987) Jarvis's Probation Officers' Manual, Fourth Edition, Butterworths.

Whitehead, P. (1987) 'Putting SNOP in Perspective', Probation Journal, 34,4.

Whitehead, P. (1988) 'Change Your Ways in 30 Days'. Report on the First Year of Schedule 11, Cleveland Probation Service.

Wilkins, L.T. (1958) 'A small comparative study of the Results of Probation', BJ Delinquency, 8, pp201-209.

Willis, A. (1986) 'Help and Control in Probation:An Empirical Assessment of Probation Practice', in: J. Pointing (ed) Alternatives To Custody, Blackwell.

Wilmot, R. (1976) 'What is Rehabilitation?', International Journal of Offender Therapy and Comparative Criminology, 20, 3.

Young, J. (1986) 'The failure of criminology:the need for a radical realism', in: R. Matthews and J. Young (eds) Confronting Crime, Sage Publications.